The Crocheter's Skill-Building Workshop

The Crocheter's
Skill-Building
Workshop

DORA OHRENSTEIN

Storey Publishing

The mission of Storey Publishing is to serve our customers by publishing practical information that encourages personal independence in harmony with the environment.

Edited by Gwen Steege and Pam Thompson
Art direction and book design by Mary Winkelman Velgos
Text production by Jennifer Jepson Smith
Technical edit and diagrams by Charles Voth
Indexed by Nancy D. Wood

Cover and interior photography by John Polak, except for © Deborah Burke/Antiquedress.com, 14; Keith Putnam, back cover (author's photo); Mars Vilaubi, 64 (bottom); Richard Bergen, 9; © Ron Zmiri/shutterstock.com, 13
Illustrations by Ilona Sherratt, illustration on page 23 adapted from a sketch by José Ortiz Téllez

Storey Publishing
210 MASS MoCA Way
North Adams, MA 01247
www.storey.com

Printed in China by R.R. Donnelley
10 9 8 7 6 5 4 3 2 1

Library of Congress Cataloging-in-Publication Data

Ohrenstein, Dora.
  The crocheter's skill-building workshop : essential techniques for becoming a more versatile, adventurous crocheter / by Dora Ohrenstein.
      pages cm
  Includes index.
  ISBN 978-1-61212-246-5 (pbk. : alk. paper)
  ISBN 978-1-61212-247-2 (ebook) 1. Crocheting. I. Title.
TT820.O36325 2014
746.43'4—dc23
                    2014028045

Contents

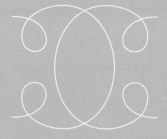

Double Crochet Decrease, p. 91

Crossed Stitches, p. 162

Shaping a Circle, p. 102

Spike Cluster, p. 191

Shaping a Multirow
Pattern, p. 122

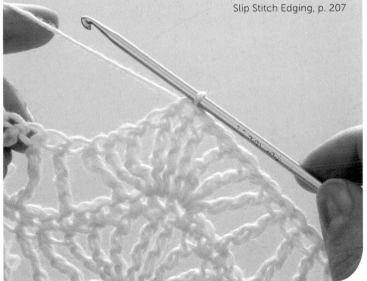

Slip Stitch Edging, p. 207

Preface

It's very exciting to be designing and writing about crochet at this moment in time. Crochet has emerged from its relatively short history — at least from the time it's been documented in the mid-nineteenth century — and appears to be in full blossom, with no signs of stopping. There is fabulous crochet on the runway every season, and amazing designs aimed at crafters too. No more is crochet confined to granny squares (although I still love them) and afghans. The great proliferation of yarns in thinner weights and fluid, silky fibers is also contributing to the crochet renaissance.

It seemed obvious to me, therefore, that the crochet community needed a book that would help crocheters move into these new areas, by providing knowledge and techniques that draw on the traditions of the past but go beyond them. If you yearn to do more sophisticated projects, or design your own, I believe you'll find many tools in this book to assist you.

As a self-taught crocheter, I've learned many things from studying books and patterns, yet I've been puzzled by the lack of information about certain aspects of crochet. One of these is how to control tension: many crocheters seem to have difficulty meeting gauge or executing certain stitches where good control is required. Others feel they crochet too tightly or loosely but don't know how to improve. Given my background as a singer and voice teacher, where training motor skills is routine, I have applied this knowledge to the topic of hand and tension control.

Another information gap seems to exist on the topic of shaping with complex stitch patterns. It's a hard one to address, because there are so many variables. Nevertheless, I have discovered guiding principles that I share in these pages. They will help you understand how shaping is accomplished and vastly improve your understanding of patterns and how to create your own designs.

The purpose of the book is to cover a broad range of techniques commonly used in crochet. I aim to provide fundamental knowledge for crucial matters such as choosing yarns and fibers and working in the round, intermediate techniques like squares and miters, and more advanced skills such as shaping with complex stitch patterns. The term *technique* includes such things as hand-and-hook maneuvers, control of tension, how and where the hook is inserted — anything you may encounter about which there might be a question, or where some bit of special knowledge could be helpful.

As you explore this book, you may realize that while you are an expert in some areas, you might be a novice in others. Crocheters tend to have a high skill level in areas of crochet they've done many times. If you love to make hats, you probably already know quite a bit about working in the round. If you are a committed maker of afghans, you know your favorite seams for attaching blocks. When approaching a different area of crochet where you have less experience, some of your skill and knowledge will apply, but unresolved questions may come up, or puzzles you haven't encountered before. This is quite common, and very few people, including me, are expert in every aspect of crochet. If you want to keep learning and growing your crochet skills, approach the less familiar areas not with trepidation, but rather with an inquisitive, open mind.

For example, if you have always done something a certain way, and you find a stitch or technique in this book that differs from your practice, *try it* — you may like it. There are very few things done only one way in crochet. You may find a particular technique that I describe works well for you, helps you adapt something you already do, suggests a new approach, or points out something you haven't thought of.

Crochet has many traditional techniques and practices that have come down over time. Some of these practices have become quite entrenched, to

Football by Norma Minkowitz

the point where anyone suggesting an alternative is seen as unorthodox. I believe that crochet is too young and rapidly evolving a craft to be restrained by convention. Many strategies I discuss are time-honored, but just as many are more recent developments or things I've discovered on my own. I believe this eclectic approach fosters continuous growth and innovation, and respects the traditions of the past no less for it. For a craft to stay vital and alive, it must evolve, as its proponents use newly developed materials and strive to create items that suit contemporary needs and tastes. Today's yarns and hooks are very different, and in some ways improved, from those of the past, and they allow us to do more with crochet than ever. We seek a different look and feel in our garments, which in turn affects the stitches and techniques used to make them. I believe our techniques change as our materials and aesthetics do.

Designers and artists around the globe are inventing fantastic new ways to do and use crochet, perhaps inspired by the amazing variety and sophistication of contemporary yarns. In the fashion world, crochet continues to be featured season after season. Fine artists are also discovering crochet's amazing possibilities.

It's impossible to cover everything in one book, so I have focused on areas that I believe appeal to most crocheters and where information is limited or hard to find in one place. My focus is on broad topics — shaping, construction, texture, and color — that apply to many different projects. My hope is that the book will be a resource to consult before tackling a pattern or developing your own designs.

You'll find patterns for 77 swatches, each meant to be a quick and effective way to learn a particular technique. Think of each one of these swatches as a lesson. If you've never used swatches in this way before, you may be surprised at what an effective teaching tool a swatch can be. People learn best by doing. Imagine learning a complicated dance step without moving your feet! It's the same in crochet. By actually working the swatches, you'll have a more satisfying learning experience, and you'll also have your swatch to refer to when the technique appears in a project.

The five projects in this book also employ many of the techniques discussed in the preceding chapters. It's often easier to understand a concept when it's put to use, so the projects here include working in the round, cable stitches, uncommon stitches, edgings, and seams.

My hope is that the material in this book will serve you for a long time to come by providing you with valuable tools and strategies for all the crochet challenges ahead.

PART I

Techniques

1

Choosing Yarns

ENTER A GOOD YARN SHOP today and you'll find a choice of yarns so lavish as to be daunting. One way of getting control of the situation is to arm yourself with knowledge about yarns, so that you know just what it is you are paying for.

Understanding the elements that combine and interact in any given yarn will help you make wise yarn choices. We'll look at what weights and fibers are best suited for a chosen project, how to compare quality and prices, how to recognize tightly and loosely spun yarns, and much more. By the end, you'll be an educated shopper.

Before going any further, let me say that there is no difference between yarn used for knitting and yarn used for crochet. Occasionally I hear stories from crocheters who are told that only certain yarns are suitable for crochet. Please don't believe such statements! Each craft produces a different result with the same yarn, and you may prefer the look of a particular yarn in crochet and another in knitting. But truly, you can crochet with any yarn!

Many crocheters limit themselves to certain weights of yarn, such as worsted or bulky, and certain fibers, such as superwash wool or acrylic, because they feel unsure of how to work with unfamiliar yarns, for budgetary reasons, or because other yarns are not easily available to them. No one can deny these concerns, but the fact is that crocheting with a wider range of fibers and yarn weights dramatically expands the quality and variety of projects you can make.

Most of the stitch patterns crocheters know and love derive from the nineteenth century, when crochet as we know it came into being. Nineteenth-century needle hobbyists enjoyed not only crochet, but tatting, knitting, and embroidery. They generally used very fine threads, thinner than anything manufactured today. During this period, intricate laces were very much in fashion, and the crochet hook turned out to be an excellent vehicle for making lace. From the middle of that century to its end, the growing popularity of crochet demanded more designs and publishers

Yarn is the elemental component from which fabric receives its shape and character. The texture and appearance of fabric is created by the composition of the threads it is made from. The amount of twist in the fibers determines the balance and drape; the number of fibers and plies determines the thickness and weight of the fabric.

— Penny Walsh, *The Yarn Book*

This Edwardian-style costume, featuring gown, parasol, purse, and straw hat with Irish crochet, was created in the 1940s for a theatrical production.

of patterns, resulting in a gradual accumulation and dissemination of literally thousands of stitch patterns, techniques, motifs, edgings, and designs. This is the vocabulary of crochet handed down by our Victorian ancestors.

While technically it's possible to crochet any stitch at any gauge, many of these intricate stitch patterns lose their charm when blown too far out of proportion. Yet so rich is the store of these patterns that it's a shame to omit them from one's repertoire. Finer yarns allow a great many more of these stitch patterns to be successfully wrought: lace stitches, motifs, and edgings look wonderful with finer yarns such as sport, fingering, or lace weight.

A range of fibers, too, is important to fully explore crochet's possibilities. Working with quality fibers that make yarns softer, more colorful, lustrous, smooth, or textured enriches the crocheting experience immeasurably. Often crocheters think of themselves merely as hobbyists, but working with a wider range of fibers, colors, and textures can bring out the hidden artist you didn't even know was there!

Following yarn from its sources through the manufacturing process shows how each step impacts the finished product and helps predict how the yarn will behave when crocheted. This knowledge helps us choose the best yarn for a particular project, match yarn with compatible

stitches, select the most appropriate hook size, and substitute yarns in a pattern when necessary.

In this chapter, we will also take a look at crocheted fabric and examine how to choose yarns and stitches that create the most suitable fabric for a project. This is an important element in upgrading the quality of your crochet.

Yarn Sources

Yarns may be made of animal, plant, or synthetic fibers. Here are some of the common yarns you may encounter, organized by source.

Animal Fibers

All animal fibers have the advantage of being somewhat elastic and breathable, trapping air and thereby creating warmth. Except for silk, animal fibers begin as hair. Wool comes from the fleece of sheep, alpaca from the South American camelid, and mohair and cashmere from special breeds of goats. Just as human hair can be silky and straight or coarse and curly, so animal hairs differ markedly, not only from one species to another, but also depending on the animal's age, location, and where the hair was on its body.

Wool has been used for textiles for many centuries, and humankind has learned to breed sheep to capitalize on those qualities that make the sheep best for this purpose. An example is the merino sheep, whose hair is very fine and soft. Merino yarns are more desirable and expensive than generic "wool" yarns, which mix hairs from a variety of different sheep and are coarser.

Wool fibers naturally have tiny scales that bind together. This is what causes wool, when subjected to hot water and agitation, to shrink and felt. To prevent this, some wool yarns are superwashed in a chlorine-based acid bath that removes the scales, or else they are coated with a polymer that prevents the scales from commingling. Sometimes both processes are used. While being able to put a wool item in a washing machine is a nice convenience, the downside is that superwashed wool is heavily processed. If you want a more natural wool, try high-quality wools that are not superwashed. These should be hand-washed in warm or cool water and air-dried.

Alpacas have been bred in Peru since prehistoric times, not as pack animals, but for their highly prized hair. Compared to wool, alpaca fiber is warmer, more lustrous, and wonderfully soft against the skin. Baby alpaca is even softer. Alpaca is fuzzier than wool and more prone to stretching; it must be blocked and washed with great care (see page 207). Because of its excellent drape, alpaca is great for making crochet garments.

FIBER TYPE		
Animal	**Plant**	**Synthetic**
Wool	Cotton	Acrylic
Mohair	Linen	Nylon
Alpaca	Hemp	Polyester
Cashmere	Rayon/Viscose	
Silk		

Wool

Alpaca

Mohair derives from the angora goat. (Note that an angora goat does not produce angora; for that, we turn to angora rabbits.) Like all animal fibers, mohair comes in a variety of grades and at its best can make a lustrous, very strong yarn. The finest quality — kid mohair — is taken from young animals and is not scratchy on the skin. Mohair can make a very light yet warm fabric, excellent for scarves and jackets. The finest-weight mohairs can also be used for indoor wearables.

Cashmere comes from another breed of goat originally from the Himalayas. This extraordinary fiber is 30 percent lighter than wool and yet eight times warmer. The animal produces a coarse outer coat not suitable for yarn and a downy undercoat. It is this remarkable downy undercoat, produced by each animal in very small quantities, that's used in cashmere. That's why cashmere is so expensive. If you can splurge on a skein or two, a cashmere scarf or hat can be quite divine!

Other animal sources include yak, buffalo, possum, qiviut, and camel, each with its own particular characteristics. If you enjoy working with new textures, keep an eye out for yarns featuring some of these less common animal fibers — they can be quite special!

Some animal fibers are more durable than others; for example, the softest cashmeres will not wear as well over time as a hardy wool. That's another point to consider when selecting yarns for a project.

Silk, which has been traced back as far as 3000 BCE, is the one animal fiber that does not begin as hair. When the silkworm forms its cocoon, it excretes a gummy liquid called sericin. By rotating its body some 200,000 times in three days, the insect coats itself in a continuous filament that, if laid out flat, would measure over a mile.

Bundles of these long strands are spun into silk yarn. For high-quality silk, the insects are cultivated and fed in a controlled environment, a labor-intensive process that drives up silk's cost. Yet such is the beauty of silk, and the power of its visual and tactile appeal, that it has commanded a high value for millennia. Silk yarns, or yarns that have a significant silk content, look and feel fantastic in crochet, and are recommended for crochet wearables of all kinds.

Silk/mohair

Mohair

Cotton

Linen

Plant Fibers

Plant fibers are composed of cellulose, a substance found in all plants in greater or lesser degrees.

Cotton fiber is 90 percent cellulose, wood 40 to 50 percent, and hemp 45 percent. Unlike animal fibers, which capture and hold heat, cellulose absorbs water at the plant's root and conveys it to the top of the stem. On humans, the cellulose fibers absorb moisture and then allow it to evaporate, drawing heat away from the body. That's why we wear plant fibers in warm weather.

While animal fibers are naturally elastic, meaning they bounce back after being stretched, plant fibers are not. Think of a cotton sweater that no longer holds its shape. Plant fibers are also denser than animal fibers, and this is significant for crochet. A worsted-weight cotton may be heavier in weight than a worsted-weight wool, and too much weight in a crochet project is something to be avoided.

Despite this, cotton, especially in finer-weight yarns, can be a great vehicle for crochet. Cotton thread has been used throughout crochet history to make lovely doilies, lace collars, Irish crochet motifs, and other refined examples of crochet. Cotton produces crisp, well-defined stitches, washes and dries easily, and does not pill. Higher quality cottons, such as pima and Egyptian, have longer fiber lengths, yielding a softer fiber. These softer cottons are excellent choices for crocheted wearables.

Linen comes from flax plants, one of the oldest sources of textiles. Linen was used in Egypt during the time of the pharaohs and dates to at least 5000 BCE. Its advantages are great: strength, durability, and luster. The fiber is naturally stiff, which gives good definition to stitches but works against drape. On the other hand, linen softens considerably over time with wear and washing, so it can make excellent wearables, depending on the weight of the yarn and the stitches used in a project.

Hemp is another fiber sometimes seen in yarns that derives from the cannabis plant. It is quite stiff and therefore is best used for items like bags or belts. It can also be rough on the fingers and hands.

Rayon and viscose are fibers made by chemically treating a substance, usually wood pulp, to soften it into a liquid. The liquid is then forced through an extruding device, something like a showerhead, from which it emerges as very long thin strands, which are spun into yarns. These fibers can be lustrous and have excellent drape, but they do not breathe well. They are often used in blended yarns to soften other stiffer fibers and to make a yarn more durable. In recent years, bamboo, milk, and a variety of other substances have been turned into yarns using this process.

Synthetic Fibers

Synthetic fibers commonly used in yarns are acrylic and nylon. Acrylic is soft and warm, but unlike natural fibers, it is not resilient or strong, cannot retain its shape, and is prone to pilling. Acrylic yarns vary in quality, with the best having a soft hand and attractive luster. As for nylon, it is generally used in sock yarns to add durability.

Yarn Manufacturing

Most yarns you see, whether in a big-box store or a small independent yarn shop, are manufactured by one of a handful of mills located in China, South America, Turkey, and Italy, with a few in the United States and Canada. These large mills make yarn for use in the textile industry; yarns for knitting and crocheting by hand are just a tiny part of their operations. Yarn companies work with these mills to create the products they think will be most enticing to consumers, changing fibers, weights, types of spin, and colors each season. With the limited number of mills across the world, inevitably you will see very similar yarns crop up across different yarn companies. Each company selects colors and packaging materials that distinguish its brand from competitors.

Yarn manufacturing for hand crochet and knitting is a relatively small industry, highly subject to that precarious segment of the economy: the consumer market. The industry's survival over the recent unstable economic period attests to the popularity of knitting and crochet.

Economy yarns are generally sold at large chain stores and represent by far the greatest segment of the yarn market. Smaller yarn manufacturers' products are sold primarily in independent yarn shops and increasingly online.

Manufacturers must balance desirable qualities in a yarn against its cost, and the price of the yarn will reflect those decisions. Yarns made to appeal to the budget-conscious shopper will use less natural fiber, which is more costly than synthetics, or else natural fibers of a lesser quality. More economical manufacturing means that color, nuance, and texture of the yarn may be sacrificed. Such workhorse yarns are made for durability and washability, with less emphasis on softness, subtle color variation, and the individual characteristics of different fibers.

A yarn shop offers a much greater selection of fibers and much more variation in price and quality than a big-box store. You will probably find shelves organized according to yarn weights. If you haven't explored many yarn shops, start by comparing yarns of the same weight and fiber from several manufacturers, choosing a popular type of yarn, such as 100 percent merino worsted or sock weight. Don't look at the price tag until you've spent some time ogling and fondling. You'll notice that color palettes vary, as does the twist and ply in the yarns, yielding many different surfaces and textures. Which ones appeal to your touch and eye? Armed with the knowledge in this chapter, choose a couple of skeins of some unfamiliar fiber and play with them!

If you enjoy buying from local artisanal producers, visit the fiber fairs and sheep festivals that happen all over the United States. There you'll find handspinners and dyers who devote a great deal of labor to every step of their production process, thereby producing yarns of great character and individuality.

> **All natural!** Some small yarn producers aim to produce more natural yarns and therefore specialize in minimally processed yarns, leaving natural substances, like lanolin, in the wool. You may also find tiny bits of foreign matter in the yarn, but this should not cause concern. Lanolin-rich wool has a characteristic feel and smell, which some people treasure and others dislike.

Spinning and Twisting

Humans have been spinning natural fibers for millennia, and the essential process has remained the same. Spinning is a process whereby millions of short lengths of fiber called staples are combined and subjected to simultaneous stretching and twisting, allowing them to adhere to one another, creating a single continuous strand of yarn.

In our modern manufacturing world, many steps turn the unprocessed animal, plant, or raw synthetic fiber into the product you buy as a ball or skein of yarn. Before being spun, natural fibers must be cleaned, then combed and carded. The carding machine separates the fibers and turns them into a thin web of fibers running more or less parallel. Other devices further elongate and tame the fibers into slivers (bundles) to make them ready for spinning.

Yarns derived from animal fibers are made by twisting these slivers. Some yarns are spun very tightly, others less so. This is largely dependent on the fibers. Shorter fibers such as merino and cashmere require more twist to hold them together; longer-staple fibers such as alpaca and silk require less. The degree of twist has a significant impact on the strength of the yarn, with more twist yielding a stronger and more compact yarn and low twist making a lighter, softer yarn. Fabric made with high-twist yarns will not wrinkle or pill as easily as those made with low twist. You can see how tightly spun a yarn is by observing the angle of twist: the closer to parallel with the strand of yarn, the looser, the more perpendicular, the tighter.

The Effect of Plying

Twisting fibers into a single continuous thread results in a single ply of yarn, often simply called a single. By convention, singles are spun with a Z twist, with the slant rising as it goes from left to right. When additional plies are added, they are twisted in the opposite direction, in an S twist, with the slant lowering as it goes from left to right.

Understanding Twist

Get to know how your yarn was made: Look closely at the yarn end to determine if it has been plied with an S or Z twist. Then notice whether it's been spun tightly or loosely by looking at the angle of the twist. Now unravel the end a little. How many plies are there?

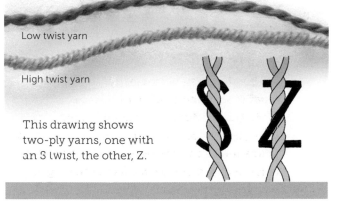

Low twist yarn

High twist yarn

This drawing shows two-ply yarns, one with an S twist, the other, Z.

Whether a yarn is spun with an S or Z twist can impact on a yarn's utility for crochet; since yarnovers are made in the direction of the S, loosely plied yarns may unravel and cause stitches to look untidy.

All yarns begin as a single ply, but only some are practical in this form; most yarns have several plies. Adding more plies improves the regularity of texture and color. But long-staple fibers such as alpaca and silk can make beautiful singles on their own, and single ply yarns are excellent in crochet. The unplied, single strand is a plain surface that allows a stitch pattern to show up very cleanly and clearly.

Yarns can have two, three, four, or more plies, with each additional ply giving the yarn more strength. The additional plies do not

Unplied single-strand yarn

necessarily make the yarn thick, though, since the strands being twisted together may be very thin. Sometimes the plies are very obvious on the yarn's surface, and sometimes they are more smoothly integrated. Note this characteristic when matching a yarn with a stitch pattern. Pronounced plies add complexity that, when combined with intricate stitch patterns, can make the surface overly busy.

Why Some Yarns Pill

Spinning and plying yarns make them less subject to pilling, though some may still occur. The problem starts with tiny ends of fibers that protrude from the surface. When fabric is subjected to friction from wear — under the arm on sweaters or on the heels of socks, for example — these tiny ends pull free from the fabric and twist around one another to form pills. Fibers composed of shorter fibers — merino, cashmere, angora, and some acrylics — are more apt to pill because there are more tiny ends that can become pills. Longer-haired fibers, like mohair, alpaca, and silk, have fewer protruding ends and fewer pills. Pills on shorter fibers can often be pulled off easily, but when they occur in long-haired fibers they should be handled with more care: if you hear a ripping sound as you try to pull off a pill, it means the fiber is still connected to the main body of the fabric. Avoid pulling out such pills; rather, cut them off with scissors or a sweater shaver.

Yarn Weights

Yarns come in a variety of weights, and the Craft Yarn Council (CYC), an industry body that aims to promote and standardize yarns, has come up with a numerical system indicating the weight of a yarn.

Bulky or super-bulky. Clearly, heavier-weight yarns yield larger stitches and a thicker fabric with more body and less flexibility than fabric made with thinner yarn. Bulky or super-bulky yarns are best for projects where thick fabric is desirable, such as a warm winter hat, a rug, or a sturdy, structured purse.

Worsted. Many crocheters consider worsted-weight yarn to be classic and use it almost exclusively for all their projects. Though worsted is more versatile than bulky yarn, it's important to consider the size of stitches and quality of fabric. Solid fabric of worsted works well for outerwear garments such as jackets, hats, and mitts, but may be too stiff for other wearables. Worsted-weight yarns are also excellent for afghans, where they provide sufficient heft. Worsted looks great in a simple traditional granny square, but more delicate or complex open stitches are often more attractive in a thinner yarn.

Double-knitting, or DK, yarn is slightly thinner than worsted, and that difference allows this weight to be more suitable for indoor

For Something Different

Some yarns are not plied at all, but rather formed out of a knitted tube, sometimes called chainette. They tend to be flatter and more tapelike than spun yarns and have the advantage of being light in weight compared to their thickness, since the center of the tube is hollow. This is good yarn for crochet, as yarn constructed this way is far less dense and heavy than its spun-and-twisted counterpart. On the other hand, the more a yarn departs from a tube shape and approaches a flat tape shape, the more distorted the crochet stitches appear.

Tube yarn

The Craft Yarn Council's numerical weight system

Balls and Skeins! Yarns are sold either in balls or skeins, and most of the high-end yarns are sold in skeins that need to be wound before using them. Yarn shops will wind the skeins into balls for you, but a swift and a winder are tools I highly recommend for those who are serious about their craft (see page 32).

If your yarn is already packaged in balls, start by drawing out the yarn from the center of the ball rather than the outside. It's much more convenient, because the ball will not roll away when handled.

garments, such as sweaters, depending on the fiber. An afghan made of DK yarn can also make a more supple fabric than one made with worsted, since the stitches are smaller and the fabric not as thick.

Sport, fingering, and lace. These remaining categories are the most crochet-friendly of all. These thinner yarns can be used in solid fabric with no holes and still have good drape, and openwork lace will be more attractive, clean, and legible with smaller stitches. For garments such as sweaters, skirts, and shawls, thinner yarns are excellent choices. Most sock yarns qualify as sport or fingering, but take note of the nylon content in sock yarns, which can make a garment that doesn't breathe well. If the nylon content is 10 percent or less it should be fine. Fingering- and lace-weight yarns are naturally the most appropriate for creating delicate, fluid fabric for shawls and will show off intricate lace patterns to best advantage.

A Few Caveats

Certain fibers, such as mohair, alpaca, and some synthetics, have a halo of fuzz around the strand of yarn. This can impart an interesting and attractive quality to the work, softening the look of the stitches. But keep in mind that even though the strand of yarn itself may appear thin, the fuzz means the yarn should be treated as a heavier weight. It may look like lace or fingering, for example, but it will behave more like worsted. Don't be tempted to work such yarns with small hooks!

While the CYC's numerical system is a helpful indication of a yarn's weight, *the categories are not always strictly adhered to by yarn manufacturers*. You will find yarns labeled "worsted" that are really more like bulky, and sport or DK yarns that are more like worsted! Even lace-weight yarns vary greatly in thickness. Do not despair, however; every yarn can be evaluated by making swatches and observing the results.

Total Yarn Weight

If you are making a project with many skeins of yarn, think about the total weight of that project when done. For an indoor wearable, more than a pound or two is not desirable. Fabric that is heavy in weight is likely to stretch out of shape, regardless of its fiber content.

When choosing yarn for a project, balance issues of drape, warmth, weight of yarn, and color selection. If you really want to use a particular stitch, then it's important to make that your starting point, and search for the yarn that shows it off best. For intricate stitches, a smooth yarn is usually the best choice. If speed is your main consideration, go with the heaviest weight that project can bear, but choose a stitch or hook size that will not make the fabric too dense. For indoor wearables, choose a lightweight fiber and a thinner yarn that feels good on the skin.

Specialty Yarns

In addition to the standard plied yarns we've examined thus far, there are yarns with special characteristics that give us even more possibilities. These yarns are usually quite complex and therefore should be used with simple stitches where the attention is on the yarn itself.

Thick-and-thin yarns are usually singles where the thickness of the strand is intentionally varied. They create great surface texture, but complex patterns will be distorted because the stitches are not of uniform size. Choose the hook size based on the thickest part of the yarn.

Bouclé yarns are created during plying by introducing one ply more quickly than another, causing a doubling back of the strand that in turn yields the characteristic loopy look. Here again, this type of yarn will add great texture but will not show individual stitches well.

Ribbon and tape yarns have strands that are not spherical in shape, but flat. Crochet stitches will not look uniform, but they can still look great in a project where the emphasis is on color and texture.

Hand-Dyed Yarns

The importance and appeal of color in yarn cannot be denied, and the past several years have seen a great flourishing of richly colored yarns made using a variety of processes. Among the yarn companies known for their beautiful hand-dyed yarns are the American companies Lorna's Laces and Madelinetosh; Malabrigo from Uruguay; and the Japanese company Noro; but there are many more. There are also smaller producers who create one-of-a-kind yarns that can be purchased at fiber festivals across the country. New techniques are constantly surfacing to enable ever more subtle and varied use of color.

A hand-dyed light merino

Crocheting with Specialty Yarns

Specialty yarns can be put to great use in crochet, as long as stitches are kept simple and the gauge is sufficiently loose to keep the fabric from becoming bulky or heavy.

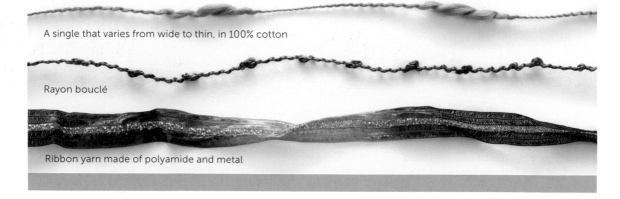

A single that varies from wide to thin, in 100% cotton

Rayon bouclé

Ribbon yarn made of polyamide and metal

Fabric and Drape

One of the reasons crochet is not always given the respect it deserves has to do with the drape of its fabric. Drape refers to the suppleness and flexibility of fabric; it is the opposite of stiff. Fabric with good drape hangs well on the body, and even an afghan is more attractive if its fabric is fluid and not rigid.

As mentioned earlier, when crochet came into its own in the nineteenth century, people worked with very thin threads, and drape was not a problem. But by the mid-twentieth century, most yarn enthusiasts were accustomed to working with fairly thick yarns, like worsted weight. Compared to knitting, crochet is thicker and bulkier — it's just the nature of the stitches, and no one is to blame! Still, if we want good drape in our crochet fabric, there are plenty of ways to get it. You just have to know how.

Projects will serve their purpose better, and look better, if the quality of drape is carefully considered when choosing yarn, hook size, and stitch pattern. Fabric of any kind, whether handmade or manufactured, can range from fluid and flexible to rigid and dense. Neither quality is good or bad, but it must suit the project you have in mind, both in terms of function and appearance.

Not every project needs drape. A more sturdy and structured fabric is well suited to *amigurumi* (usually small stuffed animals with a crocheted outer surface), bags, and often (but not always) outerwear such as hats and jackets. For *amigurumi*, though most of the structure is supplied by the filling, stiff fabric helps create a durable project that holds its shape over time. Similarly, a purse or tote with some rigidity to the fabric will maintain its shape and last with wear. Other kinds of bags, such as a market bag or backpack, can be less structured.

With outerwear, if the purpose is to provide warmth, a thicker fabric is desirable, and therefore the fabric may not be as drapey, nor need it be. Too rigid, however, and the item — whether a scarf, hat, or jacket — can be uncomfortable to wear, as it will feel heavy and can impede movement.

Projects that benefit from a fluid fabric include shawls and indoor garments such as sweaters, summer tops, and baby clothes. The fabric for these wearables should easily fold and mold around the body, making the item both more attractive and more comfortable.

Crocheters can achieve the amount of drape or structure appropriate for their project by carefully considering the factors discussed on the following pages.

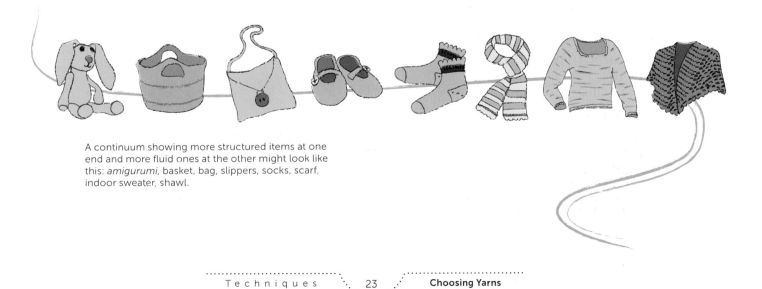

A continuum showing more structured items at one end and more fluid ones at the other might look like this: *amigurumi*, basket, bag, slippers, socks, scarf, indoor sweater, shawl.

The Effect of Yarn Weight and Fiber on Drape

Drape has a lot to do with the thickness of the fabric: the thinner it is, the more drape is likely. Working with lighter weight yarns — sport, fingering, or lace — is a simple way to achieve this quality. Yet a thin yarn composed of stiff fibers, whether cotton, linen, or certain acrylics, still may not yield sufficient drape. By contrast, a worsted or even bulky yarn consisting of alpaca, silk, or bamboo can yield a fluid fabric, especially if worked in a stitch pattern that is open and loose. The point to remember is that no one factor alone determines the quality of drape, but all of them contribute and interact with one another.

How Hook Size Affects Drape

You probably will not be surprised to learn that smaller hooks create denser fabric, and larger ones, looser and more fluid fabric. Most weights of yarn can be worked with a range of hooks, so one has considerable leeway here. If you tend to stick with the same yarn weight and hook size most of the time, you are missing out on one of the key ways to control the density or drape of your finished fabric.

Hook Size Experiment

Make this swatch with different yarn weights *and* a variety of hook sizes. It can be quite eye-opening! Compare the photos of swatches at right, and then try your own experiments.

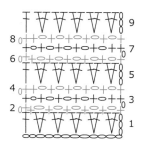

Note

> If you are unfamiliar with an abbreviation, please see Abbreviations and Basic Stitches (page 244).

Ch a multiple of 2, plus 1 end st, plus 4 for tch. (*ch 15 for swatch*)

Row 1 2 dc in 5th ch from hook, *sk 1 ch, 2 dc in next ch, rep from * across, sk 1 ch, dc in last ch, turn.

Row 2 Ch 1, sc in first dc, sc between first and second dc, *ch 1, sk 2 dc, sc between next 2 dc, rep from * across to last 3 sts, ch 1, sk 2 dc, sc in tch, turn.

Row 3 Ch 1, sc in first sc, *sc in next ch-1 sp, ch 1, rep from * across to last 2 sc, sk next sc, sc in next sc, turn.

Row 4 Rep row 3.

Row 5 Ch 3 (counts as dc), 2 dc in first ch-1 sp, *sk next sc, 2 dc in next ch-1 sp, rep from * across to last 2 sc, sk next sc, dc in last sc, turn.

Rep rows 2–5 for pattern.

High-twist DK merino worked
with a US F/5 (3.75 mm) hook

High-twist DK merino worked
with a US H/8 (5 mm) hook

High-twist DK merino worked
with a US J/10 (6 mm) hook

Stitch Density and Stitch Height

In addition to the size of the hook, density of fabric is determined by whether the stitch pattern is closed or open. Stitches that make a solid fabric with no holes are closed stitches, while lacy stitches leave gaps in the fabric and are called open. Crochet offers a wide range of stitch patterns in the open category, from those that are semisolid with just a bit of open space, to very open, with more air than fabric. The more open, the more drape. A throw made with worsted-weight yarn and a solid stitch pattern is likely to be warm and heavy, and may be just what you want; but if you're after an airy effect, as in a decorative throw that can be casually tossed over a chair or couch in luxurious folds, then a more open stitch pattern is a better choice.

The heights of stitches also affect drape. Shorter stitches yield a denser fabric; taller ones lend more drape. Single crochet is a very dense stitch, which is why it is used for *amigurumi*. Slip stitch crochet, which is gaining popularity, is the densest of all, yet it's possible to make drapey fabric with these stitches by using a very large hook. Plain rows of double or treble crochet stitches naturally lend more drape, because they create a fabric that is not really closed: the stitches are connected only at the bottom and top, and the posts of the stitches tend to separate from one another, leading to greater flexibility in the fabric. If you don't find plain rows of tall stitches appealing, there are countless stitch patterns that employ taller stitches.

On the following two pages, you'll find examples of two stitch patterns that are considered lace. Both are crocheted with a fairly stiff fingering-weight cotton, but they result in different degrees of drape.

Medium Open Lace

Work these two stitch patterns with the same yarn and hook to see how a much more open stitch affects drape.

Ch a multiple of 10, plus 1 end st, plus 1 for tch. (*ch 32 for swatch*)

Row 1 Sc in 2nd ch from hook, *sc in next ch, sk 3 ch, (2 dc, ch 3, 2 dc) in next ch, sk 3 ch, sc in next ch**, ch 1, sk next ch, rep from * ending last rep at **, sc in last ch, turn.

Row 2 Ch 2, hdc in first sc, *ch 3, sc in next ch-3 sp, ch 3**, (hdc, ch 1, hdc) in next ch-1 sp, rep from * across, ending last rep at **, 2 hdc in last sc, turn.

Row 3 Ch 4 (counts as dc, ch 1), 2 dc in first hdc, *sc in next ch-3 sp, ch 1, sc in next ch-3 sp**, (2 dc, ch 3, 2 dc) in next ch-1 sp, rep from * across, ending last rep at **, (2 dc, ch 1, dc) in tch, turn.

Row 4 Ch 1, sc in first dc, *ch 3, (hdc, ch 1, hdc) in next ch-1 sp, ch 3**, sc in next ch-3 sp, rep from * across, ending last rep at **, sc in 3rd ch of tch, turn.

Row 5 Ch 1, sc in first sc, *sc in next ch-3 sp, (2 dc, ch 3, 2 dc) in next ch-1 sp, sc in next ch-3 sp**, ch 1, rep from * across, ending last rep at **, sc in last sc, turn.

Rep rows 2–5 for pattern.

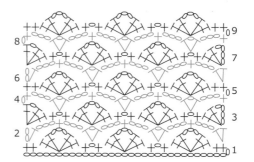

Very Open Lace

This more open pattern would be a better choice than the previous one for any project requiring excellent drape.

Ch multiple of 12, plus 3. (*ch 27 for swatch*)

Row 1 (Sc, ch 3, sc) in 3rd ch from hook, *ch 2, sk 5 ch, ([dc, ch 1] four times, dc) in next ch, ch 2, sk 5 ch, (sc, ch 3, sc) in next ch, rep from * across, turn.

Row 2 Ch 4 (counts as dc, ch 1 throughout), dc in ch-3 sp, *ch 2, [(sc, ch 3, sc) in next ch-1 sp] four times, ch 2, (dc, ch 1, dc) in next ch-3 sp, rep from * across, turn.

Row 3 Ch 1, (sc, ch 3, sc) in first ch-1 sp, *ch 3, sk next ch-3 sp, sc in next ch-3 sp, ch 3, sc in next ch-3 sp, ch 3, (sc, ch 3, sc) in next ch-1 sp, rep from * across, turn.

Row 4 Ch 4, dc in ch-3 sp, *ch 2, sk 1 sc, ([dc, ch 1] four times, dc) in next ch-3 sp, ch 2, sk 1 sc, (dc, ch 1, dc) in next ch-3 sp, rep from * across, turn.

Rep rows 2–4 for pattern.

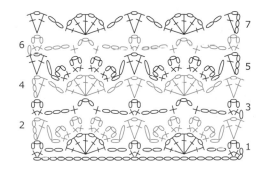

Another Key to Drape: Working in One Loop Only

Working in the front loop or back loop only, rather than the default method of working both loops of the stitch, also adds drape. (See page 66 for all the different ways to insert your hook.) You'll notice that when working under one loop, the single loop stretches much more than when working under two, adding flexibility to the fabric. Since the unworked loop may be visible on the surface or right side of the fabric, it must be considered a design element as well. If it works with the visual surface you want to create, by all means use this to add drape to your project. If not, you can find other solutions.

Strategies That Lend Drape to a Project

- Thinner yarn

- Flexible fibers, such as alpaca, bamboo, silk, viscose

- Large hook

- Open stitch pattern

- Tall stitches

- Working only in front or back loop

Suppose you are seeking not drape, but more structure for your project. You can add thickness and rigidity by doing the opposite of the strategies recommended for drape: choose a heavier yarn, a smaller hook, shorter stitches, and a closed stitch pattern. Textured stitches like bobbles, puffs, and post stitches (see chapter 8) add bulk and create a denser fabric with more structure.

A Final Thought: Yarn Substitution

It should be clear from all this information that substituting a yarn in a pattern requires careful consideration. Use the same weight yarn, but remember that each category covers a range of yarns: not all worsteds, for example, are the same thickness.

One way to see whether your chosen yarn matches the yarn used in a pattern is to check the label and see if the weight *as well as the yardage* match. This is an indication that the fibers are similar, at least as far as heaviness. If your chosen yarn is the same weight, say 3.5 ounces, but has fewer yards, it is a heavier fiber; if it has more yardage for the same weight, it is a lighter fiber. In either case, the difference may detract from the finished project. The better matched these two variables are, the more likely you'll succeed.

Other characteristics of fibers, such as shine and drape, are also important considerations. Silk lends yarn a particular sheen, as does alpaca, which also gives great drape (though it's heavy). The fuzziness of alpaca resists stitch definition, and its slipperiness means bulky stitches don't bulk. All these qualities can be assets in certain projects.

Light and dark colors affect the legibility of stitches. When you want strong stitch definition, single-ply yarns, or very high-twist soft merinos, are perfect. They'll really make cables pop. Fuzzy yarns have the opposite effect, muting the definition of each individual stitch and creating a softer look.

The more you experiment and work with different fibers, weights, spins, and plies of yarn, the better your judgments about substitutions. In fact, all the material we have considered in this chapter is important for the crocheter to understand. You'll find that as you gain experience working with a variety of yarns, you can do so much more with your crochet. Only with this kind of knowledge can you make quality wearables, create projects that perform their function well and last, and have success with any stitch or technique you try.

2

The Crochet Toolbox

JUST AS IT'S IMPORTANT TO understand and work with a variety of yarns, the well-informed crocheter should be equipped with the proper tools. The right hook can make all the difference in working with a particular yarn or stitch. Blocking boards and swifts are additional tools that are well worth investing in if your goal is to achieve outstanding results in crochet.

Hooks

Today, more manufacturers are making hooks than ever before, and we have exceptional variety in our choice of crochet hooks. They come in a range of materials, including aluminum, plastic, steel, wood, and bamboo, and each company shapes the hook to its own specifications. The hook has several parts, and small variations in how these parts are shaped can make the hook easier to work with, or more suitable for certain yarns than others.

Preference for one type of hook over another is a very personal matter, but before you decide to stick with one kind of hook, try a variety of materials and shapes so you can compare their merits. Though I have my preference for certain hooks, I still find that having a variety of hook styles is important. Here are some criteria you'll want to consider when picking a hook of one material or another:

- How light or heavy is it?

- Is it cool or warm to the touch?

- Does it slide in and out of stitches without any friction?

- Is the handle a comfortable size for you to hold?

- Is the thumb rest placed correctly for your hand?

The shaft of the hook is what determines the hook size. Having hooks in a variety of sizes allows you to work at many gauges.

There are numerous small variations in how the head of the hook is shaped, with some being very pointed at the top and others more rounded and bulbous. Each manufacturer has its own variation, and you will find a range of shapes between these two extremes. Many crocheters find this to be an important factor when choosing the best hook for a project because it affects how well the hook slides into the work when inserting the hook into stitches. Pointy hooks are useful when maneuvering the hook into small or tight stitches, but they tend to split yarn more readily. More rounded hooks do not cause splitting and are a good choice with yarns that split easily.

Some hooks are shaped with a deep angle in the throat, and others taper more gradually. You may find this feature affects the ease of making stitches, including how well yarns stay on the hook, which can be a concern when working with slippery yarn.

As you can see from this chart, the size of a hook may be indicated in several different ways. This can be confusing. Some manufacturers use letters to designate the size, some use numbers, but the crucial information is the metric measurement of the hook's shaft (see the photo on opposite page). This should appear on any hook you want to use.

HOOK SIZES	
METRIC (MM)	US
2.25	B/1
2.5, 2.75	C/2
3.0, 3.25	D/3
3.5	E/4
3.75, 4.0	F/5
4.0, 4.25	G/6
4.5	7
5	H/8
5.5	I/9
6.0	J/10
6.5, 7.0	K/10.5
8	L/11
9	M, N/13
10	N, P/15
15	P, Q
16	Q
19	S

Try a smaller hook! Learning to work with smaller hooks and thinner yarns is a definite advantage for crocheters. If you are interested in developing your skill with smaller hooks, begin by going down one hook size from what you normally use, and work with it for a while until you feel comfortable. Then proceed to the next size down. You may be amazed at how simple the adjustment is, and you will probably like the work that's coming off your hooks very much. Of course, as you decrease the size of the hook, choose thinner yarns to work with as well. If you've never worked with anything thinner than a worsted, try a DK next, then move on to sport, sock, and fingering yarns.

Many hooks are designed with a thumb rest, which is meant to provide hand comfort. Whether the grip suits your hand has to do with the size of your hand in relation to the hook. A few hooks have no thumb rest, and these are particularly useful when working small pieces in Tunisian crochet, since stitches can be left on the hook without concern about distorting the loops.

With increased interest in hand health, hooks are now offered with special handles designed to promote ease and comfort. They are very useful for those with arthritis, tendonitis, or repetitive stress injuries. The hook handles are larger so that the grip can be held more loosely, and special

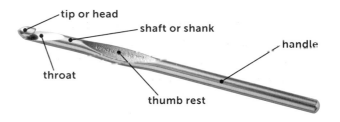

materials are used so the tool is softer to the touch. They are very pleasant to work with. If you crochet for many hours at a time, I highly recommend these ergonomically shaped hooks to promote healthy hands over the long term, even if you have no health conditions.

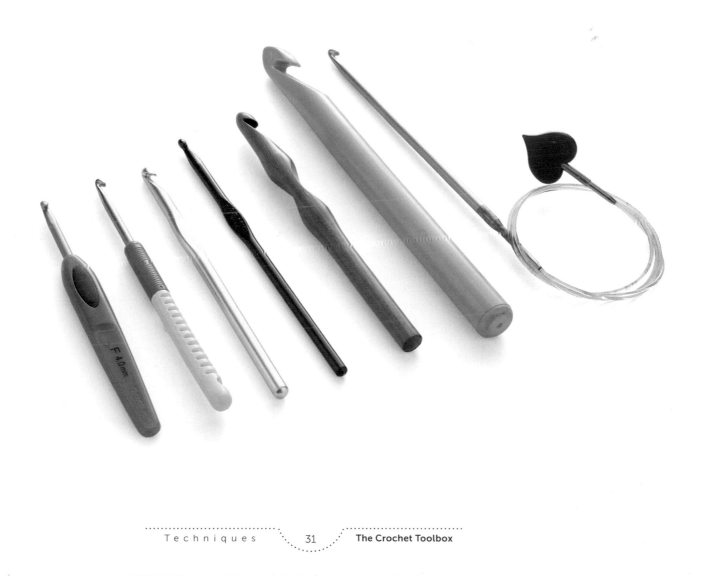

Other Tools

An essential tool for finishing crochet work is a tapestry needle. It is used for weaving in ends and for sewing seams. Tapestry needles come in different styles, some straight and others curved. The latter can help you work into tight spots. They also come in different lengths and thicknesses, and with different-sized eyes. I tend to use the shortest lengths and smallest eye that will work with the yarn at hand, but this is a matter of preference.

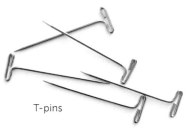

Tapestry needle

You will find patterns that require you to mark certain stitches as reference points, usually so you can count stitches on either side of that point. This can be done with a safety pin, but there are also plastic stitch markers sold at crafts stores that work well. Stitch markers for crochet are different than those used in knitting — make sure you have the kind that can be opened and attached to a stitch, rather than a closed ring. The marker can be placed anywhere on the stitch that's convenient.

While many crocheters are reluctant to block their work, I hope the Finishing Techniques chapter (page 196) will convince you to try. Blocking can improve the finished project immeasurably and is necessary for lace work. I highly recommend a commercial blocking board with a grid showing inches and/or centimeters. Blocking boards are firm surfaces with built-in padding, into which one can stick pins. Some fold up for convenient storage. The grid is important to enable blocking to precise measurements, and it can be used to get a truly accurate measurement for a blocked swatch as well.

Along with the board, you will need T-pins to hold the work in place. Find T-pins that are treated for rust resistance — most are nickel plated for this reason. If you can find some that are rust*proof*,

even better. Most on the market are rust resistant, and over time, they may show signs of rust. To avoid stains on your work, discard them and get new ones if this happens. T-pins come in various sizes, and I find the 1-inch pins are perfect, because they are thin and slide easily into the blocking board.

T-pins

Two great tools that go together are the yarn swift and ball winder. There are numerous designs for swifts, but crafters generally find an umbrella swift simpler and less costly than other options.

The swift is clamped to a table for stability. One end of the yarn is placed on a ball winder, which has a handle to turn, causing the yarn to feed from the swift to the ball winder, where it becomes a ball instead of a skein. There are also electric ball winders that turn automatically. Swifts are excellent time-saving devices that last for years, and they are well worth the investment if you use skeined yarns.

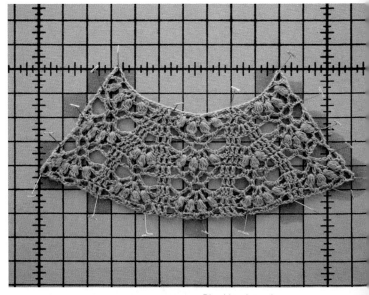

Blocking board

Controlling Tension

AN AREA OF CROCHET education that receives too little attention is developing good control of tension. People say, "I'm a tight crocheter," or the opposite, "I crochet very loosely," often with the sense that there is little to be done about it. Whichever camp you're in, please consider that it *is* possible to upgrade your control of tension with practice. Knowing how to vary your tension according to the demands of a project is a great skill to cultivate, and it can be done — once you decide change is possible.

Because this type of education is hard to come by, in this chapter I examine tension control in great detail. Practice of these stitches and techniques will improve how your crochet feels, how it looks, and how the fabric behaves. Mastering these skills will enable you to work some of the more complex maneuvers needed for stitches like cables, tapestry crochet, very tall stitches, and more.

Before we discuss this topic in greater detail, it's worth considering whether your tools and environment are suitable for optimal stitching.

Notice whether your hands and eyes are working well together to help you control the size and evenness of stitches. Can you see well where you work? Is the seating comfortable? Are you rushing, or relaxing and enjoying the process?

Notice, too, the feel of the yarn. Is it stretchy or stiff? Does it glide easily on the hook or offer resistance? Have you chosen the right hook for the project, or do you need one that's pointier or more rounded?

We discussed the characteristics of various fibers in chapter 1. Once a yarn is on the hook, you can discern some of these qualities. There are very slippery fibers, such as alpaca or silk, where you may find using a bamboo or wood hook offers a bit of helpful resistance. A yarn that splits easily can be more comfortably worked with a rounded hook. There are many variables at work, so make sure you start out comfortable with your materials and tools.

Is there an optimal tension for every yarn? Though most yarns can definitely be worked in more than one gauge, learn to notice the difference between yarn that is being worked too tightly and one that is being worked in a gauge that lets the fibers breathe and bloom. Keep in mind that while tight stitches can look very neat, they will make the fabric stiff (see pages 196 and 207).

Let's look at how the hands work best to control tension as you work. As the strand of yarn wends its way from the ball to the hand holding the yarn, then to the hook and the work itself, the degree of tension in that strand of yarn must be controlled. This job belongs to the hand, not the hook. Not everyone holds their yarn the same way, but however it's done, the yarn-holding hand feeds the yarn to your other hand at a certain tension. Thread crocheters, aiming for the type of tight, highly defined stitches used in their art, wrap thread several times around their fingers to keep the required tension.

For yarn crochet, learning to have a relaxed hand is an important skill; I've seen too many crocheters struggling to control the hook, the yarn, and the tension, and it's usually because their hands are tense. So remember, *relax*, and you can actually gain control and stop fighting with your tools!

Sometimes tight stitches occur because the crocheter tugs at each stitch with the yarn-holding hand to make it "neat." The stitches may indeed look neat, but the resulting fabric is likely to be stiff instead of fluid. See what happens if you relax, omit that tug after completing the stitch, and let each stitch breathe.

Flexible Tension

In addition to finding a relaxed position for the hands and wrists, practice varying the tension as you work stitches. The truth is, not every stitch requires the exact same degree of tension; sometimes you may have to loosen a bit, sometimes you need to tighten. I like to call this skill "flexible tension," and I encourage you to develop it. Once you are free to tighten or ease up as needed, you can really sculpt individual stitches and give a fabulous finish to your crochet. You can also handle with ease some of the more complex stitches, such as crossed and cabled stitches, if you acquire flexible control of tension.

If how you maneuver the yarn and hook is getting in the way, consider developing a different technique. It may be that your grip is too tight, or the yarn is not flowing freely through your yarn-holding hand. Some people have the opposite problem: they stitch very loosely. If you have tension issues, try the tips on the next page.

It does take time to change one's work habits, but if you have consistent trouble meeting gauge for projects, or are unable to do certain stitches and techniques, it is well worth the effort. Remember that crochet is a motor skill, like sports or playing a musical instrument. Such behaviors are acquired slowly and don't change easily, but once the change is made, it will stick, and you will be more comfortable and capable in your crochet.

Let's look at areas in which control of tension is important, so you can see how this skill will improve the look and feel of your projects.

Holding the Yarn

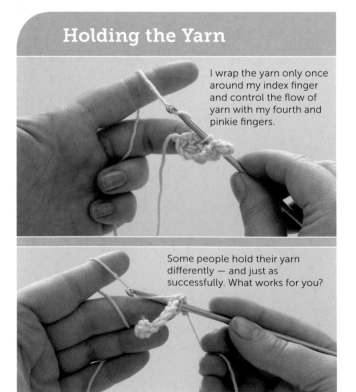

I wrap the yarn only once around my index finger and control the flow of yarn with my fourth and pinkie fingers.

Some people hold their yarn differently — and just as successfully. What works for you?

Loosen Up

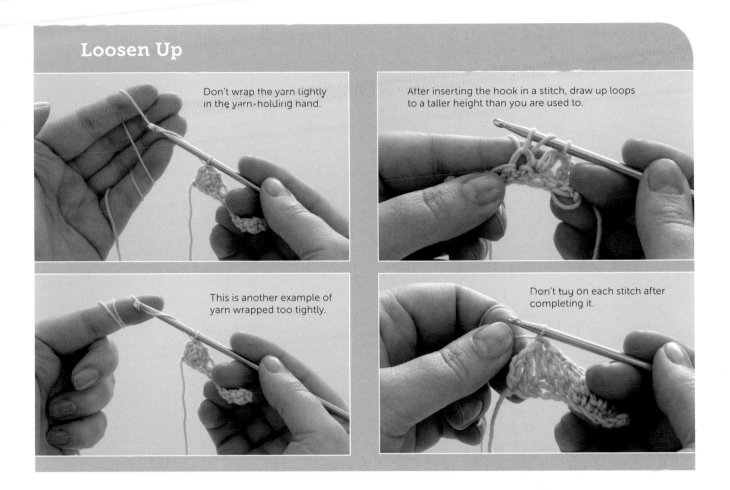

Don't wrap the yarn lightly in the yarn-holding hand.

After inserting the hook in a stitch, draw up loops to a taller height than you are used to.

This is another example of yarn wrapped too tightly.

Don't tug on each stitch after completing it.

Tighten Up

Bring your hands closer to the work. You can also use the yarn-holding hand to hold the work as you crochet. Raise the index finger of your yarn-holding hand and use it to keep the yarn more taut. You can tug slightly at the work with this finger any time you see your stitch getting too loose.

Working the Starting Chain

Where else to begin but the humble starting chain? It sets the stage for your work and must be the size of the stitches that will follow in subsequent rows or rounds. If the chains are worked very tightly, the starting edge of your work will be too short, and it will be hard to work stitches into them on the next row or round. A foundation chain worked too tightly will affect the dimensions of the finished item, for example, making the neckline of a sweater too small, or causing puckering at the edges of a throw. For all these reasons, it's wise to work starting chains at a loose tension.

Working Turning Chains

The turning chain consists of chain stitches made at the start of a new row or round, and their purpose is to bring your hook up to the proper height for the stitches that will follow. If these chains are too loose, there will be a gap between the turning chain and the second stitch of the row or round. If too tight, the edge of the work will pull the fabric and cause bulges near the edges.

> **Edges really count!** With proper control of the size of chain stitches, you can ensure that the foundation and side edges are even, stable, and match the dimensions of your work.

Loosening a Starting Chain

Insert the hook into the previous chain deep enough to get to the wider part of the hook's shaft. Make the chain, and pull it out just a bit, bringing it to the proper size to match your other rows.

You might wonder, *How do I know the size of stitches in rows I haven't worked yet?* Well, this comes with time. When you are working on projects, observe the size of the tops of stitches, and your judgment about the starting chain will become more accurate.

Pull the chain out a bit.

Tightening Chains

Sometimes tight chains are a good thing, as when they are part of a stitch pattern, as often happens in lace stitches (see page 26). Another instance in which tight chains are desirable is when working picots (see page 77).

If you have difficulty making tight chains, it may have to do with how you maneuver the hook while drawing it through a stitch. Try to swivel your hook so it points down. Lack of swiveling may be a problem that is causing other stitches to be too loose as well.

Swivel your hook so that it points down.

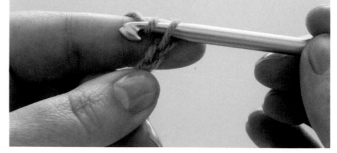

Turning Chain Tension

This is what it looks like if your turning chain is too loose . . .

too tight . . .

just right.

Adjusting Stitch Height

A common problem when trying to match gauge is that row gauge is too small compared to what's given in the pattern. This can easily be resolved by loosening up at one crucial point: right after inserting your hook in the working stitch, when pulling up the first loop of the stitch (see Loosen Up, page 35).

Tall stitches are particularly useful when working clusters and shells (see, for example, pages 68 and 138) and when working stitches taller than double crochet — trebles, double trebles, and so forth. It is that first loop that should be lengthened, not necessarily those that come after.

Treble and double treble crochet can be troublesome for those who haven't mastered tension control. In these tall stitches, the yarn is drawn through 2 loops multiple times, and if tension is not well controlled, there is extra yarn lying slack at the top of the stitch. In this case, you want to exert more tension as you work the stitch (see Tighten Up, page 35).

Experiment with varying how tautly to pull the other loops of taller stitches. It really depends on what looks best with the stitch pattern, yarn, and gauge; in other words, it is an aesthetic decision.

Beware, though, of one situation in which the first loop of a tall stitch should *not* be pulled up tall, and that's when working several of them — whether double, treble, or taller stitches — into a chain space that consists of 3 or more chains. If the first loop is very loose, the stitches will not grab well around the series of chains and look sloppy. Here you want to make the first loop tighter, and if a tall stitch is desired, pull up on other parts of the stitch. See page 45 for an example.

Skipping Stitches

Many patterns require that you skip several stitches before inserting the hook into another stitch. This may result in the loop that's on your hook stretching out to an untidy length. To avoid this, use the index finger of your hook hand to hold yarnovers on the crochet hook in place. Rather than pulling the yarn to stretch the distance from one point to the other, bring the insertion point closer to the last stitch made by bringing your hands closer together.

Don't stretch out the loop on your hook too much.

Control the tension with your index finger.

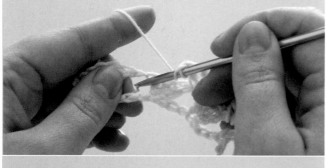

This is what you want.

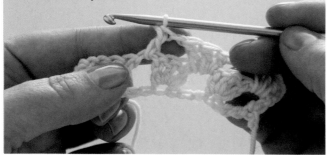

Practice with puffs and cables. As you continue to build the skill of flexible tension, try the stitch patterns in this book that involve puffs and cables. They provide excellent opportunities for practicing tension control. See pages 156 and 164 for these further opportunities to improve your stitching technique.

Hand Health

So intense is the love of crochet for many people that they lose sight of its potential to cause hand problems. Observe healthy habits that will not tire, stress, or injure your body. Because we often sit for many hours with our crochet, making the same movements repeatedly, it is an activity with the potential to cause injury. In the United States, the government agency charged with studying worker safety, Occupational Safety and Health Administration (OSHA), finds that common "ergonomic risk factors are found in jobs requiring repetitive, forceful, or prolonged exertions of the hands . . . and prolonged awkward postures." It goes without saying that if you develop serious discomfort, consult a medical professional.

If your crochet habits are causing you pain, change the way you crochet. Sure, this seems difficult and frustrating at first, but often simply changing how you grip the yarn or hook can have a very positive effect. Start by working very slowly, noticing exactly where you tend to grip and tighten — in the hand, wrist, upper arm, elbow, or even the neck and shoulders. Slowing down can also show you when the tension starts: is it while you insert the hook, while doing yarnovers, or at some other point? Once you've determined more precisely how and where the problem begins, you can coax the muscles to stay calm while you make another stitch. It certainly takes time to remove tension completely and consistently, but imagine how much better life can be if you can crochet pain-free!

Tips for Safe Crocheting

- **Find a comfortable chair.** Sit in a comfortable chair with good back support.

- **Heads up.** To avoid neck pain or strain, keep your head up rather than hanging down to peer at work in your lap.

- **Use armrests.** To raise the work closer to eye level, place an armrest or pillows under your arms.

- **Keep it light.** Work in an area that is well lit, either by natural daylight or strong bulbs.

- **Avoid tension.** Pay attention if you are feeling pain or discomfort in any part of the arm, wrist, or hand.

- **Take frequent breaks.** Do some hand and finger stretches to break from crochet.

- **Be efficient.** When crocheting, make small, efficient hand movements whenever possible. For example, if you habitually use large movements of the wrist while crocheting, see if you can accomplish the same maneuver with less movement by bringing your hands closer together, holding the work closer to your body, or changing the angle of your arms.

- **Maintain good alignment.** Try keeping the wrist and hand in line with the rest of the forearm. Wrist braces can help.

- **Notice your thumbs.** Thumbs can easily be overused in crochet, applying pressure while maneuvering the hook. Experiment with different hook holds. See if you can find a way to crochet while releasing the thumb entirely. Try wearing a hand brace that prevents the thumb from moving as much. By doing so for a period of time, you can coax your hands into using different muscles to accomplish the tasks previously done with the thumb.

- **Rest if injured.** If you have had an injury to the hand or arm, recover fully before taking up crochet.

- **Use ergonomic hooks.** These are designed especially to reduce discomfort and fatigue. There are numerous choices, some with larger grips, some more rounded, others flat; this is very dependent on the size and shape of your hand, the grip you use, and your individual style of working stitches. If the first ergonomic hook does not help, try another.

4

Fundamental Techniques

THERE ARE MANY BASIC TECHNIQUES all crocheters should have in their vocabulary, including the various ways to start and end rows or rounds, calculating the length of starting chains, working with turning chains, and inserting the hook into various parts of stitches. In this chapter we'll also examine a few stitches that are made rather differently than standard stitches, such as loops, knots, and reverse stitches. Even if you have been crocheting for a long time, it's worth reviewing this section to learn tips and tricks you may not have encountered before.

The basic stitches are the chain, single crochet, half double crochet, double crochet, treble crochet, and slip stitch. What's different about them is their height, and the technique we use to make stitches taller is the yarnover (yo). We use a true yarnover — that is, wrapping the yarn counterclockwise from back to front over the hook — before inserting the hook when making taller stitches. (Lefties wrap the yarn from back to front in a clockwise direction.) For both half double and double crochet stitches, for example, we yarnover once.

After drawing the yarn through the insertion point, instructions will say "yarnover" again, but this time we are not wrapping yarn around the hook, but grabbing the yarn with our hook to pull it through. Any wrapping at this point merely slows things down. Understanding the difference between these two moves should be fundamental to any crocheter's education.

But first, a slip knot.

Making a Slip Knot

Lesson one for all crocheters is how to form the first loop that goes on the hook, called a slip knot. Depending on how you form the slip knot, the size of the loop can be adjusted by pulling on one end or the other. Here are the steps.

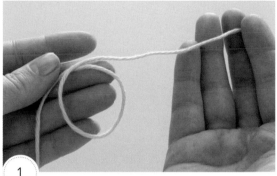

1 Form a small circle 4"–6" from the yarn end.

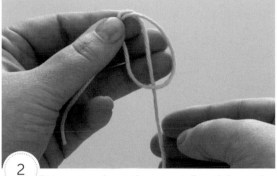

2 Bring yarn from the non-tail end through the circle.

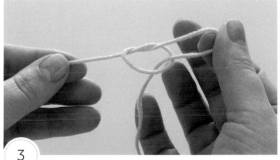

3 Draw a loop through the circle, while pulling the slip knot closed (pull on the tail end).

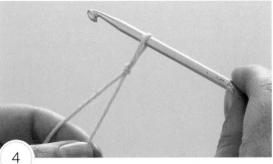

4 To make the loop smaller, pull on the non-tail end. Aim to make the loop large enough to insert the hook, as shown.

5 Tighten the loop further so it matches the size of the chains to follow.

Basic Stitches

Single Crochet (sc)

Single crochet, the shortest of the standard crochet stitches, requires no yarnover before inserting the hook.

1 Insert hook in designated stitch.

2 Draw up a loop.

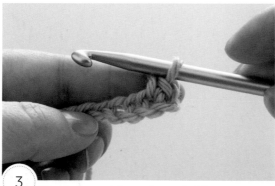

3 Yarnover and draw through 2 loops to complete the single crochet stitch.

Half Double Crochet (hdc)

Yarnover once before inserting the hook. Then draw the yarn through all 3 loops on hook.

1 Start with 1 yarnover.

2 Insert hook in designated stitch.

3 Draw up a loop.

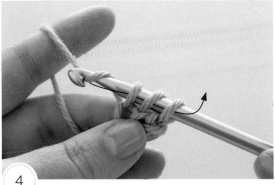

4 Yarnover and draw through all 3 loops on hook.

5 Completed half double crochet stitch.

> **Note.** I use the term *yarnover* when beginning taller stitches, but not for the move made after inserting the hook. Instead, I say "draw up a loop," which I think helps clarify the difference.

Double Crochet (dc)

Yarnover once before inserting the hook, then draw through 2 loops twice. This is why the double crochet is taller than the half double.

1 Complete steps 1–3 as for half double crochet, yarnover and draw through 2 loops on hook.

2 Yarnover and draw through 2 remaining loops.

3 Completed double crochet stitch.

Treble Crochet (tr)

For treble crochet, the yarn is wrapped twice around the hook to start, and an additional yarnover and an extra "grab the yarn with the hook and draw through" is done to work off the stitch — that is, to remove all the loops from the hook.

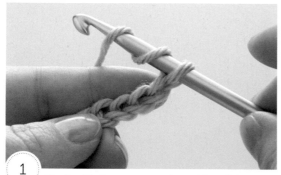

1 Start with 2 yarnovers, insert hook in designated stitch, and draw up a loop.

4 Yarnover and draw through 2 remaining loops.

2 Yarnover and draw through 2 loops on hook.

5 Completed treble crochet stitch.

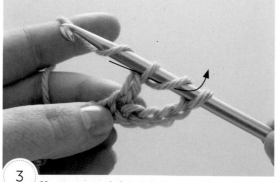

3 Yarnover and draw through 2 loops on hook again.

Double Treble Crochet (dtr)

This one has even more yarnovers!

1 Start with 3 yarnovers, insert hook in designated stitch (or 5th chain from hook), and draw up a loop.

2 Yarnover and draw through 2 loops on hook.

3 Repeat step 2.

4 Repeat step 2.

5 Repeat step 2, working off 2 remaining loops.

6 Completed double treble crochet stitch.

If your tall stitches are not coming out neat, please refer to page 37, where we discuss how to control tension on taller stitches.

It's possible to make even taller stitches than a double treble, but their uses are rare. The method is the same: make one more yarnover before inserting the hook into the stitch, and one more "grab and pull through" to work the loops of the hook. Later in this chapter we'll discuss how to make stitches with heights that are in between these standard stitch heights (see Extended Stitches Can Solve Problems, page 56).

Fastening Off

Ending work in crochet is as simple as beginning it. You will see the words "fasten off" at the end of most patterns, and all you need to do is cut yarn about 6 inches from the last stitch made and pull the end through the last loop on the hook.

The last few inches of yarn, the tail, will be woven in on the back of the work during finishing.

Fastening off does not always signal the end of a project; it is done whenever we are finished using a particular yarn and prefer a fresh start, rather than joining yarn to continue (see page 57). Fastening off forms a tighter closure than joining yarn and may be preferable when, for example, changing colors or before starting an edging.

1 Pull cut end through last stitch made.

2 If necessary, pull any unsightly knot to the back to hide it.

Counting Stitches

Stitch counts are important! Whether a certain number of stitches is required for a pattern repeat, or for shaping purposes, I highly recommend acquiring the habit of counting stitches often. There are at least two good ways to count stitches, shown here.

If your stitch count is off only by one, it's unlikely to be noticeable and you can probably correct the problem on the spot, by increasing or decreasing a stitch (see page 89). If your stitch count is off by more than one, it's probably wiser to go back and see where a stitch was inadvertently skipped or added in the row, then rip out and redo. Even when working the same number of stitches in row after row, it's easy to make a mistake every once in a while, and smarter to count regularly than catch an error many rows later.

What about counting chain stitches? This can be confusing, because when we are working, there is always a chain on the hook. The thing to remember is that the chain on the hook is *not* counted. When instructions say "dc in 4th chain from hook," begin counting in the chain right next to the hook, as shown at bottom right.

It works exactly the same if the instruction says to work in the 2nd chain from the hook, in which case you'd skip 1 chain right next to the hook and work into the next chain. The point to remember is this: begin counting in the chain closest to the hook, and count chains until you get to the one where the hook must be inserted.

> **Exception.** There is *one* instance when the loop on the hook is counted: when working off loops in taller stitches. If instructions say, "yo, draw through 3 loops on hook," one of those loops is the one on the hook you normally don't count. This does not have anything to do with the stitch count, but it is merely a way of keeping track of loops as they are removed when making taller stitches.

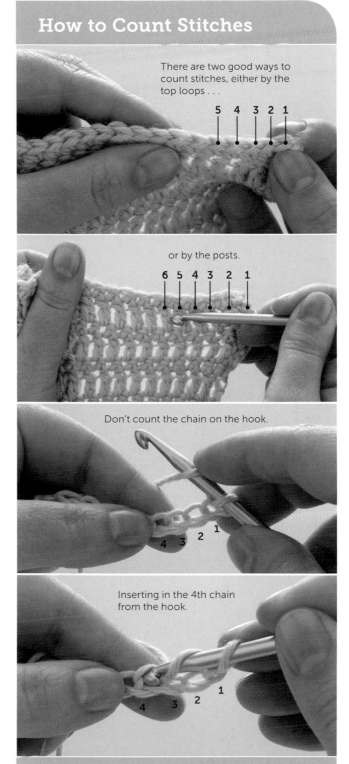

How to Count Stitches

There are two good ways to count stitches, either by the top loops . . .

5 4 3 2 1

or by the posts.

6 5 4 3 2 1

Don't count the chain on the hook.

4 3 2 1

Inserting in the 4th chain from the hook.

4 3 2 1

Number of Stitches in the Foundation Chain

One of the spots where counting is crucial is when making the foundation chain, also called the base chain. The exact number of chains is determined by the number of stitches needed for the first row or round of work.

How do you know how many chains to make? Naturally if the number of chains is specified in a pattern, just do as instructed. If you are creating your own design or altering a pattern, keep in mind the multiple of your stitch pattern, plus several additional factors. Multiples can be tricky, but once you understand how they work, you will find them very useful. Let's take a closer look.

Understanding Stitch Pattern Multiples

Stitch patterns are the lovely little groups of stitches that create shells, fans, diamonds, and hundreds of other decorative designs in crochet fabric. Many of them have been recorded in stitch dictionaries, which are excellent resources for those who enjoy learning new stitches and experimenting with different yarns, fibers, and stitches.

Some stitch patterns are small and may involve only 2 or 3 stitches, and some are much bigger, worked over as many as 20 stitches. Some stitch patterns involve only 1 row of work, others 2 or 4, and some are worked over 8 or 10 rows, as in pineapple patterns. Whether a stitch pattern is large or small, it requires a precise number of stitches, and this number is repeated over and over across the row or round. These are called pattern repeats.

When working with stitch patterns, we need to be sure that we start with the correct number of chains to suit the particular stitch pattern chosen, so that there are no extra stitches left over that don't fit into the pattern.

The number of stitches required for the stitch pattern is called a "multiple." Modern stitch dictionaries generally tell you the multiple for each stitch pattern, and this is an important number for determining the number of chains in the foundation chain. Once you've determined the number of pattern repeats needed in the first row, multiply that number by the multiple. For example, if a shell pattern requires 6 stitches for each repetition of the pattern, and the project needs 10 of those shell patterns in the first row, you will need 60 chains.

Except that's not all. Many stitch patterns have an extra stitch at the end to make the pattern symmetrical. You must add an additional chain for that end stitch. (See page 118 for an example of a pattern with a single extra stitch at the end of the row.) Some stitch patterns have an extra stitch at both ends, requiring 2 chains to be added for the starting chain.

In still other stitch patterns you'll find "half patterns" at either end; if they are exactly half the stitch count of the pattern, then your multiple remains the same, and you just need to add enough chains for one more repetition of the pattern to cover the two half patterns. But often the half patterns actually have 1 stitch more than half. (An example of this can be found on page 165.) That means you'll need to add one more pattern repeat to your calculations plus 2 more stitches to gain all the chains necessary for the first row.

Turning Chains

We have two more things to calculate to get the correct count for the starting chain; the first is the number of chains needed for the first stitch in the first row. That first stitch is called the "turning chain," and before we go further into our present topic, let's take a little detour into the question of the number of chains used in turning chains. The aim of a turning chain is to reach the height of the stitches that will follow, and the general rule of thumb for how many chains is as follows.

TURNING CHAINS

Stitch	Chains	Diagram
Slip stitch	0	
Single crochet	1	
Half double crochet	2	
Double crochet	3	
Treble crochet	4	

You may find patterns that depart from these norms, and we will go into more detail about alternative turning chains further along. But for the most part, the chart here represents the norm for crochet patterns.

Let's return to how turning chains affect the number of chains needed for the foundation chain. Many people think that you need the number of chains shown above plus another for the base chain. But in fact, for the foundation chain we *subtract* 1 from the numbers on the graph. Why? Because the turning chain on the foundation chain has no base chain. If 1 more chain is added for the base chain, a gap tends to form between the turning chain and the 2nd stitch. This is why, when the first stitch in the first row is a double crochet, instructions generally say to work a double crochet into the 4th chain. That leaves the first 3 chains to form the first double crochet stitch. If the first stitch is a half double, instructions will say to work into the 3rd chain, leaving the first 2 chains for the first half double.

You may well ask, "If a double crochet equals 3 chains, even without a base chain, why don't we add 3 chains for the turning chain?" Because we have already included that first stitch in our stitch count: it's either the first stitch of the first pattern repeat, or an end stitch at the edge. If we were to add 3 more chains for the first double crochet stitch, we would have an extra chain, since we

already counted the base stitch when calculating the multiple. So, in order to get the proper number of chains for the starting chain, *in the foundation chain only,* we calculate the number of chains as shown here:

STARTING CHAINS

Stitch	Chains to add to represent turning chains
Single crochet	1
Half double crochet	1
Double crochet	2
Treble crochet	3

When Chains Follow First Stitch

One more consideration for determining the number of chains in the starting chain arises only when the first row or round has chains immediately following the first stitch. These must also be added to the starting chain. For example, the stitch patterns on pages 115 and 120 require extra chains in the starting chain, which includes the turning chain and the number of chains after it in the first row of work. These chains are not part of the base chain and are actually part of the first row, but they need to be calculated and added to the number of chains made. Here's how to calculate:

[Stitch multiple] × [the number of pattern repeats] + extra stitches at the edges + turning chain + any other chains in the first row that come right after the first stitch = total stitches in your starting chain

Reading Patterns

When you consult modern stitch dictionaries (something I highly encourage), you find the multiple at the start of the instructions for each stitch, usually written as "multiple of 8 sts + 1" or "multiple of 14 plus 4." The first number tells you how many stitches are in the pattern repeat, and the second number represents the number of added chains needed for any of the reasons mentioned above. In this book we break it down further and tell you how many stitches are needed for the pattern repeat, how many for the turning chain, and how many for end stitches.

When might you need to calculate the number of stitches in a starting chain? Most patterns will tell you how many chains to make to begin, but you will need to recalculate if you're altering the pattern and want a longer or shorter first row. Of course, if you want to create original designs, you'll need to use these calculations to determine how to begin.

When You Count Wrong

Once you actually begin to work, it's all too easy to get the number of chains wrong. Counting errors can also occur in the first row. Don't panic! There are several strategies for correcting and preventing mistakes. A popular one is to always make more chains than you need; they are easy to pull out later. I use this strategy often, particularly with very long starting chains; who wants to work over 100 stitches in the first row and then find you come up 1 short? So, *do* calculate the number of chains carefully, and then make a few extra ones — say between 5 and 10 — just in case.

When deliberately making extra chains, start your work by making the slip knot a little looser than usual, so it can be pulled out if necessary. Later, you can undo the knot and carefully pull out the extra chains, holding your fingers on the first chain worked into. When you reach that chain, give the strand a tug and the base chain will close securely.

Another way to save the situation if you have too few chains to complete your first row is to take a separate strand of yarn, join it to the beginning of the starting chain, and make as many chains as you need. These chains will be facing the opposite direction from the rest of the starting chain, but once worked into, the difference is hard to detect.

Undoing Extra Chains

1 Extra loose chains

2 Undo slip knot.

3 Pull out extra chains, then tighten.

Working into the Starting Chain

Working into the 2 upper loops of chain stitches can be tricky and tedious. For the starting chain, most people work into either the back loop (BL) or the "bump" at the back of the stitch. Both ways produce a nice clean edge for the beginning of the work.

Some people prefer to work in the bump because the edge looks exactly like the finished edge at the end of the work. With these two strategies, you are picking up only 1 loop of the starting chain. This is fine except when the first row requires several stitches to be worked into 1 chain, as when making shells, for example (see page 122). If you pick up only 1 loop, it stretches considerably; 2 loops will stay tighter and look neater. In this case, you can insert the hook under the front and back loop of the chain, or under both the back loop and the bump. I find the second method easier.

Occasionally a pattern will instruct you to work into 1 loop of a foundation chain for the first row, say the back loop, and work into the other loop — the front loop — at a later point. When returning to the base chain to work into it a second time, you'll see 1 loop exposed: that is the one to insert your hook under. You'll use this technique when making a leaf motif, for example, where you want to have a center line with stitches extending from it on both sides.

Two Ways to Work into a Starting Chain

Working into the back loop

Working into the bump

Working into tight chains. Inserting into a chain that is not a foundation chain can be especially challenging if the chain is worked tightly. It can be helpful to think of inserting your hook above the back bump.

While it's exactly the same as picking up the top 2 loops, sometimes that thought makes it easier to maneuver the hook. If that doesn't work for you, another strategy is to pick up 1 loop at a time. In many patterns you can simply work under the back loop only, which is easier and will usually not be noticeable.

More About Turning Chains

Earlier we discussed how many chains to use at the beginning of a row in relation to the height of the stitch. Turning chains bring up a number of other issues we'll consider now.

Working into the Turning Chain

What's the best way to work into the turning chain at the end of a row? It's tricky to maneuver the hook under the top chain, and perfectly acceptable to work into other strands that are more easily accessed. When you arrive at the turning chain at the end of the row, at the top you'll see the back loop and the bump of the chain facing you; inserting the hook under these 2 loops is much easier.

I find this also keeps the turning chain close to the 2nd stitch, while working under 2 loops of the top chain can create a gap between the turning chain and the 2nd stitch.

When and How to Turn

Sometimes crochet instructions tell you to turn at the end of the row, then make the turning chain, and sometimes they say to make the turning chain and then turn. This really has to do with how a particular publisher or pattern writer prefers to write the instructions. In fact, it doesn't matter whether you turn first then chain, or chain first and then turn. It's a little easier to chain first and then turn, and that's how most crocheters do it.

Note that what is being turned is the work rather than the hook. The work can either be turned clockwise or counterclockwise. For right-handers, clockwise turning twists the turning chain, however, while counterclockwise does not, so the latter is preferable. For left-handers, the opposite is true: clockwise turning will *not* twist the chain, and counterclockwise will.

Right-handers turn counterclockwise.

Skipping the First Stitch

Unless an increase is being worked at the beginning of the row, the turning chain counts as the first stitch, and we do not work into the first stitch of the row. The exception is the single crochet stitch, where we generally chain 1 for the turning chain, but the chain-1 does *not* count as a stitch, and we *do* work into the first stitch of the row. You may find some older patterns or foreign patterns where the chain-1 *does* count as the first stitch, and you are instructed to skip the first stitch. This can work fine, or, in most cases, you can simply substitute a chain-1 and a single crochet stitch in these situations.

You will find some patterns that do not count the turning chain as a stitch, and there is usually a good reason, so follow the instructions. The turning chain may serve some other purpose in such patterns, or it may be buried in a seam during finishing.

Alternatives to Standard Turning Chains

Even when you execute a turning chain perfectly, you still tend to leave a gap between the turning chain and the second stitch, and therefore the stitches don't always form the neatest edge. It's worth knowing some alternatives. There are at least three: using fewer chains, working one long chain, and using chains and a single crochet for the first stitch.

Fewer Chains

Remember our discussion of the standard number of chains to work for the turning chain as it relates to the height of the stitch (see page 49)? Here's a reason to break with that tradition. If you're getting a gap between the turning chain and the 2nd stitch of the row, try working one less chain for the turning chain. In other words, chain 2 instead of 3 for a double crochet, 3 instead of 4 for a treble, and so on. In fact, you will find patterns that specify shorter turning chains for this reason. In such cases, feel free to use your judgment as to the number of chains to use, observing what looks best.

Work a Long Chain

By making a long chain that doesn't count as a stitch you eliminate the turning chain entirely. This technique can be used for half double and double crochet stitches, but it is not suitable for taller stitches, as it's not practical to pull up a loop to match the height of taller stitches. Working a long loop at the beginning of a row does eliminate the gap, but the elongated chain creates a bump at the side edge. You can decide which is the lesser of two evils. If you will be seaming this edge, or working an edging, the bump can probably be hidden.

1 When you begin the row, simply pull the loop on the hook up higher than normal.

2 Work the first stitch of the row into the first stitch of the previous row. The long loop does not count as a stitch.

Long Chain in First Stitch

Another alternative is to pull the loop on the hook up to the height of the first stitch and use the elongated loop as the first yarnover. Here is how it's worked with a double crochet stitch.

1 Pull the loop on the hook up to the height of a double crochet and hold in place with your index finger.

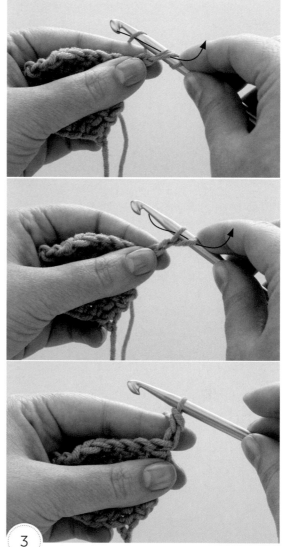

2 Bring the hook under the elongated loop so that the loop forms the first yarnover of the stitch.

3 Do not insert the hook into the stitch as you normally would; instead, draw the working yarn through 2 loops twice.

Chains and a Single Crochet for First Stitch

Sometimes turning chains can look a bit scrawny compared to other stitches in the row. This technique can be used for double crochet, treble crochet, and even taller stitches to create a heftier stitch that matches the other stitches better.

1 To use this method with a double crochet, work 2 chains.

2 Single crochet in the 2nd chain from the hook.

3 Looking at this turning chain with 2 double crochets after it, we see that it is not noticeably different from the other stitches at all. For a treble, you would chain 3, then work a single crochet in the 2nd stitch from the hook. Naturally, the chains and single crochet together count as 1 stitch.

Extended Stitches Can Solve Problems

What if the double crochet is not quite tall enough, but the treble is too tall? We do have another choice! An extra chain is made after inserting the hook and drawing yarn through the first time, and before working off the loops on the hook. These are called extended stitches.

Extended Single Crochet (Esc)

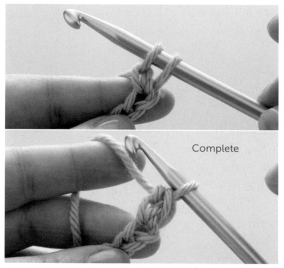

Complete

Insert hook in next stitch and draw up a loop, chain 1, yarnover and draw through 2 loops on hook.

Extended Half Double Crochet (Ehdc)

Yarnover, insert hook in next stitch and draw up a loop, chain 1, yarnover and draw through 3 loops on hook.

Extended Double Crochet (Edc)

Yarnover, insert hook in next stitch and draw up a loop, chain 1, yarnover and draw through 2 loops on hook, yarnover and draw through last 2 loops.

Creating a Smooth Transition

Extended stitches are particularly useful when making stitches of graduated heights next to one another, as they make a smoother edge without bumps. This swatch was made by going in order from the shortest to the tallest stitch.

dtr Etr tr Edc dc Ehdc hdc Esc sc

Joining and Changing Yarns

When we change from one color to the other or come to the end of a ball of yarn, we need to prevent the change from being detectable on the project's surface, or right side. The simplest way is by pulling the new yarn through the last loop of the stitch prior to the change, as shown below.

Leave tails at least 4 inches in length at the ends of both the old yarn and the new. You will find that the stitch where the change happens easily loses its shape. To avoid this, weave in the end of the old yarn right after changing yarns. In some situations, for example, when the stability of that stitch is important, you can make a tiny knot to secure the old yarn in place. Knots that lie on the back of the work are acceptable if small and tidy. If you prefer, the knots can be undone and tails woven in later.

Changing Yarn in Single Crochet

1 Insert hook in next stitch.

2 Draw loop of the new color through the 2 loops on hook.

3 Continue crocheting with the new color.

Changing Yarn in Double Crochet

1 Yarnover and insert hook in next stitch and draw up a loop, yarnover and draw through 2 loops, yarnover with the new color.

2 Draw through the last 2 loops on hook.

3 Continue with the new color.

Joining New Yarn

Sometimes a pattern will instruct us to fasten off and then start the new ball of yarn. After fastening off yarn, join a new yarn — the term often used in crochet instructions — by following these steps:

1 Insert hook under the 2 top loops of the stitch where you want to join yarn.

2 Wrap yarn around the hook with the tail away from you.

3 Draw yarn through 2 loops on the hook.

4 Continue with chains for the first stitch. Do not count the loop on the hook as a chain.

For a More Secure Join

For a more secure join, *after step 3*, remove the hook from the loop and draw the tail through to close the loop completely. Then insert your hook again as in step 1, and work steps 2–4 to continue.

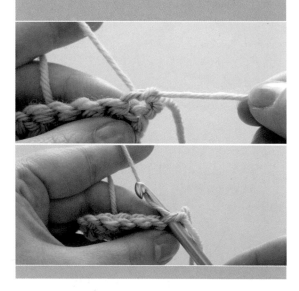

Joining into Side of Stitch

There are times when we need to join yarn into the side of a stitch, rather than under the top 2 loops, as when working an edging along the side of a throw. In such cases, the steps are the same as those described at left, except for the very first. When working into the side of a stitch, insert the hook under any two strands of the post of that stitch, then complete steps 2–4 above.

Using Standing Stitches

A standing stitch is another useful way of changing yarns at the beginning of a row or round. It's particularly helpful when changing colors in rounds of motifs, as the color change is neater. To make a standing stitch, fasten off with the old yarn, make a slip knot with the new yarn, and place it on the hook. Now make the first stitch using the new yarn in the first stitch of the row, using your index finger to hold yarnovers in place.

Using a Russian Join

Generally we change yarn at the beginning of a row, using the methods already shown. Sometimes, however, you may want to join a new yarn in the middle of a row. For such instances, a Russian join is a great technique — as long as you're using a plied yarn. Here it's shown in two colors for clarity.

1 Loop the old yarn around the new and thread the old yarn onto a tapestry needle.

2 Weave the needle back into the old yarn for 2"–3".

3 Thread the new yarn onto the tapestry needle and weave it back into the new yarn.

4 Tug on both yarns to smooth out the join. Snip any ends (or this can be done at finishing).

Foundation Stitches

There are times when you want to avoid beginning your work with a starting chain and do a chainless foundation instead. This is a method of making the first row of stitches and the starting chain at the same time, and it's done by making foundation stitches. It's a great alternative when the traditional foundation chain would be very long, or where you want to have a more flexible edge.

Foundation stitches can be used instead of a starting chain wherever the first row of work consists of solid stitches of the same height. Actually, it's even possible to use them with stitches of different heights, and to make increases within the row. The only place they can't be used is when the first row of work has chains, as is the case with many lace patterns.

When working a garment from the top down, foundation stitches create a firm, flexible edge for necklines. When working a sleeve from the bottom up, they can serve the same purpose, providing a strong but pliable edge at the cuff. Foundation stitches can also be used when adding stitches at the end of a row.

Foundation stitches are not difficult to do, but at first they may take a bit of time to read and work with proper tension. Instead of working your first row of stitches one next to the other, the row of stitches with their base chains is built up in a vertical direction. As you're working foundation stitches, the stitches lie at an angle to the chain, but once you work the next row, the angle disappears, and everything looks just as it should.

Because of the peculiar angle formed by foundation stitches, it can be tricky to keep stitch heights even since they are not lined up one next to the other. To check whether your stitch heights are staying even, stop and hold the work horizontally. It may take a bit of practice to get stitch heights even when you can't see them as you work, but it's a good exercise in kinesthetic awareness — you can judge by the feel of the stitch as you pull it up.

Another tricky issue is finding the base chain to work into as you proceed; remember that it always appears to the left of the main stitch (or to the right for left-handers). If you're having difficulty with this, try marking the chain-1 in step 3 right after completing it, and move your marker on each stitch, until you get the hang of it. To ensure that the base chain is not too tight, draw up the first loop loosely. We'll address all these issues in the following step-by-step tutorial.

Foundation Single Crochet (Fsc)

Foundation stitches can be worked into either the front or back loop of the base chain. Generally the default method is with the front loop, as shown here.

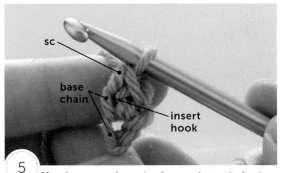

X = Foundation single crochet

1 Place a slip knot on your hook and chain 2.

4 Yarnover, draw through 2 loops.

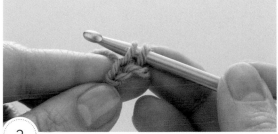

2 Insert hook in 2nd chain from hook, draw up loop.

3 Chain 1. Be sure to always make this chain-1 loosely, or the foundation chain will be tighter than the single crochet stitches.

sc

base chain

insert hook

5 You have made a single crochet stitch sitting atop a chain. It may be hard to see at first, because the single crochet sits at an angle from its chain. The chain is created by the chain-1, and as you hold the work, it appears at the left of the single crochet stitch. Turn the work so you can clearly see this chain and its 2 loops. For the next stitch, insert the hook under these 2 loops and draw up a loop.

Repeat steps 3–5. Continue in this manner until you have the required number of stitches.

Foundation Double Crochet (Fdc)

= Foundation double crochet

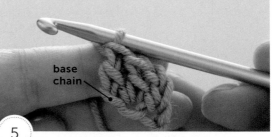

1 Place a slip knot on your hook and chain 3.

2 Yarnover, insert hook in 3rd chain from hook and draw up loop.

3 Chain 1.

4 (Yarnover, draw through 2 loops) twice. (*1 Fdc completed*)

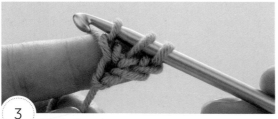

base chain

5 Turn the work so you can clearly see the double crochet stitch atop its base chain. *Yarnover, insert hook in base chain of previous st, draw up loop, chain 1, (yarnover, draw through 2 loops) twice. Rep from * for the desired number of sts. If your base chain appears to be tight, enlarge the size of the loop in step 3 by drawing it out a bit as you work.

Foundation Half Double Crochet Stitch (Fhdc) in the Back Loop

In this example, stitches are worked into the back loop (BL) of the base chains, instead of 2 loops as shown earlier. It takes a bit more maneuvering to get the hook where it belongs. If you'd like to try the Fhdc stitches without this move, simply insert the hook under 2 loops as before. Feel free to try working into the front loop only as well.

4 Chain 1.

5 Yarnover.

6 Draw through 3 loops. (*1 Fhdc completed*)

= Foundation half double crochet

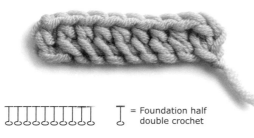

1 Chain 2.

2 Yarnover, insert hook in 2nd chain from hook.

3 Draw up a loop.

Back loop

7 *Yarnover, insert hook in back loop of base chain, draw up a loop, chain 1, yarnover, draw through 3 loops, rep from *.

Varying Heights of Foundation Stitch

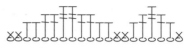

Foundation stitches need not be all the same height. Here is a swatch of the following stitches: Fsc, Fhdc, Fdc, Ftr, Fdc, Fhdc, 2 Fsc, 2 Fhdc, 2 Fdc, 2 Ftr, 2 Fdc, 2 Fhdc, 2 Fsc.

Ch 2, insert hook in 2nd ch from hook, draw up loop, ch 1, yo, draw through 2 loops (*Fsc made*); yo, insert hook in base ch of prev st, draw up loop, ch 1, draw through 3 loops (*Fhdc made*); yo, insert hook in base ch of prev st, draw up loop, ch 1, (yo, draw through 2 loops) twice (*Fdc made*); yo twice, insert hook in base ch of prev st, draw up loop, ch 1, (yo, draw through 2 loops) three times (*Ftr made*); Fdc, Fhdc, 2 Fsc, 2 Fhdc, 2 Fdc, 2 Ftr, 2 Fdc, 2 Fhdc, 2 Fsc.

Increasing in First Row with Foundation Stitches

There may be instances where you want more stitches in the first row than there are chains in the foundation. This, too, can be done when using foundation stitches. This swatch adds 1 double crochet every 3rd stitch. As you can see, increasing in this way causes the fabric to curve, a useful neckline-shaping device.

Ch 3, *work 2 Fdc, yo, insert hook in same base ch as last st and work regular dc, yo, insert hook in same base ch and work Fdc, rep from *.

For a less-pronounced curve, increase less often, for example, every 5 or 8 stitches. To increase every 5 stitches, work 5 Fdc, then increase in the last stitch by inserting the hook in the same base chain and working a normal dc. In other words, always work the number of stitches needed in Fdc, and work the increase stitch as a regular dc.

Adding Foundation Stitches at the End of a Row

If you add foundation stitches at the end of a row, you eliminate the need to work into chains on your next row. Work the last stitch of the row as a foundation stitch, at whatever height is needed. Then make the remaining stitches you intend to add as foundation stitches as well, as shown in step 2.

1 Work last stitch of row as a Fdc.

2 Add as many foundain stitches as needed.

13 Ways of Looking at Insertion Points

Throughout this chapter we've mentioned where to insert the hook, and now it's time to consider how many different types of insertion points there are. You may be amazed! It's worth noting them all, especially because some require particular attention.

1. Under the 2 top loops Inserting the hook under 2 top loops is the default method for working most stitches. When no special insertion point is indicated in instructions, insert the hook this way.

2. Under the front loop Quite often, instructions specify working under either the front or back loop, both to loosen up the fabric and to create surface texture.

3. Under the back loop

4. Under 3 loops Inserting under 3 loops may come up from time to time (as for hdc ribbing). Instructions should specify exactly which loop other than the top 2 — it might be the bump at the back of a chain, or one of the strands on the post of the stitch.

5. Between stitches Inserting between stitches is a way of increasing at a center point where the stitch count is an even number. The hook is inserted between the posts of 2 stitches. You'll notice that the stitch sits a bit lower because of the insertion point, but this minor difference shouldn't be noticeable unless you're working at a very large gauge.

6. Around the post When stitches are made by inserting the hook around the post, or stem, of a stitch they are called post stitches (see page 164).

7. Into the side of a stitch Working an edging on a finished piece often entails working into the sides of stitches. Instructions sometimes say to work into the "row-end." We discuss how to place stitches into the sides of the work on page 59. This technique is also used when changing the direction of work from horizontal to vertical rows (or vice versa). For example, you might make the body of a sweater using vertical rows, then work the yoke with horizontal rows. Rather than making two separate pieces that are sewn together, you can work the first row of the yoke into the row-ends (or sides of stitches) at the top edge.

8. Into stitches several rows below The norm for working crochet stitches is to work into the stitch directly below the working stitch. Sometimes, however, we work into a stitch in the previous row that is 1, 2, or even 3 stitches away from the current stitch. This technique is used with crossed stitches, cables, and spikes.

9. In tops of clusters It can be tricky to insert the hook into the top of a cluster stitch. (See page 68.)

10. Under groups of chains Inserting under groups of chains is very simple: just place your hook under the chains and draw yarn through. If several stitches are being worked under the same group of chains, they will not sit close to each other at the bottom as they normally do when groups of stitches are worked into 1 stitch, but will spread out. An example can be found on page 124.

11. In the horizontal strand of a post When making linked stitches (see page 74), the hook is inserted in the horizontal strand of a post.

extra strand

12. In the lower loop of a half double crochet stitch Half double crochet stitches have a unique look on the back, with an extra horizontal strand right under the top loop.

13. In the eye A few stitches in the crochet repertoire have a small hole where the hook is inserted repeatedly, usually referred to as an *eye*. The two examples in this book are the diamond stitch (page 184) and the marguerite stitch (page 77). The eye is easy to identify and work into, so other than recognizing the term, there's nothing special to learn about this insertion point.

Working Clusters

Many crochet stitch patterns involve working several stitches together, and the general term to describe these stitches is *cluster*. The stitches meant to be clustered are not completed, but worked and held on the hook until the last loop, that is, to the last yarnover and pull-through of the stitch. Then a final yarnover and pull-through bring all the stitches together.

Often when making cluster stitches the hook must be inserted in different stitches rather than in the same stitch over and over. Instructions should spell out where to insert the hook, and may be written as follows: Dc4tog over next 4 dc.

In this example, the first stitch is the turning chain, so to work dc4tog, you insert in the next 3 stitches instead of 4, counting that turning chain as 1 stitch in the group.

(Yarnover, insert hook in next st, yarnover and draw up a loop, yarnover, draw through 2 loops) three times.

Yarnover, draw yarn through all the loops on the hook.

In a more complex stitch pattern (see page 122), the instructions may read like this: Dc7tog over (next 3 dc, sc, 3 dc).

The first number tells you how many stitches are being drawn together, and the hook is inserted as described in the parenthesis. You may find variations of this wording, but essentially these are the details to look for: how many stitches are being drawn together, and where the hook is inserted for each stitch in the cluster.

Work partial stitches.

Yarnover, and draw yarn through all loops on the hook.

One tricky thing about clusters is knowing where to insert the hook when working into them on the following row. Note that the loop that closes the cluster appears to the left of the stitch when it's being worked. When you turn, however, that loop will be slightly to the right of the posts of the stitch): that's the loop to work into when working into the cluster (for left-handers, these directions are reversed. If you have trouble finding this spot, place a stitch marker or safety pin in the loop that closes the cluster right after making it, so you can see it when working the next row.

Unraveling Work

Inevitably, a mishap occurs and we have to pull out stitches, an activity sometimes called "ripping out" or "frogging" (say "rip it" repeatedly, and you'll know why!).

Most yarns pull out easily, but some have small protruding ends that catch on others as you unravel stitches. Fuzzy yarns such as mohair are the most difficult to unravel. In such cases, pull out the work in the opposite direction from how it was worked, that is, pulling the yarn *down* in the direction of the base of the stitch, not up, thereby creating the least amount of friction.

This keeps strands of yarn parallel to each other, and therefore less likely to tangle. Work slowly when pulling out fuzzy yarns, and you'll find they can be unraveled successfully and reused.

If tangles occur while you're unraveling, you can tease them apart by hand and continue unraveling. Sometimes you will need scissors. Take care to make only a small snip, so that the yarn doesn't fall apart.

Highly textured yarns like bouclés or certain novelty yarns are the only yarns that can't be unraveled. Luckily, mistakes such as a missing stitch may be less evident with these yarns, and it may be possible to hide errors without unraveling.

Unusual Stitches

A few stitches in the crochet repertoire require maneuvers that are uncommon. Too often crocheters don't quite get how they work and have trouble with these stitches forever after. Let's take them on here so you can enjoy all the stitches at a crocheter's disposal!

Loop Stitch

Loop stitches were popular in early crochet publications and were often used to create a mock-fur look on the fabric's surface.

1 Wrap yarn from back to front around the index finger of the yarn-holding hand.

2 Insert hook in next stitch and around the strand coming down in front of the index finger.

3 Draw yarn through until the loop around your finger is the desired height; remove finger. The loops can be quite small or large, depending on the effect you're after, but do strive to make them all about the same size.

4 Complete the stitch as a sc (single crochet) by drawing yarn through the 2 loops on the hook, with the long loop hanging at the back of the work.

Loop Stitch Swatch

Since the loops hang from the surface of the work, the loop stitches are usually made on alternating rows, as in this swatch, so that they only show on one side of the work.

† = Loop stitch

Ch any number of sts, plus 1 for tch. (*ch 11 for swatch*)

Row 1 (RS) Sc in 2nd ch from hook and in each ch across, turn. (*10 sc*)

Row 2 Ch 1, loop st in each sc across, turn.

Row 3 Ch 1, sc in each st across, turn.

Rep rows 2 and 3 for patt, ending with row 2. Finish with a row of sl sts to lock the loop sts in place.

Knot Stitch

Knot stitches, sometimes called Solomon's knot or lovers' knot, offer a way of making an entire fabric of long loops. Knot stitches are elongated chains, locked in place with a single crochet, and resulting in a very open fabric with excellent drape. It's a nice stitch to use when you want to show off a yarn, such as ribbon or other novelty yarns, that are hard to work in regular crochet. Like loop stitches, they can be large or small, depending on the desired effect. There is little wrapping of yarn, and the individual strands are clearly visible.

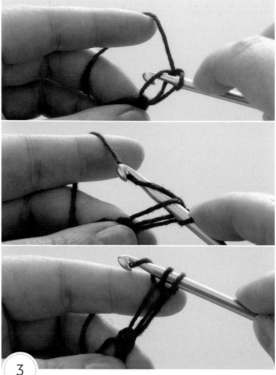

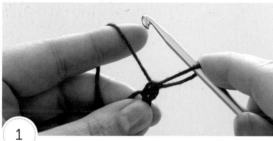

1 Draw up the loop on the hook to the desired height.

3 Insert the hook between the long loop and the strand and draw up a loop so that you have 2 loops on the hook.

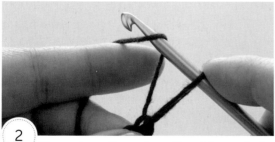

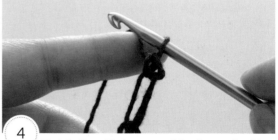

2 Draw a loop through, as if making a chain; you'll see an extra strand of yarn behind (or to the left of) the long loop.

4 Finish the stitch as a sc (single crochet) by drawing a loop through the 2 loops on the hook.

Knot evolution. Turkey has a long tradition in the needle and textile arts. Often, a border on a head scarf is stitched in tiny needlework flowers, called *oya*. I was amazed to see knot stitches interspersed with these *oya* and wondered if knot stitches are a link between laces made with a needle and those made with a hook. Needle lace dates back much earlier than crochet, so could this be a clue to how crochet evolved? It's fun to speculate!

Diamond Grid Knot Stitch

Knot stitches are usually worked in a diamond grid, where the base row and sides of the work have shorter knot stitches and the main body of the work has taller knot stitches. In the pattern below, we give the instructions for the shorter side stitches at the ends of rows. Near the beginning of row 3, the knot stitch skipped is the taller knot stitch from the previous row, not those at the side.

It's hard to make the lengths of the knot stitches match exactly, but don't let this worry you; they look good even with some variation in the size of stitches. It's also hard to weave in ends with this very open stitch. If the work has regular crochet nearby, weave ends in that section, or bury them in seams. Otherwise, just do your best to secure the ends as much as possible.

Knot stitches can also be used in combination with regular crochet, and you can find some neat-looking vintage edgings that do just that.

Ch 2.

Foundation row Sc in 2nd ch, (draw up loop to ½" and work knot st) (*short knot st made*) eight times, do not turn.

Row 1 Draw up loop to 1" and work knot st (*tall knot st made*), sc in sc between 3rd and 4th knot sts from hook, (2 tall knot sts, sk one sc, sc in next sc) three times, work 2 short knot sts for side edge, turn.

Row 2 Tall knot st, skip 1 knot st, sc in next sc, (2 tall knot sts, sk next sc, sc in next sc) three times, work 2 short knot sts for side edge, turn.

Rep row 2 for pattern.

To form a flat edge for the top of the work, work the last row as follows. Note that the term *knot st* means the long loop, not the sc that locks it in place.

Last row You ended the prev row with 2 short knot sts for the side. Sk 1 knot st, sc in next sc, (2 short knot sts, sk 2 knot sts, sc in next sc) three times.

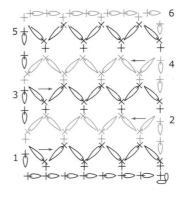

 = short knot st

= long knot st

Linked Stitch

When making a fabric of tall stitches, one stitch is connected to the other only at the top and bottom, yielding a fabric that is not really solid. Linked stitches allow us to make taller stitches that are literally linked along their posts. What's tricky about linking stitches is that there are no yarnovers before inserting the hook. Instead, the hook is inserted into the horizontal strands along the post, and loops are drawn up.

Do not work these loops tightly or you will have difficulty working into them on subsequent stitches. For working linked double crochet, follow these instructions.

① Insert the hook in the horizontal strand of prev st, yarnover and draw up a loop.

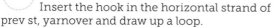

② Insert the hook in the next stitch, yarnover and draw up a loop. (*3 loops on the hook*)

③ Work off the loops as in a normal dc (double crochet): (yarnover, draw through 2 loops) twice.

The first linked double crochet of a row is worked into the turning chain. Work as follows:

- Insert the hook in the 2nd chain from the hook (it can be inserted under 1 loop, either the back loop or the bump), yarnover and draw up a loop.

- Insert the hook in the next stitch, yarnover and draw up a loop.

- Finish the dc (double crochet) as usual: (yarnover, draw through 2 loops) twice.

For a linked treble, there will be two horizontal strands along the post. Insert the hook in the horizontal strand near the top, yarnover and draw up a loop, then insert the hook in the next horizontal strand down along the post, yarnover, and draw up a loop, and then into the next stitch, yo, and draw up a loop, then complete the treble as you normally would: (yarnover, draw through 2 loops) three times.

Linked Double Crochet Swatch

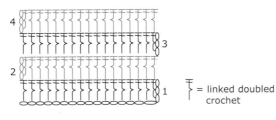

Ch any number of stitches. (*ch 19 for swatch*)

Row 1 Work 2nd linked st by drawing up loops in 2nd and 3rd ch from hook, work linked dc across, turn. (*17 sts*)

Row 2 Ch 3, work 2nd linked st by drawing up loops in 2nd and 3rd ch from hook, work linked dc across, turn.

Rep row 2.

Look familiar? You may notice a resemblance between linked trebles and Tunisian crochet. Essentially, when working linked trebles, you draw up loops exactly as in the forward row of Tunisian simple stitches, then work them off as in a return row. In effect, each linked stitch is a short little row of Tunisian simple stitches!

Linked Treble Stitch

For this swatch of linked treble stitches, I found it easier *not* to count the turning chains as stitches, as they are hard to find. After the turning chain, I worked the first linked stitch into the first stitch of each row and did not work into the turning chains at the ends of rows.

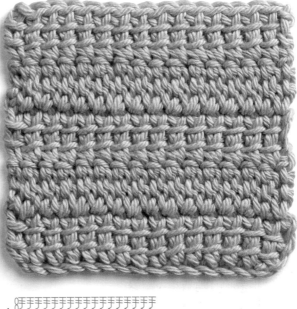

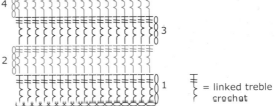

Ch any number of stitches. (*ch 20 for swatch*)

Row 1 Work first linked st by drawing up loops in 2nd, 3rd, and 4th ch from hook, work linked tr across, turn. (*17 sts*)

Row 2 Ch 4, work first linked st by drawing up loops in 2nd and 3rd ch from hook and in st at base of ch-4, work linked tr across, turn.

Rep row 2.

Reverse Single Crochet (rsc)

Sometimes called crab stitch, this is a lovely decorative stitch for an edging. It's tricky because you work backward — that's why it's a "reverse" stitch. You can stitch up one of the circles in chapter 6 (page 99) to use as a base for experimenting with this stitch.

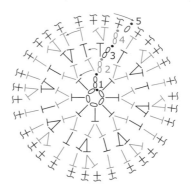

‡ = reverse sc

1 Chain 1, but do not turn.

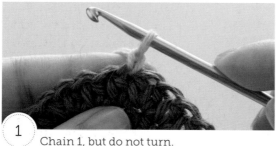

2 Insert the hook under the 2 top loops in the first stitch to the right (for left-handed crocheters, to the left).

3 Yarnover and draw up a loop.

Don't be tempted to draw the yarn through the loop on the hook, which is easy to do by accident! The new loop should be to the *left* of the loop on the hook (or right, for left-handed folks).

4 Yarnover and draw through the 2 loops on the hook to complete the rsc.

For the next stitch, insert the hook in the next stitch to the right (or left, for left-handed crocheters) and repeat steps 3 and 4. The process twists the top 2 loops of the stitch; this is what forms the decorative edge.

Picots

Picots have been an important feature of crochet work since Victorian times, because they mimic effects created by other laces that Victorian crocheters were trying to re-create with their hooks. Some find them challenging, but I believe that's because they aren't sure how to make picots neat.

Picots are usually worked into the top of a stitch (in this example, double crochet) by making 3 or 4 chains and then slip stitching into the designated stitch.

Tips for Neat Picots

There are two important things you can do to keep your picots looking their best.

• Make the chains tight.

• Work the slip stitch that closes the picot by inserting the hook into the front loop and one strand at the side of the post of the stitch below.

• Draw the loop through. This can be done no matter what height the stitch; just use the closest strand from the post of the stitch.

Marguerite Stitch

This is such a pretty stitch, but I rarely see it in patterns. It's also called star stitch, but I prefer marguerite, which is a pretty little flower that the stitch resembles. I've used the stitch in the pattern for the Marguerite Cowl on page 218.

Marguerites are formed by picking up several loops in different parts of previous stitches, then drawing yarn through all the loops to close the little flower. It's an example of putting together a stitch in a very unusual way. No other regular crochet stitch I know of gathers together several loops in this manner. In fact, when you are picking up the series of loops for this stitch, you may feel like you're doing Tunisian crochet. It's also remarkable that despite the fact that each marguerite has 5 loops, it is only a 2-stitch pattern repeat!

Rows or rounds of marguerites begin with a chain-2 and end with a half double crochet. Note that the chain-2 is hard to see once you've worked the first loops of the marguerite into it. The half double crochet that ends the row goes into the same place as the last loop of the last marguerite.

I like to work the marguerite rows alternating with rows of half double crochet stitches. These are worked into the "eye," the round hole formed when closing the flower. You may also find patterns where rows of single crochet are used instead.

Marguerite Stitch *continued*

1   Begin by chaining an even number. Inserting hook in back loop, draw up a loop in the 2nd ch from hook.

2   Inserting hook in back loop, draw up a loop in each of the next 4 chains. (*6 loops on hook*)

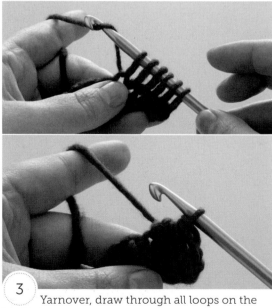

3   Yarnover, draw through all loops on the hook.

4   Chain 1. (*1 marguerite and eye made*)

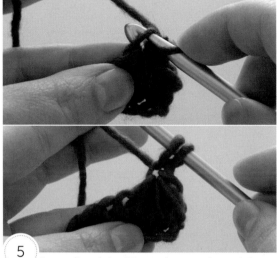

5   Insert hook in the eye just made and draw up a loop.

6   Insert hook under the last loop of marguerite just made and draw up a loop.

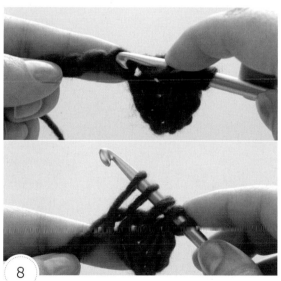

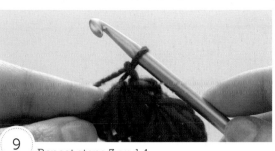

7 Insert hook in back loop of same chain as last loop of marguerite just made and draw up a loop.

8 Insert hook in back loop of next 2 chains, drawing up a loop in each. (*6 loops on hook*)

Large enough loops. Be sure to make the marguerite loops larger than the shaft of the hook. Experiment and see how large is attractive with your yarn.

9 Repeat steps 3 and 4.

10 Repeat steps 5–9 until the end of the row. Hdc (half double crochet) in last chain, which should be the same chain as the last loop of the last marguerite.

Marguerite Stitch *continued*

ALTERNATE ROWS

When working marguerites in later rows, the steps are the same, but instead of working into chains you will be inserting the hook in half double crochet stitches.

3 Draw up a loop in top of first hdc (half double crochet).

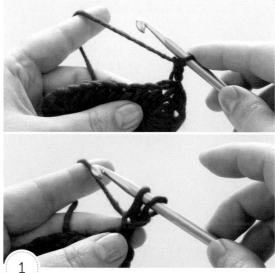

1 Chain 2, insert the hook in the front loop of 2nd chain from hook and draw up a loop.

4 Draw up a loop in each of the next 2 hdc. (*6 loops on hook*)

2 Draw up a loop in the back loop of the same chain.

5 Yarnover, draw through all loops on hook, and chain 1.

> **Marguerite variations.** Marguerites are usually worked with the right side facing and a different stitch on the alternating rows. You will find patterns for this stitch using single crochet stitches on the alternate row, but I prefer the look of half double crochet. Also, you may find marguerite stitches with different numbers of loops, but the technique will remain essentially the same.

Marguerite Stitch Swatch

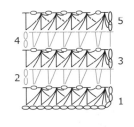

= marguerite stitch

Notes

Work under the back loop when drawing up loops in chains or half double crochet, unless otherwise noted.

The last half double in even rows is worked into the turning chain. Since it has marguerites worked into it, it can be hard to see.

Ch an even number: 2 ch for each marguerite, plus 4 for tch. (*ch 14 for swatch*)

Row 1 Draw up a loop in 2nd ch from hook, draw up a loop in each of the next 4 ch, yo, draw through 6 loops on hook, ch 1 (*marguerite made*), *draw up a loop in the eye just made, draw up a loop in last loop of prev marguerite, draw up a loop in BL of same ch as last loop of prev marguerite, draw up a loop in BL of next 2 ch, yo, draw through 6 loops on hook, ch 1 (*marguerite made*), rep from * across, hdc in same ch as last loop of last marguerite, turn.

Row 2 Ch 2, sk first hdc, 2 hdc in next ch (eye of marguerite), *2 hdc in next eye of marguerite, rep from * across, hdc in top of tch, turn.

Row 3 Ch 2, draw up a loop in FL of 2nd ch from hook, draw up a loop in BL of 2nd ch from hook, draw up a loop in first hdc, draw up a loop in next 2 hdc, yo, draw through 6 loops on hook, ch 1 (*marguerite made*), *draw up a loop in the eye just made, draw up a loop under last loop of prev marguerite, draw up a loop in same hdc as last loop of prev marguerite, draw up a loop in each of the next 2 hdc, yo, draw through 6 loops on hook, ch 1, rep from * across, hdc in same st as last loop of last marguerite, turn.

Repeat rows 2 and 3 for pattern.

Practice makes perfect! All the special stitches in this chapter deserve some practice time so you can get comfortable with them. Each time you do them, they get easier, so be patient. Not only will you have all kinds of cool new stitches to work with, but these techniques will also help you face many crochet challenges with increased skill and confidence.

5

Shaping and Construction in Crochet

YOU CAN CREATE ALMOST ANY shape imaginable in crochet, and there are usually several ways to do it. Unlike knit stitches, which must be made in rows, crochet stitches stand on their own, and this fact gives the crocheter almost limitless possibilities in creating various shapes.

The primary way shapes are achieved is by adding or subtracting stitches, a process called "shaping." When the number of stitches changes from one row to the next, we call this changing the "stitch count." Keeping track of stitch counts is important in designs with detailed shaping, such as fitted sweaters. The number of rows in any given section of a project may also change with shaping, in which case we must change the row count.

The term "construction" refers to two basic things:

- **The direction of the work.** Is the item made in rows, rounds, or on the bias (with rows running at an angle to the edges of the work)?

- **The way the design is put together.** Is the item made in one piece or several?

To look at a simple example, a rectangular scarf could be made with several constructions.

- **Horizontal rows:** Begin at the short end of the rectangle and work in rows until you reach the desired scarf length.

- **Vertical rows:** Begin along the long edge of the rectangle and work in much longer rows until you reach the desired scarf width.

- **Bias:** Begin at a corner and work on the diagonal by adding stitches at one end and subtracting them at the other.

- **In the round:** You could crochet a border around a rectangular scarf, working in the round.

- **Multipiece:** The above examples are one-piece designs, but you could also make a scarf out of a series of motifs joined together. The individual motifs could be made in the round from the center out, or they could be squares made in any number of ways, which we will explore shortly.

Scarf Construction: Direction of Work

Horizontal rows, begin at short end

Vertical rows, begin along long edge

Bias, begin at a corner

In the round, a border around a rectangular scarf

Multipiece, motifs joined

Crocheters are often bewildered about shaping and construction, hoping for formulas that will make it all simpler. Unfortunately, because crochet stitches are so varied, simple formulas just won't do the job. Nevertheless, mastering shaping does not require an advanced degree but simply an understanding of a few basic concepts; then you can build from those. This chapter provides these basic concepts, and chapter 7 amplifies them further. Even if you don't have an immediate need for these basic shapes, I urge you to experiment with the patterns given here, as the concepts

are applicable to the more complex shaping and construction used for making most crochet items, whether throws, shawls, hats, or sweaters.

Let's examine the many ways a shape can be created using crochet, starting with squares. Squares can be worked in different constructions: in rows from the bottom up, in rows from the top down, on the bias, in rounds from the center out, and in rows with a mitered corner. Circles are another basic shape that we will look at in the next chapter.

Making these simple shapes is a great way to build your crochet technique. By technique, I mean not only how well you wield the hook, but also your knowledge and understanding of how stitches behave, how placement of stitches creates different shaping effects, and how shapes can be altered or made sharper. This knowledge will be of great use when working patterns, and even more useful if you're interested in creating your own designs.

The Many Ways to Crochet Squares

It's easy to make a square in rows. Since a square by definition is the same height and width, the only issue is how many stitches and rows the square will require, and this will vary depending on how tall the stitches are. You may get a neater, more even square by mixing the heights of stitches from one row to the next to get precise measurements.

You can turn the square on its edge and work another square with rows running perpendicular to the first square, changing the direction of work and adding visual interest. This can be further elaborated with stripes, ripples, or other surface design features, a great concept to use for a throw or pillow top.

Let's look at some alternatives for making squares.

Square on the Bias

As an alternative to the horizontal and vertical grid that is formed by working conventionally in rows, we can work rows on the bias, that is, on the diagonal, by adding stitches on one half and subtracting them on the other. To make the square shape, I alternated between 3- and 2-stitch increases in the first half and 3- and 2-stitch decreases for the second half. In the decreasing section, I used a chain-2 for the turning chain for the decrease to make a nice slanted edge. Remember that in the row following a decrease, the stitches at the edge count as 1 stitch, and you don't work into the turning chain.

I changed colors after getting to the widest point of the square, to show clearly that the square is made of two triangles, but you can of course make it in one color.

To make this square larger, work additional rows after row 6, continuing to increase either 2 or 3 stitches at each side alternately, then decreasing at the same rate for the same number of rows.

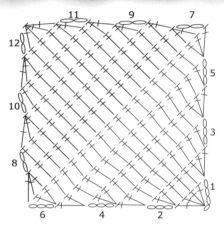

Note

Make an extra chain to begin instead of a ring.

Row 1 Ch 4 (counts as ch-1, dc), 4 dc in 4th ch from hook, turn. (*5 dc*)

Row 2 Ch 3 (counts as dc throughout), 2 dc in first dc, dc in next 3 dc, 3 dc in tch, turn. (*9 dc*)

Row 3 Ch 3, dc in first dc, dc in next 7 dc, 2 dc in tch, turn. (*11 dc*)

Row 4 Ch 3, 2 dc in first dc, dc in next 9 dc, 3 dc in tch, turn. (*15 dc*)

Row 5 Ch 3, dc in first dc, dc in next 13 dc, 2 dc in tch, turn. (*17 dc*)

Row 6 Ch 3, 2 dc in first dc, dc in next 15 dc, 3 dc in tch, turn. (*21 dc*)

Change color (optional).

Row 7 [Ch 2, dc2tog] (counts as dc3tog throughout), dc in next 15 dc, dc3tog, turn. (*17 dc*)

Row 8 [Ch 2, dc in next dc], dc in next 13 dc, dc2tog, turn. (*15 dc*)

Row 9 Ch 2, dc2tog, dc in next 9 dc, dc3tog, turn. (*11 dc*)

Row 10 Ch 2, dc in next dc, dc in next 7 dc, dc2tog, turn. (*9 dc*)

Row 11 Ch 2, dc2tog, dc in next 3 dc, dc3tog, turn. (*5 dc*)

Row 12 Ch 2, dc4tog (counts as dc3tog). (*1 st*) Fasten off.

True Squares

You can also make a square working in rounds from the center out, as is often done in square motifs. To avoid having a square with rounded corners, keep in mind this excellent observation, which I found in James Walters's brilliant *Crochet Workshop* (Sidgwick & Jackson, 1984).

> Wherever one forms an angle, as in squares, triangles or zig zag stitches, the top of the corner (the stitch at the center of the corner) and those at the edges, in theory, should be longer than the stitches along the straight edges.

Walters's solution is to make the center stitch at each corner a taller stitch, thereby lengthening that diagonal and resulting in a truer square. Here are examples of two squares, one made with double crochet stitches, the other with single crochet stitches, using this strategy.

Square from Center Out in Double Crochet

In this square, note that the corners are worked over 2 stitches, with longer stitches at the center of the increase. The square increases by 16 stitches each round.

To make the square larger, continue in pattern, working the same increase at each corner; each side edge of the square (before the increase) will have 4 more stitches than the previous round.

Rnd 1 Ch 4 (counts as ch 1, dc), 11 dc in first ch, sl st to top of starting ch. (*12 dc*)

Rnd 2 Ch 3, *(2 dc, tr) in next dc, (tr, 2 dc) in next dc**, dc in next dc, rep from * around, ending last rep at **, sl st to top of ch-3. (*28 sts*)

Rnd 3 Ch 3, dc in next 2 dc *(2 dc, tr) in next tr, (tr, 2 dc) in next tr**, dc in next 5 dc, rep from * around ending last rep at **, dc in last 2 dc, sl st to top of ch-3. (*44 sts*)

Rnd 4 Ch 3, dc in next 4 dc, *(2 dc, tr) in next tr, (tr, 2 dc) in next tr**, dc in next 9 dc, rep from * around ending last rep at **, dc in last 4 dc, sl st to top of ch-3. (*60 sts*)

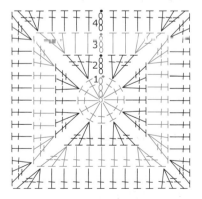

Square from the Center Out in Single Crochet

Here's another square worked from the center with single crochet stitches. It, too, uses an elongated corner stitch. When working this pattern, don't get confused by what looks like an extra stitch when you complete each round: this is the slip stitch that closes the round, left exposed because we work the first stitch of the round by inserting to the left of the slip stitch. Note that each round increases by 8 stitches; each round will have 2 more stitches between corners than did the previous round.

Rnd 1 Ch 2, 6 sc in 2nd ch from hook, sl st to top of first sc. (*6 sc*)

Rnd 2 Ch 1, 2 sc in each sc around, sl st to top of first sc. (*12 sc*)

Rnd 3 Ch 1, sc in first sc, sc in next sc, *(sc, hdc, sc) in next sc**, sc in next 2 sc, rep from * around ending last repeat at **, sl st to top of first sc. (*20 sts*)

Rnd 4 Ch 1, sc in first sc, sc in next sc, *(sc, hdc, sc) in next hdc**, sc in next 4 sc, rep from * around ending last rep at **, sc in last 2 sc, sl st to top of first sc. (*28 sc*)

Rnd 5 Ch 1, sc in first sc, sc in next 2 sc, *(sc, hdc, sc) in next sc**, sc in next 6 sc, rep from * around ending last rep at **, sc in last 3 sc, sl st to top of first sc. (*44 sc*)

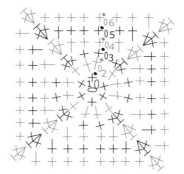

Mitered Corners

In crochet and knitting, a mitered corner is an angle created either by decreasing or increasing in the middle of a row. Commonly, this is a 45-degree angle, but angles of different degrees can also be made using this technique, and the angle can be placed somewhere other than the center point, if desired.

Mitered Square in Single Crochet

A mitered square can be made either by starting at the corner and increasing at the center on each row, or starting at the outside edge and working a decrease at the center of each row. Many patterns use mitered squares, but again, the shape is rarely a true square. Here I have adapted Walters's elongated corner technique to make the mitered square more accurate in shape. Note that the elongated stitch is used in every other row; when I elongated the corner on every row, the square was dis torted. Like many things in crochet, this may vary depending on gauge, and it may require trial and error before the shape is exactly what you wish.

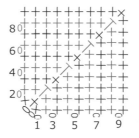

Row 1 Ch 3 (counts as 1 ch, tch), 3 sc in 2nd ch from hook, turn. (*3 sc*)

Row 2 Ch 1, sc in first sc, (sc, hdc, sc) in next sc, sc in next sc, turn. (*5 sts*)

Row 3 Ch 1, sc in first sc, sc in next sc, 3 sc in next hdc, sc in last 2 sc, turn. (*7 sts*)

Row 4 Ch 1, sc in first sc, sc in next 2 sc, (sc, hdc, sc) in next sc, sc in last 3 sc, turn. (*9 sts*)

Row 5 Ch 1, sc in first sc, sc in next 3 sc, 3 sc in next sc, sc in last 4 sc, turn. (*11 sts*)

Row 6 Ch 1, sc in first sc, sc in next 4 sc, (sc, hdc, sc) in next sc, sc in last 5 sc, turn. (*13 sts*)

To make this square larger, continue in the established pattern, making a 3-st increase at the corner on every row, alternating between using a sc and a hdc at the corner.

Mitered Square in Double Crochet

Here's another mitered square worked in double crochet, with trebles at the corners on every other row to get a better square.

Row 1 Ch 4 (counts as 1 ch, dc), 3 dc in 4th ch from hook, turn. (*4 sts*)

Row 2 Ch 3 (counts as dc throughout), (2 dc, tr) in next dc, (tr, 2 dc) in next dc, dc in tch, turn. (*8 sts*)

Row 3 Ch 3, dc in next 2 dc, (3 dc in next tr) twice, dc in next 2 dc, dc in tch, turn. (*12 dc*)

Row 4 Ch 3, dc in next 4 dc, (2 dc, tr) in next dc, (tr, 2 dc) in next dc, dc in next 4 dc, dc in tch, turn. (*16 sts*)

Row 5 Ch 3, dc in next 6 dc, (3 dc in next tr) twice, dc in next 6 dc, dc in tch, turn. (*20 dc*)

Row 6 Ch 3, dc in next 8 dc, (2 dc, tr) in next dc, (tr, 2 dc) in next dc, dc in next 8 dc, dc in tch, turn. (*24 sts*)

Row 7 Ch 3, dc in next 10 dc, (3 dc in next tr) twice, dc in next 10 dc, dc in tch, turn. (*28 dc*)

Row 8 Ch 3, dc in next 12 dc, (2 dc, tr) in next dc, (tr, 2 dc) in next dc, dc in next 10 dc, dc in tch, fasten off. (*32 sts*)

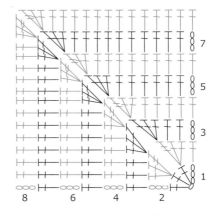

Increasing and Decreasing

Earlier we explained that shaping is usually accomplished by adding or subtracting stitches from one row to the next. Stitches can be added either at the edges of work, in the first and last stitches or a row, or at any point within a row or round of work. The latter method is called "internal shaping," and you can see an example in our mitered square. When increases or decreases are done at the edges, it will usually not disrupt the stitch pattern. In order not to interrupt the flow of a stitch pattern when doing internal shaping, the precise placement of increases or decreases must be carefully planned. To begin, we focus on shaping done at the edges, with more on internal shaping in chapter 7.

Increasing One Stitch at Each Edge

Increasing 1 stitch at each edge, single crochet

Increasing 1 stitch at each edge, double crochet

Increases at Ends of Rows

To increase by 1 stitch at the start or end of a row, make 2 stitches in the first or last stitch. This means you would *not* skip the first stitch as usual, but work into it instead. Since the turning chain is your first stitch (except in the case of single crochet stitches), you now have 2 stitches instead of one worked into the first stitch of the previous row. To increase by 1 stitch at the end of a row, work 2 stitches into the turning chain instead of one.

For single crochet stitches, to increase at the beginning of a row, work 2 stitches in the first stitch instead of one. To increase at the end of a row, work 2 stitches in the last single crochet.

You can also increase by more than 1 stitch at either end in the same way, working all the additional stitches in the first and/or last stitch of the row. The number of stitches depends entirely on the desired shape; the more stitches are added, the more rapidly the shape expands.

There are cases in which, instead of adding stitches at the edges, you want to make a longer row. To do this, you will first need to add chains for those stitches to be worked into. The chains are added to the row before the one where the additional stitches are needed. It's really quite simple: If you are adding multiple stitches at the beginning of a row, make the new chains at the end of the previous row. To do so, join yarn in the top of the first stitch of the row just before the one that needs extra stitches and chain the necessary number you'll need, then fasten off. Use a separate short strand so you needn't cut the yarn you are working with. Another alternative for adding several stitches at the end of the row is to work foundation stitches (see page 60).

Remember to use the strategies discussed on page 49 to arrive at the correct number of chains needed, including a turning chain.

Decreases at Ends of Rows

To decrease at the side edges, you can either skip stitches, slip stitch over stitches, or, most commonly, work 2 or more stitches together.

Since rows normally start with a turning chain, the first stitch already exists and can't be skipped. To skip a stitch at the beginning of the row, except in the case of single crochet stitches, skip the 2nd stitch and work into the 3rd. For single crochet, you can skip the first stitch, since the chain-1 turning chain does not count as a stitch.

To skip a stitch at the end of a row, it can be left unworked, but this will create a stair step at the edge rather than a smooth diagonal. A better alternative is to skip the second-to-last stitch.

To avoid unwanted bulk when working with thick or textured yarns, skipping stitches is often the best way to decrease. The main thing to look out for when skipping stitches is that you don't unwittingly create a hole in the fabric.

Slip stitches can be used at the beginning and ends of rows to decrease but are generally avoided because they create a stair step at the edge instead of a smooth diagonal. Instead of using slip stitches to decrease, it's preferable to either skip a stitch or work 2 stitches together. Slip stitches are used to decrease in very particular circumstances, for example, at the beginning of armholes on a garment. In this case, several slip stitches are worked at the beginning and end of the first row of the armhole, creating the flat edge that is the desired shape at the bottom of an armhole.

The most common way to decrease is to work stitches together, as shown here for single, half double, double, and treble crochet.

Single Crochet Decrease

(Insert hook in next stitch, yarnover, and draw up a loop) twice, yarnover, draw loop through 3 loops on hook.

Half Double Crochet Decrease

(Yarnover, insert hook in next stitches, yarn-over and draw up a loop) twice, yarnover, draw through 5 loops on hook.

An alternative approach. I find half double crochet stitches can get bulky when worked together the traditional way. Instead, I work as shown below. As you can see, one yarnover has been eliminated, and the stitch is more compact, but it is still the correct height. I prefer this method because it looks neater.

Yarnover, insert hook in next stitches, yarn-over and draw up a loop, insert hook in next stitches, yarnover and draw up a loop, yarn-over, draw through 3 loops on hook.

Double Crochet Decrease

(Yarnover, insert hook in next stitches, yarn-over and draw up a loop, yarnover, draw through 2 loops) twice, yarnover, draw through 3 loops on hook.

Treble Crochet Decrease

[Yarnover twice, insert hook in next stitches, yarnover and draw up a loop, (yarnover, draw through 2 loops) twice] two times, yarnover, draw through 3 loops on hook.

Some Final Thoughts on Decreases

You will notice that in order to decrease, each stitch is being worked until the last yarnover and pull-through, and then joined by drawing the last loop through the 2 incomplete stitches. We encountered this concept earlier when discussing clustered stitches (page 68).

In addition to these traditional ways to work a decrease, I believe one needs some other options. This is an area where experts do not necessarily agree, and I urge you to experiment to find the method that works best in various situations. Much depends on the yarn and gauge; when these are larger, lumps or bumps are also more obvious and may require the finesse that these alternatives afford.

At the beginning of a row, the traditional way is to not actually decrease but simply to count the turning chain and the next stitch as one in the following row. For a cleaner look, I prefer to work 1 chain less for the turning chain when making a decrease at the beginning of the row. So, for a double crochet decrease, I would chain 2, not 3, for the first stitch; when working the next row, that turning chain would not be worked into. Another alternative is to work the turning chain as usual but work the 2nd and 3rd stitches together as described above.

As you work various patterns, you may find designers have devised many interesting shaping strategies. Crochet is very much an evolving art, and rather than holding steadfastly to rules or established procedures, I encourage you to explore any new techniques you come across.

Gauge *Always* Matters

Most people encounter gauge for the first time when working patterns. There is a common misperception that gauge doesn't matter for projects where the exact dimension is not important, like a throw or a scarf. But gauge *does* matter, because it tells you much more about the project than its size. Gauge tells you about the nature of the fabric used in the project.

Gauge indicates how tightly or loosely the project was worked, and as discussed earlier (see page 23), this makes the difference between fabric that is fluid and flowing, or stiffer and more structured. If your gauge is significantly different from the original pattern, your fabric will be as well, and the item may not function as intended. If you want to obtain fabric that is similar to a pattern, not only do you need to match the gauge of the original pattern closely but also the yarn's weight and fiber.

Suppose, for example, that you found a lovely sweater worked with sport-weight yarn, but you want to make that sweater using worsted-weight yarn from your stash. If you matched the gauge of the pattern, your stitches would be very tight, and the sweater would, most likely, be boxy and stiff.

Perhaps the sweater is made with sport-weight bamboo, and you have sport-weight yarn made of cotton. Again, because bamboo is generally much softer and more flexible, your cotton at the same gauge may yield a stiffer fabric (although there are some very soft, flexible cottons). Pay attention to all the elements that contribute to the finished fabric — especially gauge.

You can adjust most patterns to make them with different yarns, but you'll have to put your math skills to use. Please stay calm, even if you are math phobic. The calculator does all the hard work!

To redo a pattern in a different gauge, start by making a swatch with your yarn, keeping in mind the kind of fabric suitable to the item. A wearable should have good drape, but a bag or hat can be more structured. Try different hooks until you have obtained the appropriate fabric, and then measure the gauge. From here, you can refigure the stitch and row counts using your new gauge instead of the gauge used in the pattern. We explain the math in detail starting on page 95.

Measuring Gauge in Stitches and Rows

To determine gauge, begin by working a swatch in the yarn and stitch pattern you want to use in the project. Make the swatch as large as you can manage, and no less than 6 by 6 inches. It's very common for gauge to change once you're working a large piece, as the weight and movement of the fabric itself can influence gauge. For this reason, a larger swatch gives a more realistic gauge measurement.

Contrary to popular belief, it is not necessary to state gauge in increments of 4 inches. This is a convention derived from knitting that many publishers use, but it is not always the best approach with crochet, where our stitches can be much larger than knit stitches. Instead, find a spot where the stitches line up either with an inch, half inch, or quarter inch, since these are easier numbers to work with. Determine separate gauges for stitches and rows. Crochet stitches are taller than they are wide, and having both gauges is critical to accuracy.

Measure the total width and height of your swatch. If the swatch measures 6 by 6 inches, you now know how many stitches and rows it takes to make a 6-inch square of fabric. This method is more precise than measuring only a few stitches, because gauge is not absolutely precise, and taking a measurement from only a small sample is not likely to be accurate. Measure the gauge in several places and determine the average.

Measuring Rows and Stitches

Measuring stitches

Measuring rows

This swatch has 24 stitches in 6 inches and 16 rows in 6 inches. This would be stated as a gauge equation, usually written as follows:

24 sts and 16 rows = 6" × 6"

Measuring Gauge in Stitch Patterns

When a project uses a repeating stitch pattern, it's more convenient to measure the gauge of the pattern repeat rather than individual stitches. The procedure is the same: measure several repeats of the pattern, and state the gauge as "X number of pattern repeats = Y inches."

Some stitch patterns are worked over several rows. In such cases, the row gauge can also be stated as a pattern repeat. Some multirow stitch patterns look fine if they stop in the middle, but

Measuring Stitch Patterns

This swatch has 2 pattern repeats across, measuring 6" and 7 rows measuring just under 2" at the narrowest point.

2 pattern repeats and 7 rows = 6" × 2"

This swatch has 6 pattern repeats and 12 rows. As you can see, the width is 5¾" and the length is 5½".

6 pattern repeats and 12 rows = 5¾" × 5½"

others need all of the rows to avoid jagged edges or asymmetry. In such cases, you will need to know the gauge of the full pattern repeat. Your gauge equation might look like this:

X patt reps = number of inches; Y rows = number of inches

(Y represents the number of rows needed in the full pattern repeat.)

These gauge equations are usually written as "X patt reps and Y rows = number of inches × number of inches."

Don't be fooled by the first pattern repeat. Sometimes it has an extra end stitch, or some other slight modification. Measure middle pattern repeats instead, to avoid trouble.

The Math: Starting with Something Simple

Once you have determined gauge, you can remake a pattern at a new gauge, or design a project from scratch, using the math steps here.

Let's start with the simple example of a scarf that is 10 inches wide and 50 inches long. Let's say your gauge is 12 stitches and 6 rows in a 4-inch square.

$$12 \text{ sts and } 6 \text{ rows} = 4" \times 4"$$

What we are trying to determine is how many of these 4-inch squares are needed to make the full 10-by-50-inch scarf. A great analogy is to think of purchasing tiles to cover a floor — you need to know the dimensions of the floor, then divide that measurement by the size of each tile. For fabric, it's the same, and your gauge swatch is the tile (thank you oftroy from the online yarn community ravelry.com for this clever analogy)!

Calculating the Number of Stitches

- Divide the desired width measurement by the measurement of the "tile":

$$10 \div 4 = 2.5$$

This tells me that I will need 2.5 "tiles" to get the 10 inches needed. My tile, or swatch, has 12 stitches in it. I need to make that tile 2.5 times. In order to do that, I need to know how many stitches this entails.

- To determine the exact number of stitches, multiply the answer obtained in step 1 by the number of stitches in the tile:

$$2.5 \times 12 = 30$$

Now you know that you will need 30 stitches for the scarf to be 10 inches wide.

Calculating the Number of Rows

For length, we work with row gauge and follow the same two-step procedure. In our hypothetical swatch, 6 rows = 4 inches.

- Divide the desired measurement by the number of inches in our tile/swatch:

$$50 \div 4 = 12.5$$

I need to make my tile 12.5 times, and there are 6 rows in each tile.

- To determine the exact number of rows, multiply the number obtained in step 1 by the number of rows in the gauge equation:

$$12.5 \times 6 = 75$$

You need 75 rows to make the scarf 50 inches in length.

Note: If you were to make this scarf with rows running along the long side of the rectangle, you would divide the length (50 inches) by the stitch gauge, and the width (10 inches) by the row gauge.

> **Remember** that when working with gauge and math, inches are always divided by the number of inches in the gauge equation, stitches are always divided by the number of stitches in the equation, and rows are always divided by the number of rows.

More Math: Complex Shaping

As mentioned earlier, to shape projects we add or subtract stitches and rows. Shaping can be done very gradually, as you would on a long sleeve, or all at once, as when adding a ruffle to a hem or neckline.

Using a sleeve as an example, let's look at all the steps involved. It may seem daunting, but once you've done this a few times, it gets much easier.

STEP 1 Determine the dimensions at the beginning and end of the shaping. To make a well-fitting sleeve, you need gradual shaping as the sleeve goes from wrist to upper arm. Suppose that the desired measurement at the wrist is 7 inches, and at the widest part of the sleeve (the bicep) it is 12 inches. I happen to know these measurements, since I design a lot of garments, but you can use a garment that fits well to obtain the measurements.

STEP 2 Determine how many stitches need to be added or subtracted. Having determined the measurements, the next step is to translate those measurements into stitches. That's where gauge comes in. Let's use this gauge equation:

$$25 \text{ sts and } 8 \text{ rows} = 6" \times 6"$$

We need to determine how many stitches at the wrist, how many at the upper arm, and how many rows over which the shaping will be accomplished. Calculate the number of stitches at the wrist, using the two steps described earlier.

- Divide the desired measurement (7") by the number of inches in the gauge equation:

$$7 \div 6 = 1.16666$$

- Multiply this number by the number of stitches in the gauge equation:

$$1.16666 \times 25 = 29.1666$$

Since we can't make a fraction of a stitch, you can use either 29 or 30 stitches. The fraction is small, so 29 stitches will be very close to 7" but a tiny bit less, and 30 stitches will be a bit more than 7". Either is close enough, since crochet fabric has a lot of give. For easier math, let's choose 30 stitches for our stitch count at the wrist.

- For the widest part of the sleeve we would calculate as follows:

$$12 \div 6 = 2$$
$$2 \times 25 = 50$$

We've determined that there should be 50 stitches for the upper part of the sleeve, and 30 at the wrist. This leaves 20 stitches between the narrowest and widest part. Everything we do from now on is aimed at figuring out exactly how and where to add those 20 stitches.

STEP 3 Determine the length over which the shaping must be completed. Now we have to address the issue of how often to make the increases, that is, establish the rate of increase. We want to add the stitches gradually over the length from the wrist to the bicep. This requires another measurement: the distance between where shaping begins to where it ends, in this case, from the wrist to the widest part of the arm. Let's use the ballpark figure of 14 inches. Again, if you don't know this measurement, measure it on something you own.

STEP 4 Determine how many rows are needed for that length. We need to do all the shaping over the span of 14 inches, and we need to know how many rows will be in this span. Here is where we use the row gauge.

- Divide the length between the beginning and end of shaping by the number of inches in the gauge equation:

$$14 \div 6 = 2.333$$

- Multiply the answer by the number of rows in the gauge equation:

$$2.333 \times 8 = 18.666$$

One could conceivably work a fraction of a row by working a shorter stitch, but let's simplify. You could either work the increases over 18 rows or 19 rows. With a sleeve, getting to the widest part a little earlier is a safer choice than getting there a little later — you don't want the sleeve to be too tight on the upper arm — so I would probably choose 18 rows. Whenever you get a fraction at this point, use your judgment as to whether to round up or down. Unless you're working at a very large gauge, 1 stitch more or less is not a big deal. If you are using very tall stitches, though, one *row* more or less can make a substantial difference. In that case, determine how much one extra row adds, and make a decision. (In working with the gauge equation, do not round up or down in the first step, as that will throw your calculations way off. Only round up or down after the second step if you get a fraction.)

Back to our sleeve example: according to the math we did earlier, the first row will have 30 stitches for the wrist, and we have 17 more rows over which to gradually add 20 stitches.

STEP 5 Determine the rate of increase or decrease. A sleeve is usually worked in one piece, and shaped on both the right and left edges, to keep the sleeve symmetrical. That means each increase adds 2 stitches. In fact, most often when garments are worked flat, 1 stitch is added at both sides, and therefore the rate of increase is 2 stitches at a time. It's the same for decreases, which are usually worked at the rate of 2 stitches at a time, one at each edge.

In other types of construction, such as top-down sweaters, you are more likely to shape at 4 or 8 points in the round, so each increase round would add either 4 or 8 stitches. In other words, the method of construction often determines the rate of increase (or decrease), that is, how many stitches are added or subtracted in each increase (or decrease) row or round.

Another factor in the rate of increase or decrease is the stitch pattern itself. Some are easy to shape 1 stitch at a time, but large stitch patterns may need to be increased by several stitches at a time (for more detail on this, see chapter 7). For the moment, let's stick with our simple rate of increase of 2 stitches at a time.

STEP 6 Determine the number of increase or decrease rows. Divide the number of stitches to be added or subtracted (step 2) by the rate of increase (step 5).

- Step 2 told us we need 20 more stitches. We divide this number by the rate of increase:

$$20 \div 2 = 10$$

This tells us we need 10 increase rows to add the correct number of stitches at the rate of 2 stitches at a time.

STEP 7 Determine how to spread out the increase or decrease rows over all the rows from where shaping begins and ends. In step 4, we determined that there are 18 rows from where shaping begins and ends. The first row has the required number of stitches (30) needed for the wrist. We want to make those 10 increases spread out evenly over the remaining 17 rows. Calculate this as follows.

- Take the total number of rows over which the shaping occurs (step 4) and subtract 1. Divide this by the number of shaping rows (step 6).

$$17 \div 10 = 1.7$$

Sometimes this math turns out very nicely and we get a whole number, such as 3 or 5, and we can simply increase every 3rd or 5th row. But often we get these pesky fractions. This fraction, since it is between 1 and 2, tells us that we will sometimes have to increase every row, and sometimes every other row. If we were to increase every row, they would take place on rows 2–11, but we would arrive at the full width of the sleeve too early — not an attractive option!

STEP 8 **If step 7 is a fraction, plot your shaping by adding or subtracting one row between shaping rows.**

Here is how I calculate how to spread out the increases. There are 10 increases to do, and 17 rows in which to do them. If an increase is made every row, we would be done by row 11, and have 7 rows (rows 12–18) with no increases. Instead, we are going to add a row between increases seven times, so that we reach the full width where it's supposed to be. This leaves us with three increases that are in adjacent rows. So, we would increase in rows 2, 4, 6, 7, 9, 11, 12, 14, 16, and 18. As you can see we skipped a row seven times, and ended up reaching the full stitch count where intended. Note that there is some leeway here; it would work just as well to have the adjacent and skipped rows in a slightly different order, so long as they are spread out over the span of the shaping.

If you were working the sleeve in the opposite direction, from the top down, you would begin with 50 stitches for the widest part of the sleeve and decrease at the same rate to end up with 30 stitches for the wrist. The math is the same, but the execution is in reverse. We would make 10 decreases of 2 stitches, three times in adjacent rows, and seven times skipping a row. Either way, the goal of making a smooth diagonal along the shaped edge is achieved.

Clearly, there is a lot of information to absorb in this chapter! My recommendation is to come back to it repeatedly, making use of the procedures you understand and building your skills and comprehension over time. It took me several years to be comfortable when confronted with shaping challenges, and I'm still learning and practicing these skills. I can assure you, it's well worth the effort!

6

Crochet in the Round

ONE OF THE ADVANTAGES of crochet is the ease of working in the round. At its most basic, crocheting in the round, as opposed to working flat, means you connect the end of a row to the beginning. This allows you to work without turning at the ends of rows, with the same side facing you at all times. You can crochet in the round to make a flat circle, a tube, or even a sweater. Most motifs are worked in the round.

There are three basic techniques you need to know for working in the round:

- How to start the circle

- How to start and finish rounds

- How to increase in each round so that the circle lies flat

Starting the Circle

There are several different ways to begin working in the round. You can make several chains (the most common method), make an adjustable ring, or use the first chain as a ring. Let's look at all of these.

Make a Ring with Chains

To make a ring with chains, work several chains, then slip stitch in the first chain to form a ring.

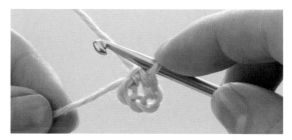

The number of chains is determined by how many stitches you intend to work into the ring and how tightly you want the ring to close.

If you are following a pattern, the number of chains will be specified. Supposing, however, that you are working a hat pattern, and after working the specified number of chains and stitches in the first round, you find you have a larger hole at the center than you'd like. Go ahead and try again with fewer chains: it will cause no harm whatsoever. For other items worked in the round, such as motifs and flowers, the size of the "hole" at the center can make a difference, as it affects the overall size of the finished piece. In these instances, it's wise to stick with the instructions as written.

Simple Adjustable Ring

The great advantage of this method is you can easily work many stitches into the ring, and the ring can be adjusted to whatever size is needed. This is somewhat offset by the fact that the method is a little fiddly, and it may take several attempts before getting it right. Persevere!

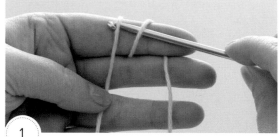

1 Holding the tail end of the yarn, wrap the yarn twice clockwise around your index finger so that the tail is closest to the point of your finger. (Lefties wrap counterclockwise.) Insert the hook under the two strands of yarn.

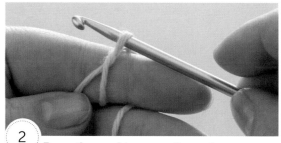

2 Draw the working yarn through.

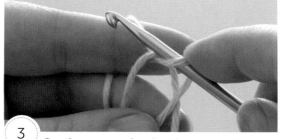

3 Gently remove the ring from your finger.

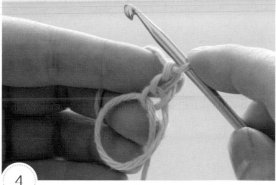

4 Do not count the loop on your hook as the first chain, and chain as necessary for the height of the first stitch.

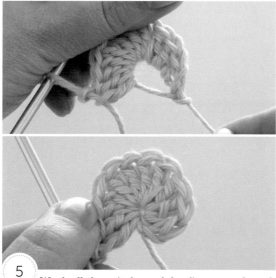

5 Work all the stitches of the first round, and then use the tail to pull the center ring as tight as you wish. Before pulling the ring tight, count the number of stitches you made in the ring to be sure it is accurate.

First Chain as Ring

This is almost as good as the adjustable ring and very easy: chain the number necessary to reach the height of the first stitch in the first round, then add one more chain. (See the chart on page 49 for how many chains are used for stitches of different heights.) Use the extra chain as the ring by working all the stitches of the first round into the first chain, leaving the remaining chains to serve as the first stitch of the round. Here's how this method works for double crochet.

1 Since double crochet stitches are equal to 3 chains, and we want one extra chain, chain 4 to begin.

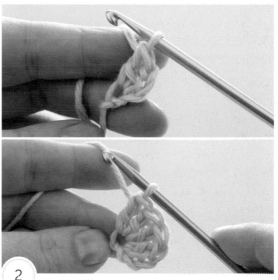

2 Work all first round stitches into the first of these 4 chains, leaving 3 chains for the first stitch.

For half double crochet, which equal 2 chains, you would chain 3 instead; with treble crochet (4 chains) you would chain 5. The chain easily stretches to accommodate all the stitches in the first round.

The one drawback with this method is that the first chain tends to stretch out too much for a tightly closed ring. If that's your aim, you may have a better result with the adjustable ring.

Starting and Ending Rounds

After making the ring to begin, the first round of stitches starts the same way as a row: chain the required number of stitches for the desired height (see chart page 49). Placing a stitch marker in the first stitch of a round can help you keep track of where you are, though it's not usually necessary unless the yarn is fuzzy or you are working at a very small gauge where stitches are hard to see.

At the end of the round, unless working in a spiral (we'll get to that shortly), the last stitch is slip stitched to the top of the starting chain. Slip stitching at the end of each round usually results in a visible "seam" line, where the joins of all the rows line up. There are various techniques for minimizing this so that the seam is less obvious. Whether they work in a project depends on various qualities in the yarn (such as fuzziness), the gauge (large-gauge joins are more visible), and the stitches used. Paradoxically, some of these techniques are the exact opposite of the other, yet one or the other strategy may work. You never know until you swatch!

- When finishing a round, slip stitch into the back loop only.

- When finishing a round, do not slip stitch into the turning chain, but into the next stitch in the round. This obscures the turning chain. With this method, do not count the turning chain in the stitch count.

- When increasing in rounds, always place your increase in the first stitch of the round.

- When increasing in rounds, always place an increase in the last stitch of the round.

Shaping a Circle

Sometime in our childhoods we learned about the relationship between the diameter and circumference of a circle, remember? In crochet circles, too, there is a relationship between the growing diameter of a circle as you work in rounds from the center out, and its circumference. Since the circumference, or outside edge, of the circle is larger than its center, you will need to add stitches as you proceed. But how many, and where?

Luckily, there is a very simple formula that works in crochet, and you are likely to encounter it repeatedly. It works like this: depending on the height of the stitch used, there is a "perfect" number to increase in each round for your circle to lie flat.

BASIC STITCH INCREASES FOR CIRCLES	
Single crochet	6
Half double crochet	8
Double crochet	11 or 12
Treble crochet	15 or 16

That means when working a circle in single crochet, you will begin with 6 stitches in the first round, make 12 in the 2nd round, 18 in the 3rd round, and so forth. For circles made with half doubles, make 8 stitches in the first round, 16 in the next round, and 24 in the 3rd round. As you can see, the taller the stitch, the more stitches need to be added in each round. That's the part that relates to diameter and π — the taller the stitch, the bigger the circle grows each round, and that's why more stitches are added.

These perfect numbers don't always work precisely, because there is variation in how people work heights of stitches. We'll give you some alternatives shortly.

The next question is where to put the increases, and here there is a standard formula, too. A simple way to explain it is as follows:

Rnd 1 Work X stitches.

Rnd 2 Work 2 stitches in each stitch.

Rnd 3 Work 2 stitches in every other stitch.

Rnd 4 Work 2 stitches in every 3rd stitch.

Rnd 5 Work 2 stitches in every 4th stitch.

When not working 2 stitches into 1, always work 1 stitch into 1 stitch.

In this method, each round has 1 more stitch between increases. To stay on track with stitch counts, always make the increase in the first increase stitch of the previous round. That way you will see the increases line up over one another.

If you make a very large circle, say for a rug or throw, many rounds of work will be required, and

Counting Tip

When you slip stitch to close the ring, you add an extra loop, making it appear that you have 1 additional stitch in the round. To stay on track, be consistent about where you work the 2nd and last stitches in the round. The first stitch will always be a chain, emerging from the turning chain of the round before, and the 2nd stitch will be an increase. Work that increase in the first stitch in each round, then skip what appears to be the last stitch in the round: that is the extra loop created by the slip stitch and not a real stitch at all.

Working first stitch of round

Working last stitch of round

the increases grow very far apart. In such cases you can place markers to help find the increase points.

To understand how circles work, there's no better way than to make some, using stitches of different heights. When trying some of the patterns for circles, remember to keep the troubleshooting tip mentioned in mind, especially this one: count the stitches at the end of each round!

These samples begin with the simplest method of creating the starting circle: chain the correct number for the stitch height plus 1 extra chain and work into the first chain for the first round. If you prefer a different method for starting the circle, feel free to use it, and remember to omit the extra chain at the start.

These circles can easily be turned into hats. Work the circle until the diameter reaches about 8 inches for an adult hat, then work even to make the sides of the hat, until the hat is as long as you like.

When Your Circle Is Not Flat

As neat as this method is for making circles, it doesn't work in all situations. You'll know because the circle will not lie flat but rather will curl or ruffle at the edges. Curling means there are not enough stitches in the round, and ruffling means there are too many. If you are following a pattern and your circle is not lying flat, it may be a problem with gauge — if it departs significantly from the original design, the rate of increase may not work. If the curling or ruffling is slight, you can block the item to lie flat. If all else fails, you may need to fudge stitch counts to make the circle lie flat. Depending on the item you're making and the complexity of the stitches used, minor tweaking of stitch counts can be an option.

Troubleshooting: Maintaining Stitch Counts

The slip stitches made at the ends of rounds do not entirely cover the top of the starting chain and therefore can appear to be an additional stitch. Because of this, it's easy to mistakenly add an extra stitch. There are several things to do that will help you avoid this error.

• Pay close attention when working the 2nd stitch of the round. If the 2nd stitch is an increase, be sure to insert the hook in the first stitch of the previous round.

• Mark the slip stitch at the end of the round right after you make it, so you are not tempted to work into it at the end of the round.

• Count your stitches at the end of each round.

Circle with Half Double Crochet Stitches

Ch 3 (counts as hdc and center ring).

Rnd 1 Work 7 hdc in ring, sl st to top of ch. *(8 hdc)*

Rnd 2 Ch 2 (counts as first hdc throughout), hdc in same hdc, 2 hdc in each hdc around, sl st to top of ch-2. *(16 hdc)*

Rnd 3 Ch 2, hdc in first hdc , *hdc in next hdc**, 2 hdc in next hdc, rep from * around ending last rep at **, sl st to top of ch-2. *(24 hdc)*

Rnd 4 Ch 2, hdc in first hdc, *hdc in next 2 hdc**, 2 hdc in next hdc, rep from * around ending last rep at **, sl st to top of ch-2. *(32 hdc)*

Rnd 5 Ch 2, hdc in first hdc, *hdc in next 3 hdc**, 2 hdc in next hdc, rep from * around ending last rep at **, sl st to top of ch-2. *(48 hdc)*

To make this circle larger, continue increasing at the same rate — 8 sts per round — always making 2 hdc in the first stitch of the increase in the previous round, which will automatically add 1 more stitch between increases in each round.

The half double crochet circle has a very nice appearance on the back. The backs of hdc stitches have a horizontal line formed by the yarnover made in each stitch, and these lines form circles outlining each round. To obtain a similar effect on the front, you can work into the back loop throughout, as was done on the next swatch, worked with double crochet. If you're not yet comfortable working into the back loop, feel free to make the circle with normal double crochet stitches.

Front

Back

Circle with Double Crochet Stitches

Ch 4 (counts as dc and center ring).

Rnd 1 Work 11 dc in ring, sl st to top of ch-3. (*12 dc*)

Rnd 2 Ch 3 (counts as first dc throughout), BLdc in same dc, *2 BLdc in next dc, rep from * around, sl st to top of ch-3. (*24 dc*)

Rnd 3 Ch 3, BLdc in same dc, *BLdc in next dc**, 2 BLdc in next dc, rep from * around ending last rep at **, sl st to top of ch-3. (*36 dc*)

Rnd 4 Ch 3, BLdc in same dc, *BLdc in next 2 dc**, 2 BLdc in next dc, rep from * around ending last rep at **, sl st to top of ch-3. (*48 dc*)

To make this circle larger, continue increasing at the same rate, in this case, 12 sts per round, by making 2 dc in the first stitch of the increase made in the previous round.

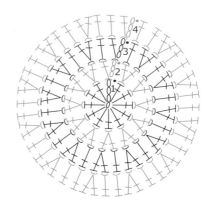

Other Methods for Shaping Circles

Suppose you don't want to use the same stitch height for the entire circle. For example, for your hat, you'd like some rounds of half double crochet stitches, others with single or double crochet You will have to adjust the increases accordingly, keeping in mind that shorter stitches need fewer increases per round, and taller ones more. You can still use the increase formula on page 102 as a guide, but also, feel free to experiment!

Improvising. If the standard formula is not working, here's how to determine when to increase as you go: Take careful note of whether the round you are working lines up nicely with the previous rounds. Wherever you find the working round pulling to the right (or left, for lefties), add a stitch, right there. Making increases as you need them, without placing them at regular intervals, will get you a flat circle. You can't use this method if you are writing a pattern (it will be tough for others to follow), but it's fine if you're making your own design. The irregular increase will not be evident in a sea of plain stitches.

Recalculate the math. On the other hand, if you prefer to establish a regular rate of increase, try this method. Work a few rounds in the improvised method described above. Determine how many additional stitches you need in each round to keep the circle flat. Add these numbers together, then divide by the number of rounds worked to obtain the average. For example, say the first round added 10 stitches, the 2nd round added 8 stitches, and the 3rd round added 6 stitches. Add the number of stitches together (24), and divide by the number of rounds (24 ÷ 3 = 8). Most likely you can use the rate of 8 extra stitches in each round. (Round fractions up or down.)

Creating a central hole. If you want a circle with a large hole at the center, how do you know how many stitches to make in the first round? Pretend you are going to start with a closed circle and work a few rounds in the yarn and stitch you plan to use. Now measure how many rounds you can eliminate at the center to create the size hole you want. For example, if the circumference after 3 rounds is just the size you want the center hole to be, start your actual piece with the number of stitches you have in round 4, and increase at the rate you would use for that particular stitch height from that point on.

A random approach. Be aware that placing increases in the manner we've been discussing actually does not produce a true circle but a polygon. In most situations that's close enough, but if you really want a circle with smooth edges and no points, place your increases more randomly throughout the round. Avoid bunching them up on one portion of the circle; spread the increases out over the entire round. One way to achieve a random effect is to use the standard increase pattern but offset it by several stitches in one direction for a round, then back in the other, avoiding placing increase points over one another.

Work is pulling to the right.

Add a stitch so that it lines up.

Working in a Spiral

To work a spiral, instead of slip stitching at the end of the round, you simply begin working the next round into the previous one. In every respect except the slip stitch at the end, you can follow the exact same methods as described earlier. It is harder to recognize where each round starts and ends; put a marker in the first stitch of the round so you can see the beginning of the round and keep track of your increases.

Spiral

Spirals work best with single crochet stitches.

Ch 2.

Rnd 1 Work 6 sc in 2nd ch from hook. (*6 sc*) Pm in first sc of rnd.

Rnd 2 Work 2 sc in each sc around. (*12 sc*)

Move marker to first sc of each round after making the st. Do this on each rnd.

Rnd 3 Work 2 sc in first sc, *sc in next sc, 2 sc in next sc, rep from * around, sc in last sc. (*18 sc*)

Rnd 4 Work 2 sc in first sc, *sc in next 2 sc, 2 sc in next sc, rep from * around, sc in next 2 sc. (*24 sc*)

Rnd 5 Work 2 sc in first sc, *sc in next 3 sc, 2 sc in next sc, rep from * around, sc in next 3 sc. (*30 sc*)

Rnd 6 Work 2 sc in first sc, *sc in next 4 sc, 2 sc in next sc, rep from * around, sc in next 4 sc. (*36 sc*)

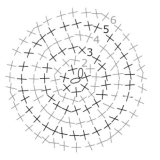

Spiral with Tall Stitches

In order to work the spiral method with taller stitches, it's necessary to make a few adjustments. This is done by using shorter stitches at the very beginning and end of the spiral. At the end, I used an extended stitch (notated with an *E* in front of the name of the stitch) to make the shape as smooth as possible, without any "bumps" or "humps" in the outside edge (see page 56).

Sc2tog (Insert hook in next st, yo, draw up a loop) twice, yo, draw through 3 loops on hook

....

Ch 2.

Rnd 1 (2 sc, 2 hdc, 8 dc) in first ch, do not join (here and throughout). Pm in first sc. (*12 sts*)

Rnd 2 2 dc in first sc, 2 dc in each st around. (*24 dc*)

Move the marker to the first st of the rnd right after making it, on every rnd.

Rnd 3 2 dc in first dc, *dc in next dc, 2 dc in next dc, rep from * around, dc in last dc. (*36 dc*)

Rnd 4 2 dc in first dc, *dc in next 2 dc, 2 dc in next dc, rep from * around, dc in last 2 dc. (*48 dc*)

Continue increasing in the same manner, following the method of increasing 12 dc per round until the spiral is the desired size.

Last round Work according to standard increase to last 2 sts of rnd. Ehdc in next 2 dc, hdc in next 2 dc, sc in next 4 dc, slip st to next dc, fasten off.

The precise number of shorter stitches at the end of the spiral can vary. The aim is to remove any stair steps or "humps" along the perimeter of the circle. Experiment until the shape looks best.

Stitch Patterns in Circular Work

There are a few considerations to keep in mind when working stitch patterns in the round. Normally, the multiple for a stitch pattern will specify the number of stitches in a pattern repeat, plus any extra stitches at the edges (see page 48). When working in the round, there are no side edges, and therefore you need only the number of stitches in the stitch pattern itself. This affects the number of chains you start out with.

Something else to consider when working in the round is whether you want to have the right side facing at all times. Most stitch patterns look fine this way, and in fact, some look even better when the right side is always facing. But other stitch patterns require you to turn in order to achieve a particular effect. For example, bobbles pop on the wrong side of the work, and therefore it's more convenient to turn so that the wrong side is facing when working a bobble round. It's perfectly fine to turn when working in rounds if this is the case.

Another reason to turn at the ends of rounds is that crochet fabric tends to bias in one direction if there is no turning. I find this particularly true with taller stitches. If the bias is not too obvious, it can usually be corrected with blocking. If it is pronounced, it's better to turn every round to avoid it.

When working cable stitches in the round, you can take advantage of the fact that the right side is facing and avoid working cables on the wrong side of the work. You'll have to go through the pattern instructions and see where back post stitches can be turned into front post stitches instead. Cables can actually look better worked in the round than flat, since all the post stitches are made in the same direction. The Colorwork Bag (page 222) is worked in this manner.

Crocheting Tubes

Hats are usually begun at the top with a small circle, but many circular projects don't begin with a circle, though they are worked in the round. Instead, we use circular crochet to form tubes, which can be shaped to make bags, cowls, ponchos, and even pullover sweaters.

When making such projects in the round, you may need quite a long foundation chain. I recommend that you don't close the chain, but wait until the end of the first round to slip stitch and close. There are two reasons: (1) you can correct a mistake in the number of chains using strategies discussed on page 50, and (2) a long chain easily twists while attempting to close it. If left open, it's easy to work into the chain correctly in round 1 without twisting. The initial chain can be closed easily with a tapestry needle when finishing the work.

Three of the patterns in this book — the Colorwork Bag (page 222), Slouchy Hat (page 212), and Marguerite Cowl (page 218) — are tubes worked in the round, and you can see how the principles discussed here are put to use. More tips on working in the round can also be found in those patterns.

7

Advanced Shaping

T'S NO SURPRISE THAT SHAPING with stitch patterns is more complicated than shaping rows of plain stitches. The sheer number and variety of stitch patterns make general rules hard to come by. Nevertheless, you will find useful strategies in this chapter to help you tackle shaping with a great many stitches, as well as principles you can use to explore this topic further.

Published information on the subject of shaping with stitch patterns is scarce. For that reason, I give a great deal of attention to it in this chapter. Some of the stitch patterns here may be new to you, so you can learn a stitch while also learning how to shape it. I've included many stitching tips that help make the patterns look their best, and analyzed the stitch patterns to show how they are put together. I hope this will expand the way you regard stitch patterns in general, uncovering links and relationships you might not have noticed in the past.

Think of shaping in the context of the types of items you want to make. Many crochet accessories are based on simple shapes like rectangles, tubes, or triangles. Hats are essentially circles and

tubes; many bags are rectangles, as are scarves; and wraps can be rectangles, triangles, or half circles. As we approach more tailored items such as sweaters, we use different shaping tools that allow us to create the more exacting shape of an armhole or a neckline.

In chapter 5 (page 82), we began discussing the need to increase or decrease in order to shape pieces to the desired dimensions. As we saw there, you can shape gradually, over a long span, as when making a sleeve that grows slowly from wrist to upper arm. On such items, we need to increase or decrease at a slow rate, perhaps 1 or 2 stitches at a time over many rows. In other circumstances, as when making circles, we increase rapidly, many stitches on each round or row.

You can shape at the edges of the work, or within a row or round. The first method is used when the project is made in a flat piece, or with several flat pieces that are seamed together. Shawls can be shaped at the edges, and sweaters made in several pieces are usually shaped at the edges too.

Circular shaping, or crochet in the round, which we began exploring in chapter 6, takes advantage of a technique called internal shaping.

In circular shaping we turn tubes into bags, capes, and even one-piece sweaters by shaping with increases and decreases within the rounds.

The distinction between these two types of construction is important, because it often dictates the choice of stitch pattern. Some stitch patterns are more adaptable than others and can be used in a variety of constructions, while others are more limited. Some stitch patterns lend themselves better than others to fine shaping, where stitches can be added or subtracted one stitch at a time, and others create strong angles because several stitches must be added or subtracted at a time.

Shaping and Stitch Patterns

Stitch patterns are often categorized by the type of stitch used (such as shells, ripples, or post stitches) or by the type of fabric produced (such as lace or textured). For our purposes, however, we need to look at other factors. What stitches are at the edges? What directions do the stitches move in? How many stitches and rows are in the pattern repeat? These factors control the type of shaping strategy best used with that particular stitch pattern.

The stitch patterns in this chapter show how these rules can be implemented, along with many other techniques you will find helpful when shaping stitch patterns. To get the most out of this section, make the swatches as you read along. You will understand this material more fully when you can see actual stitches and execute the moves with your own hands and tools. Plus, the swatches will come in handy for your own reference purposes.

Each stitch pattern here is selected because it is an iconic and beloved crochet pattern, or because it is a good example of a well-known group, such as shells and ripples. You can apply the techniques you'll learn here to other stitches in the same family, or any other stitch patterns that work similarly. There really are no rights and wrongs here, and there are always new discoveries to be made.

The easiest patterns to shape are those whose stitches align one on top of the other in a vertical direction. Let's start by looking at some that work this way.

Keep the guidelines below in mind as we explore shaping strategies and stitch patterns.

Shaping Guidelines

- When shaping at the edges, always work into the last stitch (usually a turning chain) to maintain the integrity of the side edge of the work.

- When decreasing at side edges, work 2 stitches together, rather than making slip stitches over decreased stitches. The latter produces a stair step at the edge. Instead we want smooth edges, which give a clean finish to a project.

- Keep disruption of the stitch pattern to a minimum.

- Maintain the lines of the stitches. Notice how stitches are aligned, whether they are vertical or slanted, and mimic those lines in shaping.

- If a cluster of stitches (for example, puff or bobble) or post stitch lands at the edge, turn it into a single stitch of the same height to avoid a bulky edge.

Basic Stitch with Decrease

Ch an even number. (*ch 16 for swatch*)

Row 1 Sc in 2nd ch from hook, *dc in next ch, sc in next ch, rep from * across, turn. (*15 sts*)

Row 2 Ch 3 (counts as dc), *sc in next dc, dc in next sc, rep from * across, turn. (*15 sts*)

Row 3 (dec at beg of row) Ch 1, insert hook in first dc, yo and draw up loop, yo, insert hook in next sc, yo and draw up loop, yo, draw through 2 loops, yo, draw through 3 loops (sc and dc sts have been worked together), *sc in next dc, dc in next sc, rep from * across, sc in last dc, turn. (*14 sts*)

Row 4 (dec at end of row) Ch 3, *sc in next dc, dc in next sc, rep from * across to last 3 sts, sc in next dc, yo, insert hook in next sc, yo and draw up loop, yo, draw through 2 loops, insert hook in next dc, yo and draw up loop, yo, draw through 3 loops, turn. (*13 sts*)

Rep rows 3 and 4 to continue decreasing.

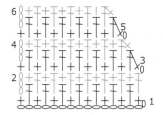

Basic Stitch with Increase

Simple Filet Increase and Decrease

Crocheters love filet patterns, usually made with a series of double crochet stitches with chain-1 or chain-2 spaces between them. It takes some ingenuity to shape them and still observe the shaping guidelines. The swatch here has 6 rows of increasing, then 2 rows worked even, then 6 rows of decreasing, and a last row worked even.

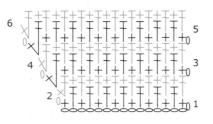

Ch an even number. (*ch 16 for swatch*)

Row 1 Sc in 2nd ch from hook, *dc in next ch, sc in next ch, rep from * across, turn. (*15 sts*)

Row 2 (inc row) Ch 1, (sc, dc) in first sc, *sc in next dc, dc in next sc, rep from * across, turn. (*16 sts*)

Row 3 (inc row) Ch 1, sc in first dc, *dc in next sc, sc in next dc, rep from * to last sc, (dc, sc) in last sc, turn. (*17 sts*)

Rep rows 2 and 3 to continue increasing.

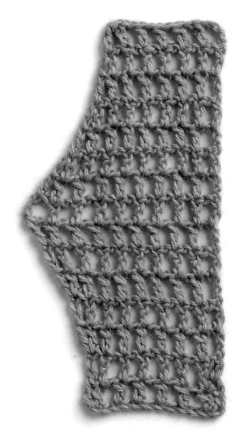

Oh, an even number. (Ch 16 for swatch)

INCREASE ROWS

Row 1 Dc in 6th ch from hook, *ch 1, sk next ch, dc in next ch, rep from * across, 2 dc in last ch, turn. (*8 dc, 6 ch-sps*)

Row 2 Ch 4 (counts as dc, ch 1 throughout), *dc in next dc, sk next ch, ch 1, rep from * across, dc in 3rd ch of tch, turn. (*8 dc, 7 ch-sps*)

Row 3 Ch 4, sk next ch, *dc in next dc, ch 1, sk next ch, rep from * across, 2 dc in 3rd ch of tch, turn. (*9 dc, 7 ch-sps*)

Rows 4 and 5 Rep rows 2 and 3 (*10 dc, 8 ch-sps*)

Row 6 Rep row 2. (*10 dc, 9 ch-sps*)

WORKING EVEN

Rows 7 and 8 Ch 4, *dc in next dc, ch 1, rep from * across, dc in 3rd ch of tch, turn.

DECREASE ROWS

Row 9 Work in patt to last 2 sts, sk next ch, dc in tch, turn. (*10 dc, 8 ch-sps*)

Row 10 Ch 2, *dc in next dc, ch 1, rep from * across, dc in tch, turn. (*9 dc, 8 ch-sps*)

Rows 11 and 12 Rep rows 9 and 10. (*8 dc, 7 ch-sps*)

Row 13 Work even in pattern

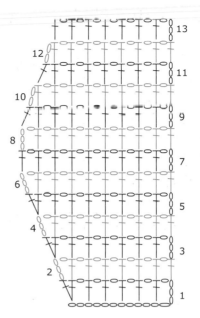

With this stitch pattern, even when there is no shaping, the chains that land at the ends of rows are not worked as chains but as double crochet stitches instead. A chain at the beginning or end of a row would leave us without a real edge — not a good thing! For increasing, we substitute a double crochet stitch for the chain, and work 2 double crochet stitches in the last stitch of the row to make the increase, as is done on all odd-numbered rows here. For the next increase (in even-numbered rows), we chain between those 2 double crochet stitches, thereby adding 1 stitch and also staying in pattern. To decrease in this pattern, work 2 double crochet stitches together when the decrease is at the end of the row. When the decrease is at the beginning of the row, substitute a chain-2 for the turning chain and leave it unworked on the following row.

Shaping the V-stitch

Our next iconic stitch pattern is the ever popular V-stitch. These can be made in several ways, but here we use the most common, where the V consists of double crochet, chain 1, double crochet. With this stitch pattern, we are no longer working with strictly vertical lines, since the V forms an angle. This will dictate some of the shaping decisions made. Our swatch begins with decrease rows, followed by increase rows.

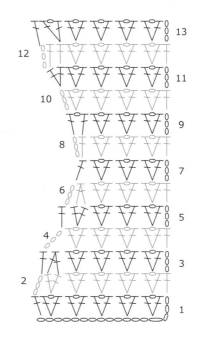

Ch a multiple of 3 plus 2 for tch. (*ch 17 for swatch*)

Row 1 (Dc, ch 1, dc) in 4th ch from hook, *sk 2 ch, (dc, ch 1, dc) in next ch, rep from * across, dc in last ch, turn. (*5 V-sts, 2 dc*)

DECREASE ROWS

Row 2 Ch 3, 2 dc in next ch-1 sp, *(dc, ch 1, dc) in next ch-1 sp, rep from * across, dc in tch, turn. (*4 V-sts, 4 dc*)

Row 3 Ch 3, *(dc, ch 1, dc) in next ch-1 sp, rep from * across to last 3 sts, dc2tog, dc in tch, turn. (*4 V-sts, 2 dc, 1 dc2tog*)

Row 4 Ch 3, sk dc2tog, *(dc, ch 1, dc) in next ch-1 sp, rep from * across, dc in tch, turn. (*4 V-sts, 2 dc*)

Row 5 Ch 3, *(dc, ch 1, dc) in next ch-1 sp, rep from * across to last 4 sts, 2 dc in next ch-1 sp, dc in tch, turn. (*3 V-sts, 4 dc*)

Row 6 Ch 3, dc2tog, *(dc, ch 1, dc) in next ch-1 sp, rep from * across, dc in tch, turn. (*3 V-sts, 2 dc, 1 dc2tog*)

Row 7 Ch 3, *(dc, ch 1, dc) in next ch-1 sp, rep from * across to last 2 sts, sk dc2tog, dc in tch, turn. (*3 V-sts, 2 dc*)

To work the first decrease in row 2, we could work as follows:

Dc2tog, ch 1, dc in next dc.

But this creates a vertical line in a pattern whose lines are slanted, except at the side edges. As mentioned in Shaping Guidelines (page 112), it's preferable to find a way of decreasing that is less disruptive of the natural lines of the stitch pattern. Instead, we eliminated the chain-1 in the first V-stitch. That way, where there were 4 stitches comprising the first edge stitch and the first V-stitch (which consists of 3 stitches), we have made a 1-stitch decrease by eliminating the chain. When we arrive at the next decrease, at the end of row 3, bring those 3 stitches down to 2, by working this:

Dc2tog, dc in tch.

This method will not disrupt the natural lines of the pattern. For the following decrease at the start of row 4, we can simply skip the 2nd double crochet of the row (which is the dc2tog just worked), and continue in pattern. We have worked 4 decrease rows of this pattern.

INCREASE ROWS

Row 8 Ch 3, dc in first dc, *(dc, ch 1, dc) in next ch-1 sp, rep from * across, dc in tch, turn. *The increase is the dc made in the first dc.* (3 V-sts, 3 dc)

Row 9 Ch 3, *(dc, ch 1, dc) in next ch-1 sp, rep from * across to last 2 sts, dc in next dc, ch 1, dc in tch, turn. *The increase is the ch-1 before the last dc.* (3 V-sts, 3 dc, 1 ch)

Row 10 Ch 3, *(dc, ch 1, dc) in next ch-1 sp, rep from * to last st, dc in tch, turn. *The increase is the dc made right after the starting ch 3.* (4 V-sts, 2 dc)

Row 11 Ch 3, *(dc, ch 1, dc) in next ch-1 sp, rep from * across, 2 dc in tch, turn. *The increase is the 2nd dc in the tch.* (4 V-sts, 3 dc)

Row 12 Ch 3, dc in first dc, dc in next dc, *(dc, ch 1, dc) in next ch-1 sp, rep from * across, dc in tch, turn. *The increase is the dc after the starting ch.* (4 V-sts, 4 dc)

Row 13 Ch 3, (dc, ch 1, dc) in next ch-1 sp, rep from * to last 3 sts, (dc, ch 1, dc) in next dc, sk next dc, dc in tch. *The increase is the last ch-1 made in the row.* (5 V-sts, 2 dc)

Increasing in this stitch pattern is more straightforward, but here there are choices to be made as well. In the first row of increase, it's easy to add a double crochet stitch at the beginning of the row. For the next increase at the end of the row, we have 3 choices:

- Work 2 dc in the 2nd-to-last stitch.

- Work 2 dc in the last stitch.

- Work (ch 1, dc) in the last stitch.

The latter looked best to me with the particular yarn and gauge of this swatch, but any of these will work. The point here is that with any stitch pattern, it's wise to explore shaping options and choose the one that looks best. In most crochet patterns there are several possible solutions to shaping, and many variables that can affect your choice, including these:

- **Smoothness of the yarn.** With yarns that have texture or fuzz, subtle shaping may not be necessary if individual stitches are obscured.

- **Gauge.** Larger stitches magnify irregularities in the lines of a pattern and may require more finesse in shaping.

Shaping a Textured Stitch

Here's a swatch that illustrates how to remove a bulky stitch from the edge when shaping. This stitch pattern makes for good practice before getting into the more complex cables featured in chapter 8. It features an interesting technique for creating a cabled texture: a post stitch and a regular double crochet stitch worked together.

It is only fair to warn you about an issue that makes this pattern tricky: with the alternating rows of double and single crochet stitches in this pattern, the stitches do not line up precisely from one row to the next. When you come to the end of row 2, before turning, take note of how the single crochet stitches sit slightly to the left of the doubles from the row before. When you turn, they will be slightly to the right. Left-handed crocheters will see the single crochet stitches slightly to the right on the working row, and slightly to the left on the following row. Keep this in mind as you work into the single crochet stitches to ensure that you are working into the right one. As you start decreasing, the misalignment can make it confusing to determine which single crochet to work into, so remember that they are always to the right of the double crochet stitches for right-handers, and slightly to the left of the double crochet stitches for left-handers.

One more note about this stitch pattern: it has half double crochet stitches on each end rather than double crochet. The FPdc/dc and dc/FPdc that are 1 stitch in from the edges will sit lower, because the posts worked into stitches 2 rows below affect the height of the stitch, and the shorter end stitches match the height of these post stitches. On decrease rows, however, there are no post stitches near the edge, so the edge stitches can be double crochet stitches.

In row 14 of the pattern, the decrease must be made over a chain-1 that is part of a chain-4 turning chain. This is done here by working the

first single crochet of the decrease under the chain-4 turning chain, and the second single crochet of the decrease in the 3rd chain of the turning chain.

dc/FPdc Yo, insert hook in next st, yo and draw up a loop, yo, draw through 2 loops, yo, insert hook around post of st 2 sts to the left and 2 rows below, yo and draw up a loop, yo, draw yarn through 2 loops, yo, draw through 3 loops.

FPdc/dc Yo, insert hook around post of st 2 sts to the right and 2 rows below, draw up a loop, yo, draw through 2 loops, insert hook in next st in current row, yo and draw up a loop, yo, draw through 2 loops, yo, draw through 3 loops.

Sc2tog (insert hook in next st, yo, draw up a loop) twice, yo, draw through 3 loops on hook.

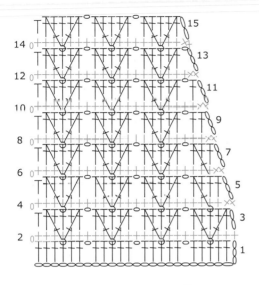

xx = sc2tog

Ch a multiple of 6, plus 1 end stitch, plus 2 for tch. (*ch 27 for swatch*)

Row 1 Dc in 4th ch from hook, dc in next 4 ch, *ch 1, sk next ch, dc in next 5 ch, rep from * across, dc in last ch, turn. (*22 dc, 3 ch-sps*)

Row 2 Ch 1, sc in each dc and ch-1 sp across, turn. (*25 sc*)

Row 3 Ch 2 (counts as hdc throughout), *dc/FPdc, dc in next 3 sc, FPdc/dc**, ch 1, sk next sc, rep from * across, ending last rep at **, hdc in last sc, turn. (*25 sts*)

To work this patt even, rep rows 2 and 3.

Row 4 (dec row) Ch 1, sc in each st to last 2 sts, sc2tog, turn. (*24 sc*)

Row 5 Ch 3 (counts as dc throughout), dc in next 3 sc, FPdc/dc, *ch 1, sk next sc, dc/FPdc, dc in next 3 sc, FPdc/dc**, rep from * across, ending last rep at **, hdc in last sc, turn. (*24 sts*)

Row 6 (dec row) Rep row 4. (*23 sc*)

Row 7 Ch 3, dc in next 2 sc, FPdc/dc, ch 1, sk next sc, cont in established patt across, turn. (*23 sts*)

Row 8 (dec row) Rep row 4. (*22 sc*)

Row 9 Ch 3, dc in next 2 sc, ch 1, sk next sc, cont in established patt across, turn.

Row 10 (dec row) Rep row 4. (*21 sts*)

Row 11 Ch 3, dc in next dc, ch 1, sk next sc, cont in established patt across, turn.

Row 12 (dec row) Rep row 4. (*20 sc*)

Row 13 Ch 4 (counts as dc, ch 1), sk next sc, cont in established patt across, turn.

Row 14 (dec row) Ch 1, sc in each st across to ch-4 tch, sc2tog, placing first sc of decrease under ch-4 and 2nd sc of decrease in 3rd ch of ch-4, turn. (*19 sc*)

Row 15 Rep row 3.

You have now decreased one full pattern repetition, at the rate of 1 stitch every other row. From this point you can continue to decrease at this rate by repeating rows 4–15. It is also possible to decrease or increase in this pattern in the double crochet rows. For a pattern like this, I would draw the decreases (or increases) by hand to visualize exactly how the shaping will work before attempting it with the hook.

Managing the Post Stitches

The post stitches in this pattern must stretch over the distance of 3 stitches and 2 rows. To make the post stitches lie flat without pulling at the work, make them long: after inserting the hook around the post, draw the next loop up high before completing the stitch. After working the first dc/FPdc, the next double crochet is worked behind the post stitch just completed, and the double crochet stitch after that goes into the same stitch where the post stitch was placed. After one more double crochet, you work the FPdc/dc, with the post stitch being worked into the same post. Insert your hook below the earlier post on that stitch.

Shaping with Half-Pattern Repeats

Shaping gets more challenging when stitches do not align vertically from one row to the next. Some of our favorite stitch patterns — shells and fans, for example — are like that. In most cases, we can shape such patterns by increasing or decreasing at the rate of one-half a pattern repeat.

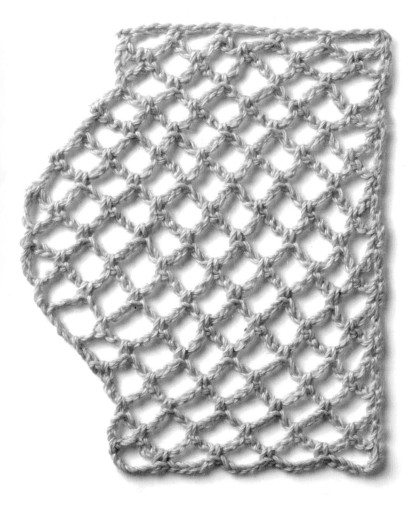

Trellis Stitch Shaping

This trellis pattern consists of a series of chained loops connected with single crochet stitches. We shape it by increasing or decreasing at the rate of a half-pattern repeat per row, thereby adding or subtracting one full pattern repeat over 2 rows.

Notes

At the end of row 11, do not work the dc into the 3rd ch of the tch, but insert the hook under the ch-5 loop. The dc here counts as the final 3 ch of the ch-5 space. By working it as described, we bring the working yarn to the place where the next row must start. In the next row, we will treat this (dc, ch 2) as if it were a ch-5 sp.

Ch a multiple of 4 sts, plus 1 for end st, plus 1 for tch. (*ch 22 for swatch*)

Row 1 Sc in 2nd ch, *ch 5, sk 3 ch, sc in next ch, rep from * across, turn. (*6 sc, 5 ch-5 sps*)

Row 2 Ch 5 (counts as dc, ch 2), *sc in next ch-5 sp**, ch 5, rep from * across, ending last rep at **, ch 2, dc in last sc, turn. (*2 dc, 5 sc, 4 ch-5 sps, 2 ch-2 sps*)

Row 3 Ch 1, sc in first dc, *ch 5, sc in next ch-5 sp, rep from * across placing last sc in 3rd ch of tch. (*6 sc, 5 ch-5 sps*)

To increase, do not turn yet.

INCREASE ROWS

Row 4 Ch 5 (counts as dc, ch 2), turn, sc in BL of 2nd ch from hook (to keep from twisting), *ch 5, sc in next ch-5 sp, rep from * across, ch 2, dc in last sc, turn. (*6 sc, 2 dc, 5 ch-5 sps, 2 ch-2 sps*)

Row 5 Ch 1, sc in first dc, *ch 5, sc in next ch-5 sp, rep from * across, ch 5, dc in side of last sc, turn. (*6 sc, 1 dc, 6 ch-5 sps*)

Rows 6 and 7 Rep rows 4 and 5. (*7 sc, 1 dc, 7 ch-5 sps*)

Row 8 Ch 1, sc in first dc, *ch 5, sc in ch-5 sp**, rep from * across, ending last rep at **, ch 2, dc in last sc, turn. (*8 sc, 1 dc, 7 ch-5 sps, 1 ch-2 sp*)

WORKING EVEN

Row 9 Ch 1, sc in first dc, *ch 5, sc in next ch-5 sp, rep from * across, turn. (*8 sc, 7 ch-5 sps*)

Row 10 *Ch 5, sc in next ch-5 sp**, rep from * across, ending last rep at **, ch 2, dc in last sc, turn. (*2 dc, 2 ch-2 sps, 7 sc, 6 ch-5 sps*)

DECREASE ROWS

Row 11 Work as in row 9, up to last ch-5. Instead of working last ch-5, work (ch 2, dc in ch-5 sp), turn. (*7 sc, 7 ch-5 sps*)

Row 12 Ch 1, work sc inserting hook under (dc, ch 2), *ch 5, sc in next ch-5 sp**, rep from * across, ending last rep at **, ch 2, dc in last sc, turn. (*7 sc, 1 dc, 6 ch-5 sps, 1 ch-2 sp*)

Row 13 Rep row 11. (*6 sc, 6 ch-5 sps*)

Row 14 Rep row 12. (*6 sc, 1 dc, 6 ch-5 sps, 1 ch-2 sp*)

End of dec rows. There are 3 rows worked even at the top of this swatch.

Rows 15 and 17 Rep row 3. (*6 sc, 5 ch-5 sps*)

Row 16 Rep row 2. (*2 dc, 2 ch-2 sps, 4 ch-5 sps, 5 sc*)

Last Row Ch 1, sc in first dc, *ch 3, sc in next ch-5 sp, rep from * across, placing last sc in 3rd ch of the chain. This creates a flat edge.

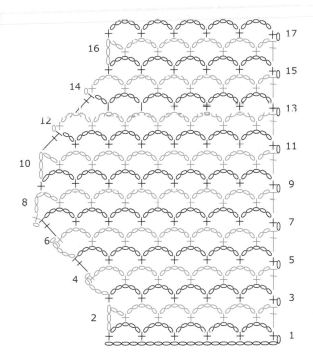

Shaping a Multirow Pattern

Here's an example of a 4-row pattern that can be shaped in half-pattern repeats. To prevent a stair step at the edge, I made a small alteration in the pattern at the end of row 5, working only one single crochet at the outside edge. Another interesting maneuver occurs in the increase portion (row 9): adding chains at the end of a row. This is a great stitch to practice making tall stitches really tall, as discussed on page 37. It's also an example of a stitch using clusters worked over several stitches, as mentioned on page 68.

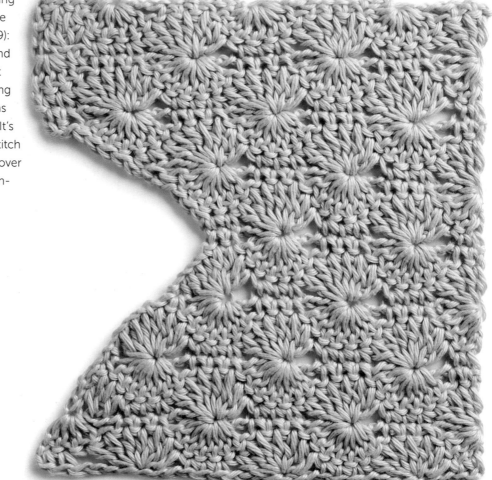

On the finished swatch, you can see how the shaping follows an angle that is formed by the stitch pattern. Searching for such natural angles in a stitch pattern is a great way to shape with more complex stitch patterns.

One important point to make about shaping at the rate of a half pattern is that we are adding or removing several stitches at a time. This results in a more steeply angled edge than we get when shaping at the rate of 1 stitch at a time. Some of these angles are very useful for making armholes and necklines, but less suitable for the subtle shaping needed on sleeves, skirts, shawls, or any items requiring gradual shaping. Another important thing to keep in mind is that steeply angled edges are not suitable for seams, because the angled edge is longer than the straight edge. This is why, when making items that require gradual shaping at the edges, one must choose stitch patterns carefully.

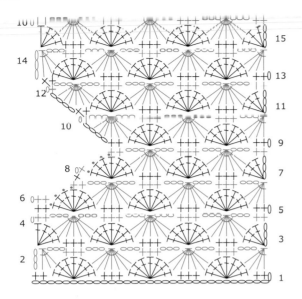

Note

Work all dc3tog, dc7tog, and dc4tog as in row 2.

....

Ch a multiple of 10, plus 1 for end st, plus 1 for tch. (*ch 32 for swatch*)

Row 1 Sc in 2nd ch from hook, sc in next ch, *sk 3 ch, 7 dc in next ch, sk 3 ch**, sc in next 3 ch, rep from * across, ending last rep at **, sc in last 2 ch, turn. (*10 sc, 3 shells*)

Row 2 Ch 3 (counts as dc throughout), dc3tog over (sc, 2 dc), *ch 3, sc in next 3 dc, ch 3**, dc7tog over (2 dc, 3 sc, 2 dc), rep from * across, ending last rep at **, dc4tog over (2 dc, 2 sc), turn. (*9 sc, 4 Cl, 6 ch-sps*)

Row 3 Ch 3, 3 dc in dc4tog, *sc in next 3 sc**, 7 dc in next dc7tog, rep from * across, ending last rep at **, 4 dc in last dc3tog, turn. (*9 sc, 2 shells, 2 half shells*)

Row 4 Ch 1, sc in first 2 sts, *ch 3, dc7tog, ch 3**, sc in next 3 sc, rep from * across, ending last rep at **, sc in last 2 sts, turn. (*10 sc, 3 Cl, 6 ch-sps*)

Row 5 Ch 1, sc in first 2 sc, *7 dc in next dc7tog**, sc in next 3 sc, rep from * across, ending last rep at **, sc in last 2 sc, turn. (*10 sc, 3 shells*)

DECREASE ROWS

Row 6 Ch 1, sc in first 2 sc, sl st over next 3 dc, (sl st, sc) in next dc, sc in next dc, ch 3, *dc7tog, ch 3, sc in next 3 sc, rep from * across, dc4tog, turn. (*10 sc, 4 sl sts, 5 ch-sps, 3 Cl*)

Row 7 Ch 3, 3 dc in dc4tog, *sc in next 3 sc**, 7 dc in next dc7tog, rep from * across to 2 sc before sl sts, sk next sc, sc in next sc, leave rem sts unworked, turn. (*7 sc, 2 shells, 1 half shell*)

Row 8 Ch 1, sc in first sc, sl st over next 3 dc, (sl st, sc) in next dc, sc in next dc, ch 3, *dc7tog, ch 3, **sc in next 3 sc, rep from * across, ending last rep at **, sc in last 2 sc, turn. (*8 sc, 4 sl sts, 4 ch-sps, 2 Cl*)

Rep rows 6–8 to decrease.

INCREASE ROWS

Row 9 Rep row 5, at end of row ch5, turn. (*7 sc, 2 shells, 5 ch*)

Row 10 Ch 1, sc in 2nd ch from hook, ch 3, dc7tog, ch 3, sc in next 3 dc, cont in patt across. (*7 sc, 5 ch-sps, 3 clusters*)

Row 11 Ch 3, 3 dc in dc4tog, *sc in next 3 sc, 7 dc in next dc7tog, rep from * across, 2 sc in last sc, ch 5, turn. (*8 sc, 2 shells, 1 half shell, 5 ch*)

Row 12 Rep Row 10. (*9 sc, 6 ch-sps, 3 Cl*)

Row 13 Rep Row 9. (*10 sc, 3 shells, 5 ch*)

WORKING EVEN

Rows 14 and 15 Rep rows 2 and 3.

Row 16 Rep row 2.

Blocks in a Circle Decrease

Here's another example of a pattern shaped at the rate of half a pattern at a time. I chose this one because the shaping strategy is less obvious than on a shell pattern like the previous one. Work several rows even so you can become familiar with the stitch pattern before shaping it. Decreases start in row 11. You'll see that the shaping strategy takes advantage of the natural angle built into the pattern by the groups of 3 double crochets.

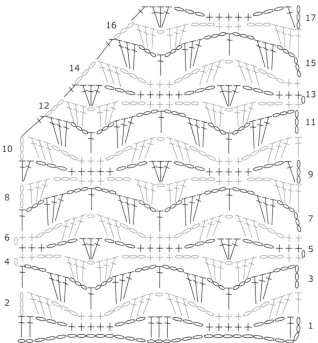

Ch a multiple of 14, plus 1 for end stitch, 2 for tch. (ch 31 for swatch)

Row 1 Dc in 4th ch from hook, *ch 3, sk 3 ch, sc in next 5 ch, ch 3, sk 3 ch**, dc in next 3 ch, rep from * across, ending last rep at **, dc in last 2 ch, turn. (7 dc, 10 sc, 4 ch-sps)

Row 2 Ch 3 (counts as dc at beg of rows), *3 dc in next ch-3 sp, ch 3, sk next sc, sc in next 3 sc, ch 3, 3 dc in next ch-3**, ch 1, sk 3 dc, rep from *, ending last rep at **, dc in tch, turn. (14 dc, 6 sc, 5 ch-sps)

Row 3 Ch 6 (counts as dc, ch 3), sk 3 dc, *3 dc in next ch-3 sp, ch 3, sk next sc, dc in next sc, ch 3, 3 dc in next ch-3 sp, ch 3**, dc in ch-1 sp between 3-dc groups, ch 3, rep from * ending last rep at **, dc in tch, turn. (17 dc, 8 ch-sps)

Row 4 Ch 1, sc in dc, *sc in next ch-3 sp, ch 3, sk 3 dc, 3 dc in next ch-3 sp, ch 1, 3 dc in next ch-3 sp, ch 3**, sc in next ch-3 sp, sc in next dc, rep from * across, ending last rep at **, sc in ch-6 sp, sc in 3rd ch of tch, turn. (7 sc, 12 dc, 6 ch-sps)

Row 5 Ch 1, sc in first sc, sc in next sc, *sc in next ch-3 sp, ch 3, 3 dc in ch-1 sp between 3 dc groups, ch 3, sc in next ch-3 sp**, sc in next 3 sc, rep from * across, ending last rep at **, sc in last 2 sc, turn. (11 sc, 6 dc, 4 ch-sps)

Row 6 Ch 1, sc in first sc, sc in next sc, *ch 3, 3 dc in next ch-3 sp, ch 1, 3 dc in next ch-3 sp, ch 3, sk next sc,** sc in next 3 sc, rep from * ending last rep at **, sc in last 2 sc, turn. (7 sc, 12 dc, 6 ch-sps)

Row 7 Ch 6 (counts as dc, ch 3), *3 dc in next ch-3 sp, ch 3, dc in ch-1 sp between 3-dc groups, ch 3, 3 dc in next ch-3 sp, ch 3, sk next sc, dc in next sc**, ch 3, rep from * ending last rep at **, turn. (17 dc, 8 ch-sps)

Row 8 Ch 3, 3 dc in next ch-3 sp, *ch 3, sc in next ch-3 sp, sc in next dc, sc in next ch-3 sp, ch 3, 3 dc in next ch-3 sp**, ch 1, 3 dc in next ch-3 sp, rep from * across, ending last rep at **, dc in tch, turn. (6 sc, 14 dc, 5 ch-sps)

Row 9 Ch 3, dc in first dc, *ch 3, sc in next ch-3 sp, sc in next 3 sc, sc in next ch-3 sp, ch 3**, 3 dc in next ch-1 sp, rep from * across, ending last rep at **, 2 dc in tch, turn. (10 sc, 7 dc, 4 ch-sps)

Row 10 Rep row 2.

DECREASE ROWS

Row 11 Rep row 3 to last 4 sts, sk last 3 dc, dc in tch, turn. (14 dc, 7 ch-sps)

Row 12 Ch 3, sk 3 dc, *3 dc in next ch-3 sp, ch 1, 3 dc in next ch-3 sp, ch 3**, sc in next ch-3 space, sc in next dc, sc in next ch-3 sp, ch 3, rep from * across, ending last rep at **, sc in ch-6 sp, sc in 3rd ch of tch, turn. (5 sc, 13 dc, 5 ch-sps)

Row 13 Rep row 5 to last 4 sts, sk 3 dc, dc in top of tch, turn. (8 sc, 7 dc, 3 ch-sps)

Row 14 Ch 3, sk 3 dc, 3 dc in next ch-3 sp, ch 3, sk next sc, sc in next 3 sc, ch 3, 3 dc in next ch-3 sp, ch 1, 3 dc in next ch-3 sp, ch 3, sk next sc, sc in last 2 sc, turn. (5 sc, 10 dc, 4 ch-sps)

Row 15 Ch 6, 3 dc in ch-3 sp, ch 3, dc in ch-1 sp, ch 3, 3 dc in next ch-3 sp, ch 3, sk next sc, dc in next sc, ch 3, 3 dc in ch-3 sp, sk 3 dc, dc in tch, turn. (13 dc, 5 ch-sps)

Row 16 Ch 3, 3 dc in first ch-3 sp, ch 1, 3 dc in next ch-3 sp, ch 3, sc in next ch-3 sp, sc in next dc, sc in next ch-3 sp, ch 3, 3 dc in next ch-3 sp, dc in tch, turn. (3 sc, 11 dc, 3 ch-sps)

Row 17 Ch 3, dc in first dc, ch 3, sc in next ch-3 sp, sc in next 3 sc, sc in next ch-3 sp, ch 3, 3 dc in next ch-1 sp, sk 3 dc, dc in tch, turn. (5 sc, 6 dc, 2 ch-sps)

Row 18 Rep row 2.

Rep rows 11–18 to continue decreasing.

Notice how this example follows these guidelines:

- The decrease follows the natural slant of the stitches.

- The last stitch of the row is always worked in the turning chain of the previous row.

Blocks in a Circle Increase

Here's the same stitch pattern as on page 124 with increases, which start in row 2.

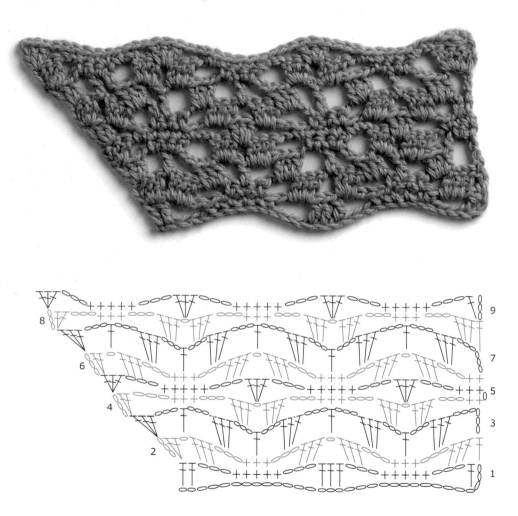

Ch a multiple of 14, plus 1 for end st, 2 for 2 ch. (ch 31 for swatch)

Row 1 Dc in 4th ch from hook, *ch 3, sk 3 ch, sc in next 5 ch, ch 3, sk 3 ch**, dc in next 3 ch, rep from * across, ending last rep at **, dc in last 2 ch, turn. (7 dc, 10 sc, 4 ch-sps)

Row 2 Ch 3 (counts as dc at beg of rows), 2 dc in first dc, *ch 1, 3 dc in next ch-3 sp, ch 3, sk sc, sc in next 3 sc, ch 3, 3 dc in next ch-3 sp, rep from * across, dc in tch, turn. (6 sc, 16 dc, 7 ch-sps)

Row 3 Ch 6 (counts as dc, ch 3), *3 dc in next ch-3 sp, ch 3, sk next sc, dc in next sc, sk next sc, ch 3, 3 dc in next ch-3 sp, ch 3 dc in ch-1 sp between 3-dc groups, ch 3, rep from * ending sk 2 dc, 3 dc in last tch, turn. (17 dc, 9 ch-sps)

Row 4 Ch 3, 2 dc in first dc, *ch 3, sc in next ch-3 sp, sc in next dc, sc in next ch-3 sp, ch 3, 3 dc in next ch-3 sp, ch 1, 3 dc in next ch-3 sp, rep from * across, ch 3, sc in ch-6 sp, sc in 3rd ch of ch-6, turn. (8 sc, 15 dc, 7 ch-sps)

Row 5 Ch 1, sc in first 2 sc, sc in next ch-3 sp, *ch 3, 3 dc in ch-1 sp between 3-dc groups, ch 3, sc in next ch-3 sp, sc in next 3 sc, sc in next ch-3 sp, rep from * across, ch 3, sk 2 dc, 3 dc in tch, turn. (13 sc, 9 dc, 5 ch-sps)

Row 6 Ch 3, 2 dc in first dc, *ch 1, 3 dc in next ch-3 sp, ch 3, sk next sc**, sc in next 3 sc, ch 3, 3 dc in next ch-3 sp, rep from * across, ending last rep at **, sc in last 2 sc, turn. (8 sc, 18 dc, 8 ch-sps)

Row 7 Ch 6 (counts as dc, ch 3), *3 dc in next ch-3 sp, ch 3, dc in ch-1 sp between 3-dc groups, ch 3**, 3 dc in next ch-3 sp, ch 3 sk next sc, dc in next sc, sk next sc, ch 3 rep from * ending last rep at **, 3 dc in tch, turn. (24 dc, 11 ch-sps)

Row 8 Ch 3, 2 dc in first dc, *ch 3, sc in next ch-3 sp, sc in dc, sc in next ch-3 sp, ch 3**, 3 dc in next ch-3 sp, ch 1, 3 dc in next ch-3 sp, rep from * across, ending last rep at **, 3 dc in ch 6, dc in 3rd ch of ch-6, turn. (9 sc, 19 dc, 8 ch-sps)

Row 9 Ch 3, dc in first dc, *ch 3, sc in next ch-3 sp, sc in next 3 sc, sc in next ch-3 sp, ch 3**, 3 dc in ch-1 sp between 3-dc groups, rep from * ending last rep at **, sk 2 dc, 3 dc in tch, turn. (15 sc, 11 dc, 6 ch-sps)

Rep rows 2–9 to continue increasing.

Adaptable Stitch Patterns

Let's look at a stitch pattern that can be shaped in several ways. The one here can be shaped at an angle, decreasing one half pattern over 2 rows, as shown in this swatch, and also in smaller increments, shown in the next one. The pattern begins with half patterns at each edge, and requires 4 rows to complete the full pattern.

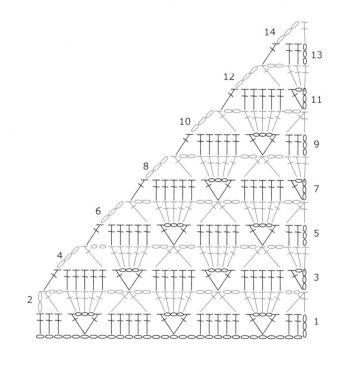

Note

In this pattern, all the clusters are made of dc2tog. Sometimes they are over a group of 5 sts, sometimes a group of 3 or 4. Here's how to work the cluster:

....

Cl (cluster) Yo, insert hook in first dc of group, yo, draw through 2 loops, sk the required number of dc, yo, insert hook in last dc of group, yo, draw through 2 loops, yo, draw through 3 loops on hook.

If you are working the Cl over 5 dc, you skip 3 dc; if over 4 dc, skip 2 dc; if over 3, sk 1 dc.

(Dc, ch 3, dc) in next Cl: Insert hook in space under Cl.

....

Ch a multiple of 10, plus 1 for end st, plus 2 for tch. (*ch 33 for swatch*)

Row 1 Dc in 4th ch from hook, dc in next ch, *sk 2 ch, (dc, ch 3, dc) in next ch, sk 2 ch**, dc in next 5 ch, rep from * across, ending last rep at **, dc in next 3 ch, turn. (*31 sts*)

Row 2 Ch 2, dc in 3rd dc (counts as Cl over 3 sts), *ch 2, 5 dc in ch-3 sp, ch 2**, Cl over 5 dc, rep from * across, ending last rep at **, Cl over next dc and tch, turn.

> **Stitch tip.** This is a good pattern to practice controlling tension when skipping several stitches. In order to avoid stretching stitches, keep yarn fairly taut while working the 2nd double crochet of the clusters. If you find the double crochet stitches at the decrease edges are pulling at the work, either lengthen them, or use treble stitches instead, and chain 4 when a decrease begins the row.

DECREASE ROWS

Row 3 Ch 4 (counts as dc, ch 1), dc in first Cl, *dc in next, 5 dc**, (dc, ch 3, dc) in next Cl, rep from * across, ending last rep at **, dc in tch, turn. (*29 sts*)

Row 4 Ch 3, sk 4 dc, dc in next dc, ch 2, *5 dc in ch-3 sp, ch 2, Cl over 5 dc, ch 2, rep from * across, 2 dc in ch-1 sp, dc in tch, turn. (*27 sts*)

Row 5 Ch 3, dc in next 2 dc, *(dc, ch 3, dc) in next Cl, dc in next 5 dc, rep from * across, dc in tch, turn. (*24 sts*)

Row 6 Ch 3, sk 4 dc, dc in next dc, *ch 2, 5 dc in ch-3 sp, ch 2**, Cl over 5 dc, rep from * across, ending last rep at **, Cl over last 2 dc and tch, turn. (*22 sts*)

Row 7 Ch 4 (counts as dc, ch 1), dc in first Cl, dc in next 5 dc, (dc, ch 3, dc) in next Cl, dc in next 5 dc, dc in tch, turn. (*19 sts*)

Row 8 Ch 3, sk 4 dc, dc in next dc, ch 2, 5 dc in next ch-3 sp, ch 2, Cl over next 5 dc, ch 2, 2 dc in ch-1 sp, dc in tch, turn. (*17 sts*)

Row 9 Ch 3, dc in next 2 dc, (dc, ch 3, dc) in next Cl, dc in next 5 dc, dc in tch, turn. (*14 sts*)

Row 10 Ch 3, sk 4 dc, dc in next dc, ch 2, 5 dc in next ch-3 sp, ch 2, Cl over last 3 sts, turn. (*12 sts*)

Row 11 Ch 4 (counts as dc, ch 1), dc in Cl, dc in next 5 dc, dc in tch, turn. (*9 sts*)

Row 12 Ch 3, sk 4 dc, dc in next dc, ch 2, 2 dc in last ch-4, dc in 3rd ch of tch, turn. (*7 sts*)

Row 13 Ch 3, dc in next 2 dc, dc in tch, turn. (*4 sts*)

Row 14 Ch 3, dc in tch, fasten off. (*2 sts*)

Shaping in Smaller Increments

With a little ingenuity, the same stitch pattern on the previous page can be increased in smaller increments, making a more gradual slope.

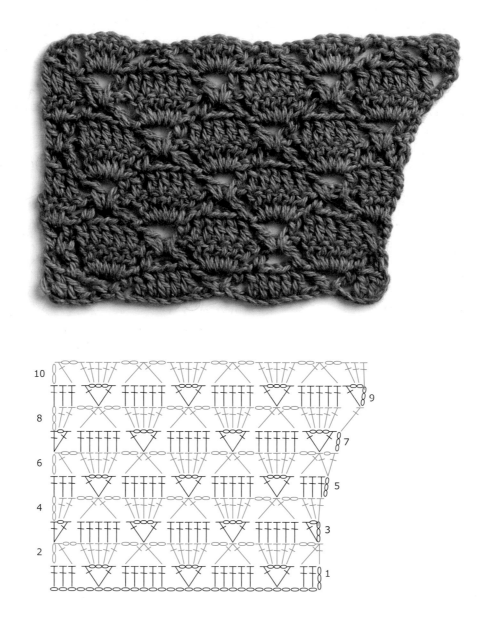

Note

In this pattern, all the clusters are made of dc2tog. Sometimes they are over a group of 5 sts, sometimes a group of 3 or 4. See notes on page 129 for how to work the cluster.

....

Ch a multiple of 10, plus 1 for end st, plus 2 for tch. (*ch 33 for swatch*)

Row 1 Dc in 4th ch from hook, dc in next 2 ch, *sk 2 ch, (dc, ch 3, dc) in next ch, sk 2 ch**, dc in next 5 ch, rep from * across, ending last rep at **, dc in next 3 ch, turn. (*31 sts*)

Row 2 Ch 2, dc in 3rd dc (counts as Cl over 3 sts), *ch 2, 5 dc in next ch-3 sp, ch 2**, Cl over next 5 dc, rep from * across, ending last rep at **, Cl over next dc and tch, turn.

Row 3 Ch 4 (counts as dc, ch 1), dc in Cl, *dc in next 5 dc**, (dc, ch 3, dc) in next Cl, rep from * across, ending last rep at **, (dc, ch 1, dc) in top of tch, turn.

Row 4 Ch 3, 2 dc in ch-1 sp, ch 2, *Cl over next 5 dc, ch 2**, 5 dc in ch-3 sp, ch 2, rep from * across, ending last rep at **, 2 dc in last ch-1 sp, dc in 3rd ch of tch, turn.

INCREASE ROWS

Row 5 Ch 3, dc in first dc, dc in next 2 dc, *(dc, ch 3, dc)** in next Cl, dc in next 5 dc, rep from * across, ending last rep at **, dc in last 3 dc, turn. (*32 sts*)

Row 6 Ch 2, dc in 3rd dc, *ch 2, 5 dc in ch-3 sp, ch 2**, Cl over next 5 dc, rep from *, ending last rep at **, Cl over next 3 dc and tch, ch 1, dc in tch, turn. (*33 sts*)

Row 7 Ch 3, *(dc, ch 3, dc) in next Cl, dc in next 5 dc, rep from * across, dc in next Cl, ch 1, dc in ch-2, turn. (*34 sts*)

Row 8 Ch 3, 2 dc in ch-1 sp, *ch 2, Cl over next 5 dc, ch 2, 5 dc in ch-3 sp, rep from * across, dc in tch, turn.

Row 9 Ch 5 (counts as dc, ch 2), dc in first dc, *dc in next 5 dc, (dc, ch 3, dc) in next Cl, rep from * across, dc in last 3 sts, turn. (*37 sts*)

Row 10 Work as in row 2 to last (dc and ch 5), 2 dc in ch-5 (tch), dc in 3rd ch of tch, turn. (*36 sts*)

Don't be worried that this stitch count is smaller than that of the row before, even though you are increasing. It's simply a quirk of the pattern.

To continue increasing, rep from row 5.

Shaping Two Legged Stitches

Here's one more sample with an angled stitch pattern that's made with a type of cluster stitch some-times called a *split cluster*. The cluster works 2 stitches together in the usual way by working each stitch up to the last loop, then working the 2 stitches together by drawing through all the loops on the hook. What's special about split clusters is that one leg of the cluster is separated from the second leg by sev-eral stitches, and the next split cluster begins in the same stitch as the 2nd leg of the previous cluster. You will encounter numerous variations on this type of split cluster pattern in patterns and stitch dictionaries.

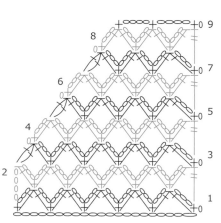

Make it, mark it. If you are not sure where to insert the hook when working into clusters, use a safety pin to mark the top of the last cluster on row 1 right after you finish it so you can tell where to insert the hook on the next row.

Split clusters can be used to form a grid of dia-monds, as in this stitch pattern, with groups of chains running parallel to the legs of the clusters. In order to follow the angled lines of the pattern while decreasing, the last chain-3 of the row is changed to a double crochet that can be worked together with the split cluster. This brings the hook to the correct place to start the next row and allows us to decrease half a stitch pattern on each row. This is a 2-row pattern where every other row begins and ends with half a pattern (one leg of a cluster). At the edges, taller stitches provide a straight side edge and match the height of the diamonds.

Notes

Clusters at the start and end of a row are spelled out as dc2tog. All other clusters are made with the first leg in the same cluster as the second leg of previous cluster, and the 2nd leg in the next cluster. Always insert hook in the top of the cluster. Clusters are followed by chain-3 and single crochet, with the single crochet worked into the same cluster as the second leg of cluster.

Dc2tog Yo, insert hook in designated st, yo, draw up loop, yo, draw through 2 loops, yo, insert hook in next designated st, yo, draw up loop, yo, draw through 2 loops, yo, draw through 3 loops on hook.

Cl (cluster) Yo, insert hook in same st as 2nd leg of last Cl, yo, draw up loop, yo, draw through 2 loops, yo, insert hook in next Cl, yo, draw up loop, yo, draw through 2 loops, yo, draw through 3 loops on hook.

Ch a multiple of 4, plus 1 end st, plus 1 tch. (*ch 22 for swatch*)

Row 1 Sc in 2nd ch from hook, *ch 3, dc2tog (inserting hook in same ch as sc just made, sk 3 ch, insert hook in next ch), ch 3, sc in same ch, rep from * across. (*5 split clusters, 6 sc*)

Row 2 Ch 4 (counts as tr throughout), dc in first Cl, ch 3, sc in same Cl, *ch 3, Cl, ch 3, sc in same Cl, rep from * across, ch 3, dc in same Cl, tr in last sc, turn. (*6 split clusters, 5 sc, 1 tr*)

To continue even with this pattern, work row 3 as row 1, inserting into clusters instead of chains, and repeat rows 2 and 3.

DECREASE ROWS

Row 3 Ch 1, sc in first tr, ch 3, dc2tog (inserting hook in same tr, then into next Cl), *ch 3, sc in same Cl, ch 3**, Cl, rep from * across, ending last rep at **, dc3tog (inserting hook in same Cl for first leg, then into last st for 2nd and 3rd legs, yo and draw through 4 loops on hook), turn. (5 split clusters, 5 sc)

Row 4 Ch 1, sc in dc3tog, ch 3, Cl (beg in dc3tog), *ch 3, sc in same Cl**, ch 3, Cl, rep from * across, ending last rep at **, ch 3, dc in same Cl, tr in last sc, turn. (*5 split clusters, 5 sc, 1 tr*)

Rep rows 3 and 4 to continue decreasing.

To provide a straight edge on this stitch pattern, end with a row 4 and work last row as follows:

Last row Ch 1, sc in tr, *ch 4, sc in next Cl, rep from * across. (*3 sc, 2 ch-sps*)

Finding shape. From these examples, I hope you can see how the movement and lines of stitches can lead you to shaping strategies. Sometimes you can tell from a stitch diagram where such natural shaping points are in a stitch pattern. Other times it becomes clear after you've made a large swatch. With experience, you can learn to read stitch patterns for these natural shaping points and create all kinds of great shapes for garments, toys, and home items.

If you already have a diagram of the pattern, or can make one, experiment by drawing in the increase you want to make.

Even if it's not clear exactly how you will do the increase or decrease, draw a line showing the 1 or 2 stitches you are trying to add or subtract. Then work a few rows of the pattern even, and start experimenting — there is usually a way to make it work.

Shaping Ripples

Have you ever tried to shape a ripple pattern? It's quite a challenge! Ripples are the result of clever placement of increases and decreases within a row. What's hard is shaping ripple stitches at the rate of one stitch at a time without losing the ripple.

Decreasing Ripples

The following swatch shows how to decrease by one stitch per row, though it's certainly not the only way to do so.

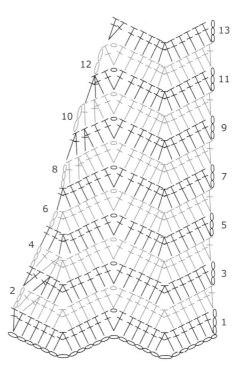

Ch a multiple of 12, plus 2 end sts, plus 2 for tch. (*ch 28 for swatch*)

Row 1 Dc in 4th ch from hook, *dc in next 4 ch, dc2tog over (next ch, sk next ch, next ch), dc in next 4 ch**, (dc, ch 1, dc) in next ch, rep from * across, ending last rep at **, 2 dc in last ch, turn. (*25 sts*)

DECREASE ROWS

Row 2 Ch 3 (counts as dc throughout), dc in first dc, dc2tog, dc in next 2 dc, *dc2tog over (dc, sk dc2tog, dc), dc in next 4 dc**, (dc, ch 1, dc) in next ch-1 sp, dc in next 4 dc, rep from * across, ending last rep at **, 2 dc in tch, turn. (*24 sts*)

Row 3 Ch 3, dc in first dc, *dc in next 4 dc, dc2tog over (dc, sk dc2tog, dc)**, dc in next 4 dc, (dc, ch 1, dc) in next dc, rep from * ending last rep at **, dc in next dc, dc2tog, 2 dc in tch, turn. (*23 sts*)

Row 4 Ch 3, dc in first dc, dc2tog, dc2tog over (dc, sk dc2tog, dc), dc in next 4 dc, cont in established patt across, turn. (*22 sts*)

Row 5 Ch 3, dc in first dc, *dc in next 4 dc, dc2tog over (dc, sk dc2tog, dc)**, dc in next 4 dc, (dc, ch 1, dc) in next dc, rep from * ending last rep at **, dc in next dc, dc in tch, turn. (*21 sts*)

Row 6 Ch 2, dc2tog over (next dc, sk dc2tog, next dc), dc in next 4 dc, cont in established patt across, turn. (*20 sts*)

Row 7 Ch 3, dc in first dc, *dc in next 4 dc**, dc2tog over (dc, sk dc2tog, dc), dc in next 4 dc, (dc, ch 1, dc) in next ch-1 sp, rep from * ending last rep at **, dc2tog over (next dc, sk dc2tog, ch 2), turn. (*19 sts*)

Row 8 Ch 3, dc in next dc, dc2tog, dc in next 2 dc, (dc, ch 1, dc) in ch-1 sp, cont in patt across, turn. (*18 sts*)

Row 9 Work in patt to last ch-1 sp, (dc, ch 1, dc) in ch-1 sp, dc in next dc, dc2tog, dc2tog over (dc2tog, sk next dc, tch), turn. (*17 sts*)

Row 10 (Ch 2, dc in next dc) (counts as dc2tog), dc2tog, (dc, ch 1, dc) in ch-1 sp, cont in patt across, turn. (*16 sts*)

Row 11 Work in patt to last ch-1 sp, (dc, ch 1, dc) in ch-1 sp, dc3tog over last 3 sts, turn. (*15 sts*)

Row 12 Ch 2, dc in ch-1 sp, ch 1, dc in same ch-1 sp, cont in patt across, turn. (*14 sts*)

Row 13 Work in patt to last ch-1 sp, sk ch-1 sp, 2 dc in last dc2tog, turn. (*13 sts*)

Rep rows 2–13 to continue decreasing in pattern.

You can adapt this method to other ripple stitches, as long as they begin and end with an increase, as most do. Just follow these guidelines:

- Maintain the increases at the start of the row.

- Make a decrease in the 2 stitches right after the starting increase, until you get to the decrease part of the ripple.

- From this point on, work 2 stitches together at the edge; this keeps the slant of the ripple intact, while also working 2 stitches together right next to the edge.

While it may seem counterintuitive, we have to decrease twice after the increase part of the ripple in order to maintain the overall decrease at the edge. I had to find some creative strategies to keep the decrease going in this swatch. Still, even though the rate of increase remains the same, the swatch does not have a perfectly smooth slant along the edge. The inherent slant of the ripple, which goes first in one direction and then in the other, has an effect on the slant at the edge. Of course, I only learned this from swatching! I would nevertheless use this method with a ripple stitch, and I doubt it would mar the overall effect.

My attempts to *increase* the ripple pattern were not successful, because the up-and-down movement of the ripple worked against the smooth slant at the edge. If increasing were necessary with a ripple stitch, I would change to plain stitches at the edges. Perhaps some adventurous crocheter will figure out a better solution!

As we've mentioned, the more the natural lines of a stitch pattern stray from a vertical axis, the harder it is to shape at the edges. On the plus side, many patterns that move with angles and curves can be shaped within the row or round, using internal increases or decreases.

Internal Shaping

Internal shaping happens not at the edges of the fabric, but within the row or round, and is particularly apt for garment designs worked top down, with rapid increases to shape the garment from the smaller neck area to the larger shoulder area. Of the many strategies for internal shaping, some make it easier to shape gradually, while others work when you want to shape more quickly. Some change the stitch pattern in an obvious way; others affect drape. It's important to consider all these factors when choosing a shaping method.

Building a Pattern Repetition Internally: Method #1

An excellent way to increase internally is to add a pattern repeat gradually, beginning at a convenient midpoint in the stitch. Build the repetition gradually, to avoid sudden bulking of the fabric. This stitch pattern takes 4 rows to complete. There's no shaping in the first 7 rows.

Shell (3 dc, ch 1, 3 dc) in designated st.

V-st (dc, ch 1, dc) in designated st.

Ch a multiple of 10, plus 1 for end st, plus 1 for tch. (*ch 32 for swatch*)

Row 1 (RS) Sc in 2nd ch from hook, sc in next ch, *sk 3 ch, shell in next ch, sk 3 ch**, sc in next ch, ch 1, sk next ch, sc in next ch, rep from * across, ending last rep at **, sc in last 2 ch, turn. (*8 sc, 3 shells*)

Row 2 Ch 3 (counts as dc throughout), dc in first sc, *ch 3, sc in ch-1 sp of next shell, ch 3**, V-st in ch-1 sp between 2 sc, rep from * across, ending last rep at **, 2 dc in last sc, turn. (*3 sc, 2 V-sts, 4 dc, 6 ch-3 sps*)

Row 3 Ch 3, 3 dc in first dc, *sc in next ch-3 sp, ch 1, sc in next ch-3 sp**, shell in ch-1 space of next V-st, rep from * across, ending last rep at **, 4 dc in tch, turn. (*6 sc, 2 shells, 2 half shells*)

Row 4 Ch 1, sc in first dc, *ch 3, V-st in ch-1 sp between 2 sc, ch 3**, sc in ch-1 sp of next shell, rep from * across, ending last rep at **, sc in tch, turn. (*4 sc, 3 V-sts, 6 ch-3 sps*)

Row 5 Ch 1, sc in first sc, sc in next ch-3 sp, *shell in ch-1 sp of next V-st, sc in next ch-3 sp**, ch 1, sc in next ch-3 sp, rep from * across, ending last rep at **, sc in tch, turn. (*8 sc, 3 shells*)

Rows 6 and 7 Rep rows 2 and 3.

INCREASE ROWS

Row 8 Ch 1, sc in first dc, ch 3, V-st in ch-1 sp between 2 sc, ch 3, sc in ch-1 sp of next shell, ch 3, (dc, ch 1, dc, ch 1, dc) in next ch-1 sp, ch 3, sc in ch-1 sp of next shell, ch 3, V-st in next ch-1 sp, ch 3, sc in tch, turn. (*4 sc, 2 V-sts, 1 double V-st, 6 ch-3 sps*)

Row 9 Ch 1, sc in first sc, sc in ch-3 sp, shell in ch-1 sp of next V-st, sc in next ch-3 sp, ch 1, sc in next ch-3 sp, [(2 dc, ch 1, 2 dc) in next ch-1 sp] twice, sc in next ch-3 sp, ch 1, sc in next ch-3 sp, shell in next ch-1 sp, sc in ch-3 sp, sc in last sc, turn. (*8 sc, 2 shells, 2 half shells*)

Row 10 Ch 3, dc in first sc, ch 3, sc in ch-1 sp of next shell, ch 3, V-st in next ch-1 sp, ch 3, sc in next ch-1 sp, ch 3, V-st inserting hook between next 2 shells, ch 3, sc in next ch-1 sp, ch 3, V-st in next ch-1 sp, ch 3, sc in next ch-1 sp, ch 3, 2 dc in last sc, turn. (*4 sc, 4 dc, 3 V-sts, 8 ch-3 sps*)

Row 11 Ch 3, 3 dc in first dc, sc in next ch-3 sp, ch 1, sc in next ch-3 sp, shell in next ch-1 sp, sc in next ch-3 sp, ch 1, sc in next ch-3 sp, shell in next ch-1 sp, cont in patt to end, turn. (*8 sc, 3 shells, 2 half shells*)

Row 12 Ch 1, sc in first dc, ch 3, V-st in next ch-1 sp, ch 3, sc in next ch-1 sp, ch 3, [(dc, ch 1, dc, ch 1, dc) in next ch-1 sp, ch 3, sc in next

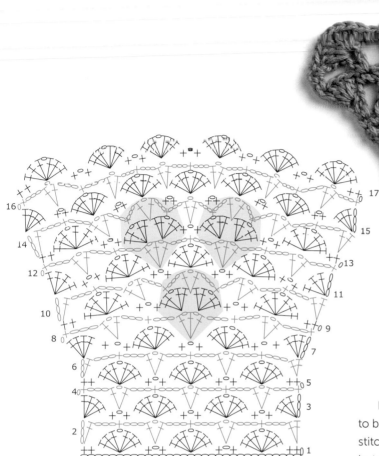

ch-1 sp, ch 3] twice, V-st in next ch-1 sp, ch 3, sc in tch, turn. (*5 sc, 2 V-sts, 2 double V-sts, 8 ch-3 sps*)

Row 13 Ch 1, sc in first sc, sc in ch-3 sp, shell in next ch-1 sp, sc in next ch-3 sp, ch 1, sc in next ch-3 sp, [(2 dc, ch 1, 2 dc) in next ch-1 sp] twice, sc in next ch-3 sp, ch 1, sc in next ch-3 sp, [(2 dc, ch 1, 2 dc) in next ch-1 sp] twice, cont in patt to end, turn. (*10 sc, 2 shells, 4 half shells*)

Row 14 Ch 3, dc in first sc, ch 3, sc in next ch-1 sp, ch 3, [V-st in next ch-1 sp, ch 3, sc in next ch-1 sp, ch 3, V-st between next 2 shells, ch 3, sc in next ch-1 sp, ch 3] twice, V-st in next ch-1 sp, ch 3, sc in next ch-1 sp, ch 3, 2 dc in last sc, turn. (*6 sc, 4 dc, 5 V-sts, 12 ch-3 sps*)

Rows 15–17 Rep rows 3–5.

Here are various strategies I used in this swatch to build the stitch pattern incrementally. Many stitch patterns lend themselves to these strategies, but since no set procedures exist, each designer can invent his or her own method. It's fun!

- **Row 8 (shell center):** Work a double V-stitch (dc, ch 1, dc, ch 1, dc) instead of a V-stitch.

- **Row 9:** Work (2 dc, ch 1, 2 dc) in each chain-1 space of the double V-stitch. (A partial shell allows fabric to grow gradually.)

- **Row 10:** Work 1 single crochet in the chain-1 space of the partial shells, as if they were full shells. This completes a full pattern repetition in the row, which will be clearer after finishing the next row.

- **Row 11:** Use the V-stitch to begin building additional pattern repetitions. For a symmetrical increase, make a double V-stitch on either side of the newly added shell, then continue the increases as done earlier, resulting in two more full pattern repetitions.

Changing the Size of a Pattern Repeat

Another method of internal shaping involves changing the number of stitches in the pattern repeat. Shell patterns are particularly adaptable to this method, but it works with other patterns too. This example shows the same stitch pattern as on the previous pages, but instead of adding a pattern repetition, we are decreasing by changing the size of the shells. The first 4 rows are worked even in pattern, and decreasing begins in row 5.

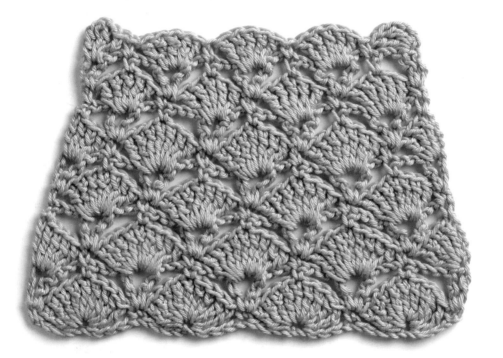

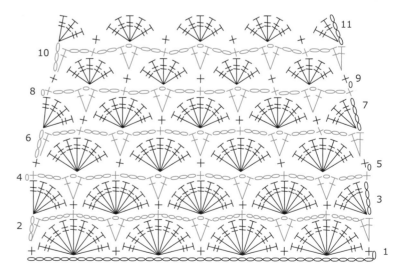

Note

When working into a V-st, always work into the ch-1 sp.

....

V-st (Dc, ch 1, dc) in indicated st.

....

Ch a multiple of 10, plus 1 end st, plus 1 for tch. (*ch 42 for swatch*)

Row 1 Sc in 2nd ch from hook, *sk 4 ch, 9 tr in next ch, sk 4 ch, sc in next ch, rep from * across, turn. (*5 sc, 36 tr*)

Row 2 Ch 3 (counts as dc throughout), dc in first sc, *ch 4, sc in center tr of next shell, ch 4**, V-st in next sc, rep from * across, ending last rep at **, 2 dc in last sc, turn. (*4 dc, 3 V-sts, 4 sc, 8 ch-4 sps*)

Row 3 Ch 4 (counts as tr throughout), 4 tr in first dc, *sc in next sc**, 9 tr in next V-st, rep from * across, ending last rep at **, 5 tr in tch, turn. (*4 sc, 37 tr*)

Row 4 Ch 1, sc in first tr, *ch 3, V-st in next sc, ch 3, sc in center tr of next shell, rep from * across, placing last sc in tch, turn. (*5 sc, 4 V-sts, 8 ch-3 sps*)

DECREASE ROWS

Row 5 Ch 1, sc in first sc, *7 tr in next V-st, sc in next sc, rep from * across, placing last sc in tch, turn. (*5 sc, 28 tr*)

Row 6 Ch 3, dc in first sc, *ch 3, sc in center tr of next shell, ch 3**, V-st in next sc, rep from * across, ending last rep at **, 2 dc in last sc, turn. (*4 dc, 3 V-sts, 4 sc, 8 ch-3 sps*)

Row 7 Ch 4, 3 tr in first dc, *sc in next sc**, 7 tr in next V-st, rep from * across, ending last rep at **, 4 tr in tch, turn. (*4 sc, 29 tr*)

Row 8 Ch 1, sc in first sc, *ch 2, V-st in next sc, ch 2, sc in center tr of next shell, rep from * across, placing last sc in tch, turn. (*5 sc, 4 V-sts, 8 ch-2 sps*)

Row 9 Ch 1, sc in first sc, *5 tr in next V-st, sc in next sc, rep from * across, turn. (*5 sc, 20 tr*)

Row 10 Ch 3, dc in first sc, *ch 2, sc in center tr of next shell, ch 2**, V-st in next sc, rep from *, ending last rep at **, 2 dc in last sc, turn. (*4 dc, 4 sc, 3 V-sts, 8 ch-2 sps*)

Row 11 Ch 4, 2 tr in first dc, *sc in next sc**, 5 tr in next V-st, rep from * across, ending last rep at **, 3 tr in tch, turn. (*4 sc, 21 tr*)

This stitch pattern has two main elements — shells and V-stitches. The two elements are alternated from one row to the next, making a 4-row pattern repetition. The size of the shells is decreased every other row of shells, that is, every 4th row. For the alternating element (the V-stitch) to match, the number of chains between V-stitches is reduced as well. Note that the shells are always an odd number of stitches to provide a stitch at the exact center of the shell.

To increase with this method, you would start with smaller shells and fewer chains between V-stitches, and add stitches to the shells and chains.

When putting this method to use, it's quite possible to shape more quickly, by changing the stitch count in every shell row, or more slowly, by placing the decreases farther apart. It's also possible to change the count only in certain shells and not others. By shaping at different rates of increase, one can create tailored shapes in garments for hips, shoulders, waist, and sleeves.

Shaping in Columns

Now let's examine shaping with stitch patterns that have a different structure, what I call a "panel" stitch pattern. Unlike stitch patterns where two elements overlap, here the two elements are in distinct columns.

Columns of Fans and Double Crochet

This swatch is made of panels of fans and panels of plain double crochet stitches, with chains creating space in between so that the two elements are distinct. This stitch pattern could conceivably be decreased at the side edge, shaping along the diagonal formed by the fan and decreasing 3 double crochet stitches at once to continue the same diagonal. But let's look at several different ways this stitch pattern can be shaped internally. First is the pattern with no shaping.

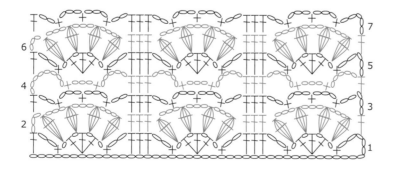

1 dc bobble (YO, insert hook in designated sp, yo and draw up loop, yo, draw through 2 loops) four times in same sp, yo, draw through 5 loops on hook.

Ch a multiple of 14, plus 13 for partial panel, plus 3 for tch, plus 2 for first ch-2 in row 1. (*ch 46 for swatch*)

Row 1 Sc in 9th ch from hook, *ch 1, sk 2 ch, (dc, ch 1, dc, ch 1, dc) in next ch, ch 1, sk 2 ch, sc in next ch, ch 2, sk 2 ch**, dc in next 3 ch, ch 2, sk 2 ch, sc in next ch, rep from * across, ending final rep at **, dc in last ch, turn. (*6 sc, 17 dc, 18 ch-sps*)

Row 2 Ch 3 (counts as dc here and throughout), *sk (ch 2, sc) [bobble in next ch-1 sp, ch 3] three times, bobble in next ch-1 sp, sk (sc, ch 2)**, dc in next 3 dc, rep from * across, ending last rep at **, dc in next ch, turn. (*8 dc, 12 bobbles, 9 ch-sps*)

Row 3 Ch 5 (counts as dc, ch 2), *(sc in next ch-3 sp, ch 3) twice, sc in next ch-3 sp, ch 2**, dc in next 3 dc, ch 2, rep from * across, ending last rep at **, dc in tch, turn. (*9 sc, 8 dc, 12 ch-sps*)

Row 4 Ch 8 (counts as dc, ch 5), *sk (ch 2, sc), sc in next ch-3 sp, ch 3, sc in next ch-3 sp, ch 5, sk 2 ch**, dc in next 3 dc, ch 5, rep from * across, ending last rep at **, dc in 3rd ch of tch, turn. (*6 sc, 8 dc, 9 ch-sps*)

Row 5 Ch 5 (counts as dc, ch 2), *sc in ch-5 sp, ch 1, (dc, ch 1, dc, ch 1, dc) in next ch-3 sp, ch 1, sc in next ch-5 sp, ch 2**, dc in next 3 dc, ch 2, rep from * across, ending last rep at **, dc in 3rd ch of tch, turn. (*6 sc, 17 dc, 18 ch-sps*)

Rep rows 2–5 for patt ending with row 3.

Shaping by Adding Chains

The example below is shaped by increasing the number of chain stitches between the two panels.

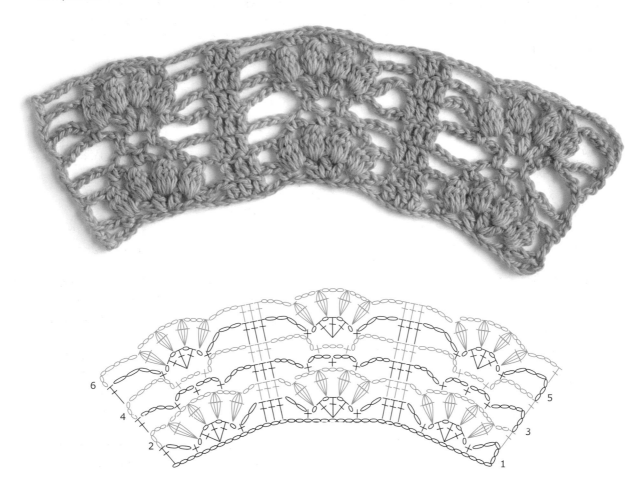

Ch a multiple of 14, plus 13 for partial panel, plus 5 for tch. (*ch 46 for swatch*)

Row 1 Sc in 9th ch from hook, *ch 1, sk 2 ch, (dc, ch 1, dc, ch 1, dc) in next ch, ch 1, sk 2 ch, sc in next ch, ch 2, sk 2 ch**, dc in next 3 ch, ch 2, sk 2 ch, sc in next ch, rep from * across, ending final rep at **, dc in last ch, turn. (*6 sc, 17 dc, 18 ch-sps*)

INCREASE ROWS

Row 2 Ch 5 (counts as dc, ch 2), *sk (ch 2, sc), [bobble in next ch-1 sp, ch 3] three times, bobble in next ch-1 sp, ch 2, sk (sc, ch 2)**, dc in next 3 dc, ch 2, rep from * across, ending last rep at **, dc in 3rd ch of tch, turn. (*8 dc, 12 bobbles, 15 ch-sps*)

Row 3 Ch 7 (counts as dc, ch 4), *(sc in next ch-3 sp, ch 3) twice, sc in next ch-3 sp, ch 4**, dc in next 3 dc, ch 4, rep from * across, ending last rep at **, dc in 3rd ch of tch, turn. (*9 sc, 8 dc, 12 ch-sps*)

Row 4 Ch 10 (counts as dc, ch 7), *sk (ch 4, sc), sc in next ch-3 sp, ch 3, sc in next ch-3 sp, ch 7, sk 4 ch**, dc in next 3 dc, ch 7, rep from * across, ending last rep at **, dc in 3rd ch of tch, turn. (*6 sc, 8 dc, 3 ch-3 sps, 6 ch-7 sps*)

Row 5 Ch 7 (counts as dc, ch 4), *sc in ch-7 sp, ch 1, (dc, ch 1, dc, ch 1, dc) in next ch-3 sp, ch 1, sc in next ch-7 sp, ch 4**, dc in next 3 dc, ch 4, rep from * across, ending last rep at **, dc in 3rd ch of tch, turn. (*6 sc, 17 dc, 6 ch-4 sps, 12 ch-1 sps*)

WORKING EVEN

Row 6 Ch 7 (counts as dc, ch 4) *sk (ch 4, sc), (bobble in next ch-1 sp, ch 3) three times, bobble in next ch-1 sp, ch 4, sk (sc, ch 4)**, dc in next 3 dc, ch 4, rep from * across, ending last rep at **, dc in 3rd ch of tch. (*8 dc, 9 ch 3 sps, 6 ch-4 sps, 12 bobbles*)

This stitch pattern requires 4 rows to work. We add 2 chains beginning in row 2, and the remaining 3 rows of the pattern repeat all have 2 extra chains. When using this method, be sure to keep track of the number of chains in the original pattern, which usually differs from one row to the next. For a gradual increase, keep that extra number of chains constant until the beginning of the next pattern repetition. In this example, where the next repetition of the pattern repeat begins in row 5, add 2 more chains, and remember to add them in the next 3 rows as well. As you can see, longer lines of chains change the character of the pattern, making it more open, which can be very attractive. One could also combine this with other shaping strategies to get a longer span of shaping. For example, start the pattern with only one double crochet stitch between fans, then add the double crochet stitches gradually over two pattern repeats, then continue the increase using chains.

Shaping the Double Crochet Panel

Another option for increasing this stitch pattern is to add to the double crochet panel, as shown here in two colors: 2 double crochet stitches are added in each row. This changes the character of the stitch pattern, creating a solid triangular element. If the increase were continued, the new visual element would become more pronounced. It would be particularly effective for the last few rows on a shawl, where the triangular double crochet panels could be finished off with a point or scallop.

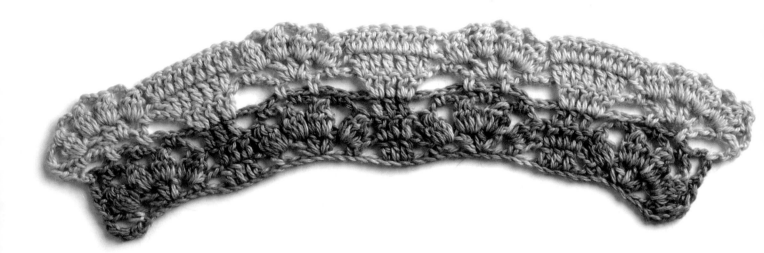

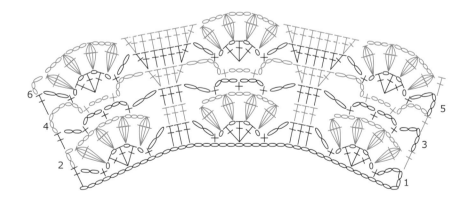

Ch a multiple of 14, plus 13 for partial panel, plus 5 for tch. (ch 60 for swatch)

Rows 1–3 Follow instructions for rows 1–3 of Columns of Fans and Double Crochet swatch (page 140).

Row 4 Ch 8 (counts as dc, ch 5), *sk (ch 2, sc), sc in next ch-3 sp, ch 3, sc in next ch-3 sp, ch 5, sk 2 ch**, 2 dc in next dc, dc in next dc, 2 dc in next dc, ch 5, rep from * across, ending last rep at **, dc in 3rd ch of tch, turn. (*12 dc, 6 sc, 9 ch-sps*)

Row 5 Ch 5 (counts as dc, ch 2), *sc in ch-5 sp, ch 1, (dc, ch 1, dc, ch 1, dc) in next ch-3 sp, ch 1, sc in next ch-5 sp, ch 2**, 2 dc in next dc, dc in next 3 dc, 2 dc in next dc, ch 2, rep from * across, ending last rep at **, dc in 3rd ch of tch, turn. (*25 dc, 6 sc, 18 ch-sps*)

Row 6 Ch 3 (counts as dc), *sk (ch 2, sc), [bobble in next ch-1 sp, ch 3] three times, bobble in next ch-1 sp, sk (sc, ch 2)**, 2 dc in next dc, dc in next 5 dc, 2 dc in next dc, rep from * across, ending last rep at **, dc in 3rd ch of tch, turn. (*20 dc, 12 bobbles, 9 ch-sps*)

Building a Pattern Repetition Internally: Method #2

We could also use the method explored earlier (page 136), where a new pattern is built starting in the middle of a pattern repeat. This is a more organic approach that keeps the two elements balanced and therefore doesn't change the pattern as much. Here the column of double crochet stitches is split in half with a V-stitch, and the fan pattern is inserted a few stitches at a time in the space created, until we reach the full pattern repetition in row 8.

V-st (dc, ch 1, dc) in designated st.

....

Ch a multiple of 14, plus 13 for partial panel, plus 5 for tch. (*ch 46 for swatch*)

Row 1 Sc in 9th ch from hook, *ch 1, sk 2 ch, (dc, ch 1, dc, ch 1, dc) in next ch, ch 1, sk 2 ch, sc in next ch, ch 2, sk 2 ch**, dc in next 3 ch, ch 2, sk 2 ch, sc in next ch, rep from * across, ending final rep at **, dc in last ch, turn. (*6 sc, 17 dc, 18 ch-sps*)

Row 2 Ch 3 (counts as dc here and throughout), *sk (ch 2, sc), [bobble in next ch-1 sp, ch 3] three times, bobble in next ch-1 sp, sk (sc, ch 2)**, dc in next dc, V-st in next dc, dc in next dc, rep from * across, ending last rep at **, dc in 3rd ch of tch, turn. (*10 dc, 12 bobbles, 11 ch-sps*)

Row 3 Ch 5 (counts as dc, ch 2), *(sc in next ch-3 sp, ch 3) twice, sc in next ch-3 sp, ch 2**, dc in next 2 dc, V-st in ch-1 sp, dc in next 2 dc, ch 2, rep from * across, ending last rep at **, dc in tch, turn. (*9 sc, 14 dc, 12 ch-sps*)

Row 4 Ch 8 (counts as dc, ch 5), *sk (ch 2, sc), sc in next ch-3 sp, ch 3, sc in next ch-3 sp, ch 5, sk 2 ch**, dc in next 3 dc, ch 3, dc in next 3 dc, ch 5, rep from * across, ending last rep at **, dc in 3rd ch of tch, turn. (*6 sc, 14 dc, 11 ch-sps*)

Row 5 Ch 5 (counts as dc, ch 2), *sc in ch-5 sp, ch 1, (dc, ch 1, dc, ch 1, dc) in next ch-3 sp, ch 1, sc in next ch-5 sp, ch 2**, dc in next 3 dc, (dc, ch 1, dc, ch 1, dc) in next ch-3 sp, dc in next 3 dc, ch 2, rep from * across, ending last rep at **, dc in 3rd ch of tch, turn. (*29 dc, 22 ch-sps*)

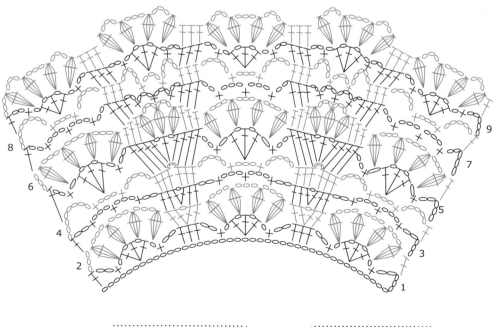

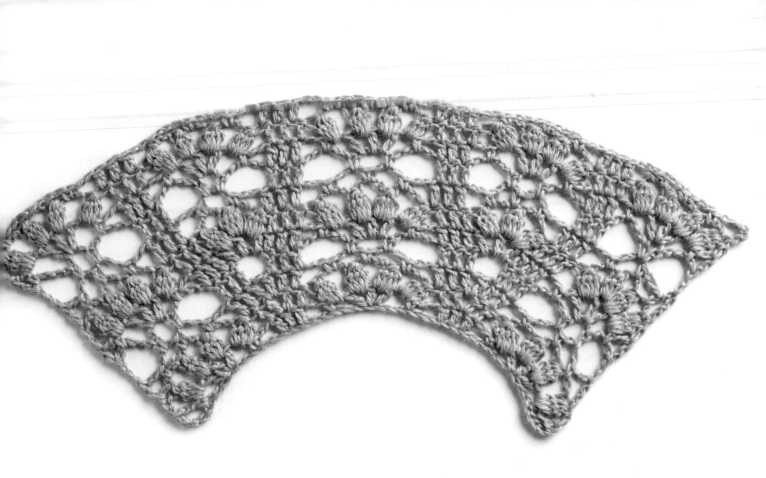

Row 6 Ch 3 (counts as dc here and through-out), *sk (ch 2, sc), [bobble in next ch-1 sp, ch 3] three times, bobble in next ch-1 sp, sk (sc, ch 2)**, dc in next 3 dc, bobble in next ch-1 sp, ch 3, bobble in next dc, ch 3, bobble in next ch-1 sp, dc in next 3 dc, rep from * across, ending last rep at **, dc in next ch, turn. (*14 dc, 18 bobbles, 13 ch-sps*)

Row 7 Ch 5 (counts as dc, ch 2), *(sc in next ch-3 sp, ch 3) twice, sc in next ch-3 sp, ch 2**, dc in next 3 dc, ch 2, sc in next ch-3 sp, ch 3, sc between ch-3 sps, ch 3, sc in next ch-3 sp, ch 2, dc in next 3 dc, ch 2, rep from * across, ending last rep at ** dc in tch, turn. (*15 sc, 14 dc, 20 ch-sps*)

Row 8 Ch 8 (counts as dc, ch 5), *sk (ch 2, sc), sc in next ch-3 sp, ch 3, sc in next ch-3 sp, ch 5, sk (sc, 2 ch)**, dc in next 3 dc, ch 5, (sc, ch 3, sc) in next 2 ch-3 sps, ch 5, dc in next 3 dc, ch 5, rep from * across, ending last rep at **, dc in next ch, turn. (*10 sc, 14 dc, 15 ch-sps*)

Row 9 Ch 5 (counts as dc, ch 2), *sc in ch-5 sp, ch 1, (dc, ch 1, dc, ch 1, dc) in next ch-3 sp, ch 1, sc in next ch-5 sp, ch 2**, dc in next 3 dc, ch 2, rep from * across, ending last rep at **, dc in 3rd ch of tch, turn. (*10 sc, 29 dc, 30 ch-sps*)

To work even from here, continue as for Columns of Fans and Double Crochet swatch (page 140), starting with row 2.

If you've enjoyed exploring this stitch pattern and its variations, check out the Lace Capelet pattern on page 228, which uses this stitch and some of these shaping methods.

Shaping Complex Lace

Pineapple stitches and other complex lace patterns (stitch patterns covering many rows and a variety of stitches) can be shaped in various ways, adapting the techniques we've been discussing. Sometimes portions can be increased or decreased by only 1 stitch at a time, while others can be shaped at an angle or in panels. Although this chapter will help you see shaping opportunities in any stitch pattern, some resist shaping, so save those for items where a simple rectangle works.

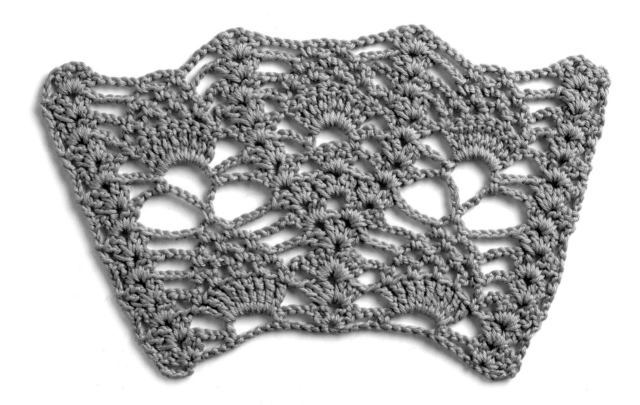

Pineapples and Shells Stitch

This stitch pattern features two panels: one of pineapples and a second of paired little shells [(3 dc, ch 2, 3 dc) in 1 stitch]. The paired shells form a nice frame for the pineapple panels, separated from them with chain stitches. In this sample, shaping begins in row 2, and the full pattern repetition is added by row 9. The remaining rows are worked even in the pineapple and shells pattern. Depending on the shape you're making and how rapidly it must expand, you can make the increase between every pineapple panel, or after every third one, or even farther apart.

Double V-st (2 dc, ch 2, 2 dc) in designated sp.

Ch a multiple of 15, plus 7 end sts, plus 3 for tch. (*ch 40 for swatch*)

Row 1 Double V-st in 7th ch from hook, *ch 3, sk 4 ch, sc in next ch, ch 6, sk 4 ch, sc in next ch, ch 3, sk 4 ch, double V-st in next ch, rep from * across, sk 2 ch, dc in last ch, turn. (*4 sc, 2 dc, 3 double V-sts*)

Row 2 Ch 3 (*counts as dc here and through-out*), double V-st in next ch-2 sp, *ch 1, 9 tr in next ch-6 sp, ch 1**, (3 dc, ch 2, 3 dc) in next ch-2 sp, rep from * across, ending last rep at **, double V-st in last ch-2 sp, dc in tch, turn. (*2 double V-sts, 18 tr, 8 dc, 5 ch-sps*)

Row 3 Ch 3, double V-st in next ch-2 sp, *ch 3, [(sc, ch 3) in next tr, sk next tr] four times, sc in next tr, ch 3**, (4 dc, ch 2, 4 dc) in next ch-2 sp, rep from * across, ending last rep at **, double V-st in next ch-2 sp, dc in tch, turn. (*10 sc, 10 dc, 2 double V-sts, 13 ch-sps*)

Row 4 Ch 3, double V-st in next ch-2 sp, *ch 3, (sc in next ch-3 sp, ch 3) three times, sc in next ch-3 sp, ch 3**, (2 dc, ch 1, 2 dc, ch 1, 2 dc) in next ch-2 sp, rep from * across, ending last rep at **, double V-st in last ch-2 sp, dc in tch, turn. (*8 sc, 8 dc, 2 double V-sts, 11 ch-sps*)

Row 5 Ch 3, double V-st in next ch-2 sp, *ch 4, (sc in next ch-3 sp, ch 3) twice, sc in next ch-3 sp, ch 4**, double V-st in next ch-1 sp, ch 2, double V-st in next ch-1 sp, rep from * across, ending last rep at **, double V-st in last ch-2 sp, dc in tch, turn. (*6 sc, 4 double V-sts, 9 ch-sps*)

Row 6 Ch 3, double V-st in next ch-2 sp, *ch 5, sc in next ch-3 sp, ch 3, sc in next ch-3 sp, ch 5**, (double V-st in next ch-2 sp) three times, rep from *, ending last rep at **, double V-st in last ch-2 sp, dc in tch, turn. (*4 sc, 5 double V-sts, 2 dc, 6 ch-sps*)

Row 7 Ch 3, double V-st in next ch-2 sp, *ch 8, sc in next ch-3 sp, ch 8**, (double V-st in next ch-2 sp, ch 1) twice, double V-st in next ch-2 sp, rep from * across, ending last rep at **, double V-st in last ch-2 sp, dc in tch, turn. (*2 sc, 2 dc, 5 double V-sts, 6 ch sts*)

Row 8 Ch 3, double V-st in next ch-2 sp, *ch 4, sc in ch-8 sp, ch 6, sc in next ch-8 sp, ch 4**, double V-st in next ch-2 sp, ch 4, sk next ch-1 sp, sc in next dc, ch 6, sk next (dc, ch 2, dc), sc in next dc, ch 4, double V-st in next ch-2 sp, rep from *, ending last rep at **, double V-st in last ch-2 sp, dc in tch, turn. (*6 sc, 4 double V-sts, 2 dc, 9 ch-sps*)

Row 9 Ch 3, *double V-st in next ch-2 sp, ch 1, 9 tr in ch-6 sp, ch 1, rep from * across, double V-st in last ch-2 sp, dc in tch, turn. (*27 tr, 2 dc, 4 double V-sts, 6 ch-sps*)

Row 10 Ch 3, *double V-st in next ch-2 sp, ch 3, (sc in next tr, ch 3, sk next tr) four times, sc in next tr, ch 3, rep from * across, double V-st in last ch-2 sp, dc in tch, turn. (*4 double V-sts, 2 dc, 15 sc, 18 ch-sps*)

Row 11 Ch 3, *double V-st in next ch-2 sp, ch 3, (sc in next ch-3 sp, ch 3) three times, sc in next ch-3 sp, ch 3, rep from * across, double V-st in last ch-2 sp, dc in tch, turn. (*4 double V-sts, 2 dc, 12 sc, 15 ch-sps*)

Row 12 Ch 3, *double V-st in next ch-2 sp, ch 4, (sc in next ch-3 sp, ch 3) three times, ch 1, rep from * across, double V-st in last ch-2 sp, dc in tch, turn. (*4 double V-sts, 2 dc, 9 sc, 12 ch-sps*)

Row 13 Ch 3, *double V-st in next ch-2 space, ch 5, sc in next ch-3 sp, ch 3, sc in next ch-3 sp, ch 5, rep from * across, double V-st in last ch-2 sp, dc in tch, turn. (*4 double V-sts, 2 dc, 6 sc, 9 ch-sps*)

Short Rows

Before leaving the fascinating subject of shaping, let's not forget the option of short-row shaping. This shaping technique is popular with knitters and can be used in crochet as well. Short rows are just what they seem — a row deliberately made shorter than those around it. They can create extra fabric at a crucial shaping point, for example, near the neckline at the top of the shoulder (for shoulder slope), or to make a skirt flair. In crochet, since our stitches are taller than they are wide, it can be tricky to do these in such a way as to completely integrate them into the fabric. Note that the row after a short row is worked partially into the short row, and partially into the row that precedes the short row. The trick when using short rows is to avoid creating a hole or a pucker in the fabric, and you'll see how in this swatch.

Ch 20.

Row 1 Hdc in 3rd ch from hook, hdc in each ch to end, turn. (*19 hdc*)

Row 2 (short row) Ch 2 (counts as hdc throughout), hdc in next 5 hdc, sc in next hdc, sl st in next hdc, turn, leaving remaining sts unworked.

Place a marker in the same st where you made the sl st.

Row 3 (short row) Ch 1, sk sl st, sc in next sc, sc in next hdc, hdc in next 4 hdc, hdc in tch, turn.

Row 4 Ch 2, hdc in next 4 hdc, hdc in next 2 sc (from this point you will be working into the stitches of row 1), hdc in next hdc (in the same st as the sl st in row 2 where you placed the marker), hdc in each hdc across, turn.

Row 5 Ch 2, hdc across.

Basic Short Rows

This strategy brings the ends of the short rows to a point, leaving no obvious hole in the fabric. To accomplish this, I removed any unnecessary slip stitches or turning chains to create a smooth melding of the rows. Other methods might yield a similar effect, so feel free to experiment. Do be sure to maintain the overall stitch count so that you don't inadvertently add or lose stitches in the course of making the short rows.

Before resorting to short-row shaping, however, keep in mind that it can be much more challenging — if not impossible — to do short rows with complex stitch patterns. Fortunately, we have many other ways to shape in crochet, but this is one more tool for your collection. Short rows can, however, be very useful when working with rows of plain stitches.

This extended study of shaping techniques is sure to enhance your understanding of patterns, allow you to make alterations in them, and create designs from scratch. When you encounter different stitch patterns, think about how they can be shaped, how stitches align, what angles and lines you see in the stitches, and whether they work better to shape at the edges, internally, or both. Then try out your ideas by experimenting on a swatch or two or three, and remember to be bold in your experiments! Swatches are tools for discovery and learning, and each time you have an idea that doesn't work, it's as valuable as one that does!

8

Texture

TEXTURE IS SOMETHING CROCHET does superbly well. To define it broadly, texture adds dimension to the surface of the fabric. Using a variety of stitches and techniques that are well established in crochet, we can create either subtle or very pronounced textures.

Texture can be created by bunching stitches together, as in clusters, bobbles, and puffs, by working in the front or back loop only, by placing 2 stitches of different heights next to one another, or with post stitches, crossed stitches, or spikes. Crochet cables are textured stitches that use post stitches to re-create the look of knitted cables.

These textured surfaces can be very attractive, but keep in mind that they add weight to the project. Sturdy items like hats and purses can benefit from the weight and structure offered by textured stitches. For other projects where fabric needs to be light and flexible, use lighter weight, lofty yarns when working textured stitches.

In this chapter we will investigate a variety of textured stitches: clusters, bobbles, puffs, popcorns, post stitches, crocodile stitch, and several different cable stitches. For each, we address technical issues, stitching tips, hand maneuvers, tension, shaping, and fabric. Some of the stitches require excellent control of tension, and they can help you advance that skill if you practice them.

Please choose some favorites among these stitches and dive into them immediately! The variety and technical challenges make for some of the most enjoyable stitches in crochet, and they open up a fantastic world of textured effects.

Texture is increasingly an important design feature in fashion, knits, and crochet wear, and it looks like a trend with great sticking power. Just remember when using it in crochet wearables to work with thinner yarns so that your garments don't get too heavy and stiff.

Forked Clusters

The forked cluster is a favorite cluster stitch that I like to alternate with single crochet rows for texture. It is almost like working 2 double crochet stitches together, but not quite. The front and back of the fabric are different, because the back of the clusters create stronger texture than the front, but both sides look great, and you can choose either one for the right side of the work. The single crochet rows are worked in the front loop only to add another subtle layer of texture.

Reverse

Note
The last dc in FCl rows is worked into the same stitch as second leg of previous FCl.

FCl (forked cluster) Yo, insert hook in same st as second leg of prev FCl, yo and draw up a loop, yo, insert hook in next st, yo and draw up a loop, (yo, draw through 3 loops) twice.

Ch any number. (*ch 18 for swatch*)

Row 1 Yo, insert hook in 4th ch from hook, yo, insert hook in next st, yo and draw up a loop, (yo, draw through 3 loops) twice, FCl across, dc in last ch, turn. (*14 FCl, 2 dc*)

Row 2 Ch 1, FLsc in each st across.

Row 3 Ch 3 (counts as dc), beg in 2nd sc, FCl across, dc in last sc, turn.

Rep rows 2 and 3 for patt, ending with row 2.

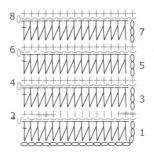

Tall/Short Texture

This swatch features a stitch that alternates single and double crochet stitches in each row. Just for fun, I added a row of alternating single and trebles at the bottom and top of this swatch, to highlight the difference in texture one extra yarnover makes. If you want to use the more subtle pattern only, begin with row 3 of the pattern after making your starting chain. It's a very pretty closed stitch.

Ch an odd number of sts, plus 1 for tch. (*ch 18 for swatch*)

Row 1 (WS) Sc in 2nd ch from hook, *tr in next ch, sc in next ch, rep from * across, turn. (*9 sc, 8 tr*)

Row 2 Ch 2 (counts as hdc throughout), hdc in each st across, turn. (*17 hdc*)

Row 3 Ch 1, sc in first hdc, *dc in next hdc, sc in next hdc, rep from * across, turn. (*9 sc, 8 dc*)

Row 4 Ch 3 (counts as dc), *sc in next dc, dc in next sc, rep from * across, turn. (*9 dc, 8 sc*)

Row 5 Ch 1, sc in first dc, *dc in next sc, sc in next dc, rep from * across, turn. (*9 sc, 8 dc*)

Rows 6–9 Rep rows 4 and 5.

Row 10 Ch 2, hdc in each st across, turn.

Row 11 Ch 1, sc in first hdc, *tr in next hdc, sc in next hdc, rep from * across, fasten off.

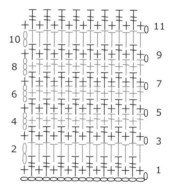

Puffs, Bobbles, and Popcorns

Ever-popular puffs and bobbles are great vehicles for adding textural interest. So are popcorns, but they are less common, probably because they require an extra step. All these stitches are created by working many stitches into one stitch, but each one has a slightly different look. Unfortunately, their names are not standardized, so you will find them called different things in different publications. We define them as follows:

- **Puffs** are the same as working a group of half double crochet stitches together: (Yo, insert hook in designated stitch, yo and draw up a loop) multiple times, yo, draw through all loops on hook.

- **Bobbles** are similar to working a group of double crochet stitches together, except all the stitches are made in 1 stitch: (Yo, insert hook in designated stitch, yo and draw up a loop, yo, draw through 2 loops) multiple times, yo, draw through all loops on hook.

- **Popcorns** are a series of double crochets worked normally, all in the same stitch, then the first and last stitches are slipped together: Work several double crochets in the next stitch, remove hook from working stitch, insert hook in first stitch of group, draw unworked loop through.

It is possible to work bobbles and popcorns with treble crochet, and possibly even taller stitches, though I haven't ever tried. Puffs, on the other hand, are, by definition, the height of a half double crochet. They can be made taller by drawing up the loops to a greater height.

A pattern should always tell you how many stitches to make; it may say 5-double crochet bobble, or 4-stitch puff, for example. Detailed instructions will also include a breakdown of how to execute the stitch, spelling out all the yarnovers and insertion points, in the definition section of the pattern.

One of the nifty things about these dimensional stitches is that you can work additional stitches in your puff, bobble, or popcorn to make them pop out more. This gives you considerable leeway to get just the right effect. If you are using a softer yarn, for example, you may find that you need more stitches in a bobble than is given in a pattern. Or the opposite — if your yarn has a lot more body, you may want to use fewer stitches to soften the effect. In many instances a puff, bobble, or popcorn can be substituted for each other if you determine that another works better with your yarn or hook size for achieving the desired effect.

Keep in mind that puffs, bobbles, and popcorns always count as one stitch, no matter how many stitches are used to make them. On the other hand, if they're made very poofy, they can crowd out other stitches. If you find this happening, try loosening tension on the stitches near the bobble. They may just need some breathing room so they can adapt around it.

A technical question arises with these stitches: should you make an extra chain after completing the stitch? This serves to tighten the top of the stitch and make it pop more. Pattern instructions should specify whether or not this was done. But even if it is not in the pattern, if you like the effect, by all means use it. Just make sure not to work into the extra chain in the subsequent row.

When shaping a design that includes dimensional stitches, avoid placing them right at the edge of the work, as a bulky edge does not look as neat and makes seaming difficult. Substitute a plain stitch of the correct height instead.

Puffs

Puffs look very cute, but they can be tricky to make well. In order for the puff to be neat and pleasingly plump, you need good control of tension.

Puffs can be made with 2, 3, 4, or more loops. Naturally, the more loops, the more puff. Here are typical instructions for a 4-stitch puff, which will give you 8 loops on the hook.

(Yo, insert hook in designated st, draw up a loop) four times, yo, draw through 8 loops on hook.

Let's break it down so you understand how each move contributes to the look of the puff.

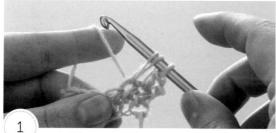

1 Yarnover, insert hook in designated stitch and draw up a loop. Bring up the loop to a good height — over 1". This is a crucial step in allowing enough "slack" yarn to work the puff loosely.

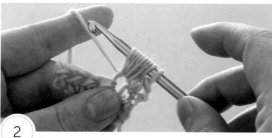

2 Repeat step 1 three times more. These loops are less stretchy than the first, and that's okay; pull them up as best you can. You should have 8 loops on the hook. Before completing the last yarnover that is pulled through all the loops, slide the loops down a bit on the shaft of the hook and pull up on all the loops again. This move helps make all the loops match in size.

3 Now yarnover and draw through all 8 loops. If you pull too tightly, your nice long loops will get squished. If you have trouble maneuvering your hook through all the loops, try swiveling the hook so that it faces down and doesn't catch the yarn. This may take a few trials to fully master, so don't give up too soon.

4 Chain 1 to tighten the top of the puff.

Just 1 stitch. No matter how many stitches you put into your bobble or puff, it still counts as 1 stitch.

Puff Flower

Here's a superfun little motif to practice your puffs. You will find that puffs look a little different on the front and back of the work, usually neater on the front. Following the instructions above and the tips below should help the appearance on both sides. To "fatten up" the petals of this flower, the puffs are worked with 6 stitches, and there will be 12 loops on the hook before finishing the puff. Use this motif to create a necklace, or apply it to a hat or purse for decoration.

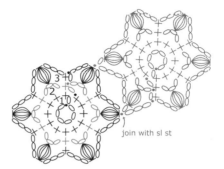

join with sl st

Puff (Yo, insert hook in designated st, draw up a loop to ½") six times, yo, draw through 13 loops on hook.

FIRST FLOWER

Ch 6, sl st to first ch to close ring.

Rnd 1 Ch 1, work 12 sc in ring, sl st to top of first sc. (*12 sc*)

Rnd 2 Ch 1, sc in first sc, *ch 3, sk next sc, sc in next sc, rep from * around, sl st to top of first sc. (*6 ch-3 sps*)

Rnd 3 Ch 1, sc in first sc, *ch 3, puff in ch-3 sp, ch 1 to close puff, ch 3, sc in next sc, rep from * around, sl st to top of first sc, fasten off. (*6 puffs*)

SECOND FLOWER

Rnds 1 and 2 Rep rnds 1 and 2 of First Flower.

Rnd 3 Ch 1, sc in first sc, *ch 3, puff in ch-3 sp, ch 1 to close puff, ch 3, sc in next sc, rep from * three more times, ch 3, puff in next ch-3 sp, ch 1, sl st to top of puff on first flower, ch 3, sc in next sc, ch 3, puff in next ch-3 sp, ch 1, sl st to top of next puff on first flower, ch 3, sl st to first sc, fasten off. (*6 puffs*)

Stitching Tips

- **Work the puffs** loosely.

- **Work the chains** tightly.

- **When connecting** one flower to the next, be careful that both flowers end up with the right side facing. To facilitate this, you can experiment with the connecting slip stitch, either inserting the hook from front to back or back to front. You may find one way makes it easier for you than the other, or that one way makes a more pleasing join than the other.

Ripple and Puff

Here's a stitch pattern that combines ripples and puffs.

Note

The backs of puffs will show on the right side in this pattern.

....

Puff (Yo, insert hook in designated st and draw loop up to ½") four times, yo, draw through 9 loops on hook.

....

Ch a multiple of 12. (*ch 24 for swatch*)

Row 1 (RS) Dc in 4th ch from hook, dc in next 3 ch, ch 2, dc in next 5 ch, sk 2 ch, *dc in next 5 ch, ch 2, dc in next 5 ch, rep from * across, turn.

Row 2 Ch 4 (counts as dc, ch 1), sk 2 dc, dc in next dc, ch 1, sk next dc, *(dc, ch 1, puff, ch 1, dc) in ch-2 sp, (ch 1, sk next dc, dc in next dc)** twice, sk 2 dc, (dc in next dc, ch 1, sk next dc) twice, rep from * across, ending last rep at **, ch 1, sk last 2 dc, dc in tch, turn.

Row 3 Ch 3, sk ch-1, *(dc in next dc, dc in next ch) twice, ch 2, sk puff, (dc in next ch, dc in next dc) twice**, dc in next ch, sk 2 dc, dc in next ch, rep from * across, ending last rep at **, sk 1 ch, dc in 3rd ch of tch, turn.

Row 4 Ch 3 (counts as dc throughout), sk next dc, dc in next 3 dc, *(dc, ch 1, puff, ch 1, dc) in ch-2 sp**, dc in next 4 dc, sk 2 dc, dc in next 4 dc, rep from * across, ending last rep at **, dc in next 3 dc, sk next dc, dc in tch, turn.

Row 5 Ch 3, sk next dc, dc in next 3 dc, *dc in ch-1 sp, ch 2, dc in ch-1 sp, dc in next 3 dc**, dc in next dc, sk 2 dc, dc in next 4 dc, rep from * across, ending last rep at **, sk next dc, dc in tch, turn.

Rep rows 2–5 for pattern.

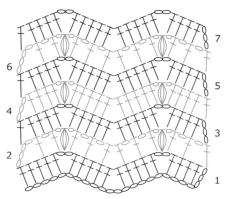

Bobbles

Bobbles are created by gathering several stitches together in the same way we gather stitches for decreasing. The difference is that when making bobbles, the hook is always inserted in the same stitch. Each stitch is worked until the last loop, then a final yarnover is drawn through all the loops on the hook. The hook holds as many loops as there are stitches in the bobble, plus one: the loop already on the hook from the last stitch made. So, if you are making a 5-double crochet bobble, the instructions will tell you to draw through 6 loops on the hook to complete the bobble.

Curiously, the bobble pops on the opposite side of the work, so they are worked with the wrong side facing. It is possible to push them through to the other side, should the need arise, as when you are working in the round with the right side facing at all times. Once you have finished the row or round, use your fingers to push the bobble to the other side of the work.

One fun use of bobbles is to create a design on the fabric's surface. Here's a pattern that demonstrates the concept.

> **Make them pop.** If you want your bobbles to really pop, place them next to shorter stitches, such as single or half double crochet. Making more stitches in the bobble will also give it more pop.

Bobble (Yo, insert hook in designated st, yo and draw up loop, yo, draw through 2 loops) five times, yo, draw through 6 loops on hook. Note that this is a 5-dc bobble.

Ch a multiple of 11, plus 2 end sts, plus 1 for tch. (*ch 14 for swatch*)

Row 1 Sc in 2nd ch from hook and in each ch across. (*13 sts*)

Row 2 Ch 1, sc in next 6 sc, bobble in next sc, sc in next 6 sts, turn.

Row 3 Ch 1, sc across.

Row 4 Ch 1, sc in next 4 sc, bobble in next sc, sc in next 3 sc, bobble in next sc, sc in each sc to end.

Row 5 Rep row 3.

Row 6 Ch 1, sc in next 2 sc, bobble in next sc, sc in next 3 sc, bobble in next sc, sc in next 3 sc, bobble in next sc, sc in each sc to end.

Row 7 Rep row 3.

Row 8 Rep row 4.

Row 9 Rep row 3.

Row 10 Rep row 2.

Row 11 Ch 1, sc in each st across.

Popcorn

Popcorns pop more than bobbles and puffs. When the first and last stitches of the popcorn are brought together, the stitches between them jump out from the surface.

1 Work 5 double crochet (dc) in designated stitch.

2 Remove hook from working loop, insert hook in first double crochet (dc) of group.

3 Draw unworked loop through.

Two Color Popcorn

This two-color pattern is like a whole garden of popcorns. It's a great pattern for a project done in the round because the right side needs to be facing on all rows. If worked flat, it requires joining new yarn every row and leaves many ends to weave in. (For joining new yarn, see page 58.)

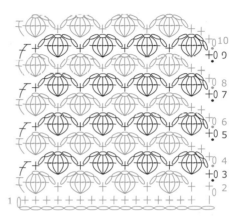

This swatch is worked with two colors (A and B).

With A, ch a multiple of 8, plus 2 for end sts. (*ch 18 for swatch*)

Row 1 Sc in 2nd ch from hook and in each ch across, turn.

Row 2 (RS) Ch 1, sc in first sc, *sc in next sc, ch 2, sk next sc, popcorn in next sc**, ch 2, rep from * across, ending last rep at **, dc in last sc, do not turn, fasten off.

Row 3 With RS facing, join color B in first sc, ch 1, sc in same sc, ch 2, *popcorn in next sc, ch 2, sc in next popcorn**, ch 2, rep from * across, ending last rep at **, dc in last dc, do not turn, fasten off.

Row 4 With RS facing, join color A in first sc, ch 1, sc in first sc, sc in ch-2 sp, *sc in next popcorn, ch 2, popcorn in next sc**, ch 2, rep from * across, ending last rep at **, dc in last dc, do not turn, fasten off.

Rep rows 3 and 4 for pattern.

Crossed Stitches

This next stitch helps you become accustomed to crossing one stitch over another. Crossed stitches are used frequently in cables and involve working behind or in front of another stitch, which can be tricky. In this stitch, one stitch wraps around another. Try it — it's fun and a good warm-up for more complex cabling. To make this easier, use a very flexible yarn.

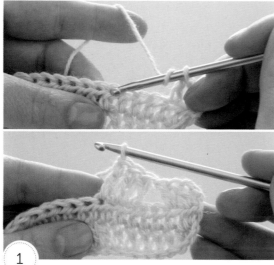

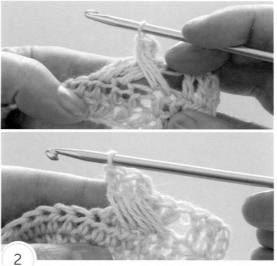

① Skip 3 sts, work 1 double crochet (dc) in each of the next 3 sts.

② Work 1 double crochet (dc) in each of the skipped sts, pulling up the first loop very tall so it easily wraps around the previously made stitches. When working the crossed stitches, you will see them wrap around the 3 stitches just completed. It can be hard to find the skipped stitches to work into, but go ahead and use your fingers to pull other stitches out of the way to find them.

Crossed Stitches

Because the loops of the crossed stitches are quite long, this is a nice stitch for showing off a yarn with special characteristics.

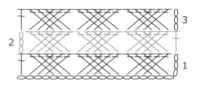

Ch a multiple of 6, plus 2 for end sts, plus 2 for tch. (*ch 22 for swatch*)

Row 1 Sk 6 ch (3 ch for tch and 3 ch for crossing), *dc in next 3 ch, dc in 3 sk ch**, sk 3 ch, rep from * across, ending last rep at **, dc in last ch, turn.

Row 2 Ch 3 (counts as dc),* sk 3 dc, dc in next 3 dc, dc in 3 sk dc, rep from * across, dc in tch, turn.

Rep row 2 for pattern.

Cabling Techniques and Stitches

Many crocheters are interested in cables but are not secure with the technical challenges, such as working behind stitches. We'll go over techniques you'll need to work a great variety of different cable stitches, some easier than others. Some stitch patterns require working posts only on the right side, and others are done on both sides.

In all cable stitches, it's important to elongate the post stitches so that the fabric isn't pulled. If your tendency is to crochet tightly, these stitch patterns will be good practice for loosening up, letting your eye judge the distance and guide your tension accordingly.

When working with cables in a project that requires shaping, you should generally avoid placing cables at the edges to avoid bulk. Instead, just as with bobbles and puffs, substitute a plain stitch of the correct height. Keep in mind that post stitches are shorter because they are worked into the post of a stitch, not the top. That means that if you're working with double crochet post stitches, use a half double crochet at the end of the row and a chain 2 at the beginning; if the post stitches are treble crochet, use a double crochet at the end and chain 3 to start the row.

Once you're comfortable making post stitches, you'll want to master a few additional techniques common to cabling. One is how to work a back post stitch. These are used to continue cabling while you are on the work's wrong side. Instructions usually tell you to insert the hook from back to front around the post. It may sound hard, but it's really easy. I find the simplest way to do this is as follows.

Step-by-Step Back Post Stitch

1 Flip the work so you are looking at the back upside down. Yarnover and insert the hook from right to left under the post.

2 Complete the stitch, in this case a dc (double crochet).

3 Turn the work back so you can continue working on the wrong side.

> **Front post stitch.** To make these, start from the front and simply insert hook from front to back around the post, as shown on page 66.

Back Post Stitch with Open Fan

Practice your back post stitch in this pattern, a nice example of how post stitches can be combined with openwork.

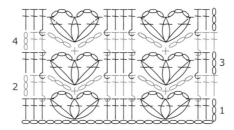

Dc2tog (double crochet 2 stitches together) (Yo, insert hook in designated st, yo and draw up a loop, yo, draw through 2 loops) twice, yo draw through 3 loops on hook.

Open fan (Dc2tog, ch 3, dc2tog, ch 3, dc2tog) in designated st or sp.

FPdc (front post double crochet) Yo, insert hook from front to back around post, yo and draw up a loop, (yo, draw through 2 loops) twice.

BPdc (back post double crochet) Yo, insert hook from back to front around post, yo and draw up a loop, (yo, draw through 2 loops) twice.

Ch a multiple of 11, plus 2 for edge sts, plus 2 for tch. (*ch 26 for swatch*)

Row 1 Dc in 4th ch from hook, dc in next ch, *sk 3 ch, open fan in next ch, sk 3 ch**, dc in next 4 ch, rep from * across, ending last rep at **, dc in last 3 ch, turn.

Row 2 (RS) Ch 3 (counts as dc throughout), dc in next dc, *FPdc in next dc, ch 3, sc in center st of open fan, ch 3, FPdc in next dc**, dc in next 2 dc, rep from * across, ending last rep at **, dc in next dc, dc in tch, turn.

Row 3 (WS) Ch 3, dc in next dc, *BPdc in next dc, open fan in next sc, BPdc in next dc**, dc in next 2 dc, rep from * across, ending last rep at **, dc in next dc, dc in tch, turn.

Rep rows 2 and 3 for pattern.

Cabled Lace

In this stitch, the cable is worked on every row, requiring front post stitches on odd-numbered rows and back post stitches on even-numbered rows.

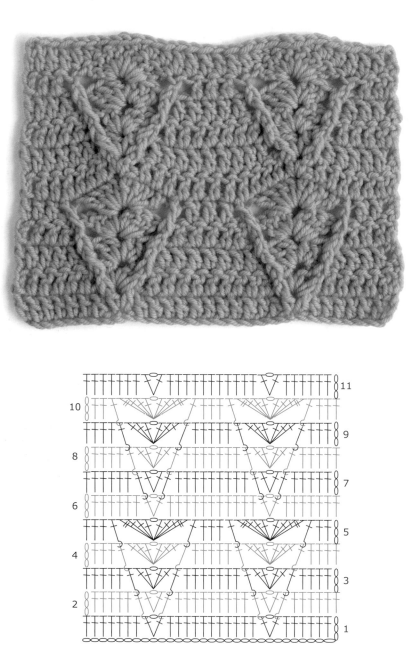

BPdc (back post double crochet) Yo, insert hook from back to front around post, yo and draw up a loop, (yo, draw through 2 loops) twice.

FPdc (front post double crochet) Yo, insert hook around post of designated st, yo and draw up a loop, (yo, draw through 2 loops) twice.

Ch multiple of 14, plus 3 for end sts, plus 2 for tch. (ch 33 for swatch)

Row 1 Dc in 4th ch from hook, dc in next 5 ch, *sk next ch, (dc, ch 1, dc) in next ch**, dc in next 11 ch, rep from * across, ending last rep at **, dc in last 7 sts, turn.

Row 2 Ch 3 (counts as dc throughout), dc in next 5 dc, *sk next dc, BPdc in next dc, (dc, ch 1, dc) in next ch-1 sp, BPdc in next dc, sk next dc**, dc in next 9 dc, rep from * across, ending last rep at **, dc in last 6 sts, turn.

Row 3 Ch 3, dc in next 4 dc, *sk next dc, FPdc in next dc, sk next dc, (2 dc, ch 1, 2 dc) in ch-1 sp, sk next dc, FPdc in next dc, sk next dc**, dc in next 7 dc, rep from * across, ending last rep at **, dc in last 5 sts, turn.

Row 4 Ch 3, dc in next 3 dc, *sk next dc, BPdc in next dc, sk 2 dc, (3 dc, ch 1, 3 dc) in ch-1 sp, sk 2 dc, BPdc in next dc, sk next dc**, dc in next 5 dc, rep from * across, ending last rep at **, dc in last 4 sts, turn.

Row 5 Ch 3, dc in next 2 dc, *sk next dc, FPdc in next dc, sk 3 dc, (tr, 3 dc, ch 1, 3 dc, tr) in ch-1 sp, sk 3 dc, FPdc in next dc, sk next dc**, dc in next 3 dc, rep from * across, ending last rep at **, dc in last 3 sts, turn.

Row 6 Ch 3, dc in next 6 sts, *sk next dc, (dc, ch 1, dc) in next ch-1 sp, sk next dc**, dc in next 11 sts, rep from * across, ending last rep at **, dc in last 7 sts, turn.

Row 7 Ch 3, dc in next 5 dc, *sk next dc, FPdc in next dc, (dc, ch-1, dc) in next ch-1 sp, FPdc in next dc, sk next dc**, dc in next 9 dc, rep from * across, ending last rep at **, dc in last 6 sts, turn.

Row 8 Ch 3, dc in next 4 dc, *sk next dc, BPdc in next dc, sk next dc, (2 dc, ch 1, 2 dc) in ch-1 sp, sk next dc, BPdc in next dc, sk next dc**, dc in next 7 dc, rep from * across, ending last rep at **, dc in last 5 sts, turn.

Row 9 Ch 3, dc in next 3 dc, *sk next dc, FPdc in next dc, sk 2 dc, (3 dc, ch 1, 3 dc) in ch-1 sp, sk 2 dc, FPdc in next dc, sk next dc**, dc in next 5 dc, rep from * across, ending last rep at **, dc in last 4 sts, turn.

Row 10 Ch 3, dc in next 2 dc, *sk next dc, BPdc in next dc, sk 3 dc, (tr, 3 dc, ch 1, 3 dc, tr) in ch-1 sp, sk 3 dc, BPdc in next dc, sk next dc**, dc in next 3 dc, rep from * across, ending last rep at **, dc in last 3 sts, turn.

Row 11 Ch 3, dc in next 6 sts, *sk next dc, (dc, ch 1, dc) in next ch-1 sp, sk next dc**, dc in next 11 sts, rep from * across, ending last rep at **, dc in last 7 sts, turn.

Rep rows 2–11 for patt, ending with row 10. To make flat top edge, work one more row as follows:

Last row Ch 3, dc in next 3 sts, *hdc in next 2 sts, sc in next st, sl st in next 3 sts, sc in next st, hdc in next 2 sts**, dc in next 5 dc, rep from * across, ending last rep at **, dc in last 4 sts.

Step-by-Step Working Post Stitches Together

The next stitch pattern uses post stitches to form a network of diamond shapes. This is accomplished by working 2 post stitches together over several stitches that lie between them.

1 Yarnover, insert hook as instructed, yarnover and draw up a loop, yarnover, draw through 2 loops leaving 2 loops on hook.

2 Skip the required number of stitches, yarnover, insert the hook as instructed, yarnover and draw up a loop.

3 Yarnover and draw through 2 loops; you now have 3 loops on the hook.

4 Yarnover and draw yarn through 3 loops once more.

Crossed Cables

If you'd like to work the pattern in color, as shown in this swatch, work color A for 4 rows, change to color B, then change color at the end of every even-numbered row until the last 3 rows, working the last 3 rows in color A.

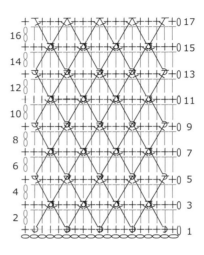

Note

Always skip the stitch behind the post stitch.

Cl FPdc (cluster front post double crochet) (Yo, insert hook around post of st 2 rows below and 2 sts to the right, yo and draw up loop, yo, draw through 2 loops), sk 3 sc, (yo, insert hook around post of st 2 rows below and 2 sts to the left, yo and draw up loop, yo, draw through 2 loops), yo, draw through 3 loops on hook. Left-handers will work the first part of the cluster 2 sts to the left and second part of cluster 2 sts to the right.

Ch a multiple of 4, plus 3 for end sts, plus 1 for turning chain. (*ch 24 for swatch*)

Row 1 Sc in 2nd ch from hook and in each ch across, turn. (*19 sc*)

Row 2 Ch 2, hdc in each sc across, turn.

Row 3 Ch 1, sc in next 3 hdc, Cl FPdc over sc 2 sts to the right and 2 sts to the left, *sc in next 3 hdc, Cl FPdc over (second leg of last Cl, sk 3 sc, next sc) rep from * across, sc in last 2 hdc, sc in tch, turn. (*15 sc, 4 Cl FPdc*)

Row 4 Ch 2, hdc across.

Row 5 Ch 1, sc in first hdc, FPdc in next Cl, *sc in next 3 hdc, Cl FPdc over (same st as last Cl made, sk 3 sc, next Cl), rep from * across to last 2 sts, FPdc in same st as last Cl made, sc in tch, turn. (*14 sc, 3 Cl FPdc, 2 FPdc*)

Rep rows 2–5 for pattern.

6-Stitch Twisted Cable

Cables that twist around each other are particularly appealing. The 6-Stitch Twisted Cable pattern consists of 2 cabling rows, one with treble stitches that cross each other, and the other with double crochet stitches in a straight vertical line. Alternate rows between cabling rows are worked in plain single crochet. All the cabling occurs on the right side of the work.

The main challenges are placing post stitches in the correct stitch, and working into hidden stitches. Don't be tempted to use your eye, as stitches that appear to be aligned one over the other are actually not! Here are some pointers to keep you on track.

- In row 3, you will be working post stitches into single crochet stitches, where the post is short. To make sure you are placing post stitches in the correct stitch, count single crochet stitches in the row where you are working posts. The first post stitch should be placed in the 7th single crochet stitch in the row below: make sure you don't miss the very first stitch and count 7 stitches to place your first post stitch. After completing the first set of 6 post stitches, you work 4 more half double crochets, then the next group of 6 stitches begins again 7 stitches from where the last post stitch was worked.

- In even-numbered rows, be sure that you have worked the correct number of stitches. Count them at the end of the row.

- In row 5, post stitches are worked into the crossed trebles. The 3rd of these post stitches will be hard to see, but pull it out from behind, as shown, so you can get your hook around it properly.

- In rows 7 and 9, after completing the 6 post stitches, count 6 skipped stitches behind the post stitches, to make sure you are working the next half double crochet in the correct place. Because the stitches do not line up directly over one another, the eye is easily deceived, so do count.

- Finally, don't pull the post stitches tight, but rather observe whether the stitch is lying flat along the surface or pulling at it. If the latter, make your stitches taller by drawing up each loop as you work the stitch.

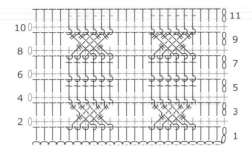

Ch a multiple of 10, plus 4 for end sts, plus 1 for tch. (*ch 25 for swatch*)

Row 1 Hdc in 3rd ch from hook and in each ch across, turn. (*24 hdc*)

Row 2 (and subsequent even-numbered rows) Ch 1, sc across, turn.

Remaining instructions are for odd-numbered rows only.

Row 3 Ch 2 (counts as hdc throughout), hdc in next 3 sc, sk 3 sts, *FPtr in next 3 hdc, FPtr in 3 skipped hdc, hdc in next 4 sc, rep from * across, turn.

Row 5 Ch 2, hdc in next 3 sc, *FPdc in next 6 tr, hdc in next 4 sc, rep from * across, turn.

Row 7 Ch 2, hdc in next 3 sc, *FPdc in next 6 dc, hdc in next 4 sc, rep from * across, turn.

Row 9 Ch 2, hdc in next 3 sc, hdc/FPtr tog, FPtr in next 2 tr, FPtr in 2 skipped sts, FPtr/hdc in next tr, hdc in next 4 sc, rep from * across, turn.

Rep rows 2–9 for pattern.

FPtr (front post treble crochet) Yo twice, insert hook around post of designated st, yo and draw up a loop, (yo, draw through 2 loops) three times.

FPdc (front post double crochet) Yo, insert hook around post of designated st, yo and draw up a loop, (yo, draw through 2 loops) twice.

Hdc/FPtr tog (half double and front post treble together) Yo, insert hook in next sc, yo and draw up a loop (3 loops on hook), yo twice, sk 3 sts, insert hook around post of next stitch and draw up a loop, (yo, draw through 2 loops) twice, yo and draw through 4 loops on hook.

Step 1, Hdc/FPtr tog

Completed Hdc/FPtr tog

FPtr/hdc tog (front post treble and half double together) Yo twice, insert hook in indicated st, yo and draw up a loop, (yo, draw through 2 loops twice — *2 loops on hook*), sk 4 sc, yo, insert hook in next sc, yo and draw up loop, yo, draw through 4 loops on hook.

Mind the gap. People are often bothered by the gap that appears next to cables. The gaps occur when cable stitches are angled; since the stitch behind the cable is unworked, an open space is exposed. Look at the bottom of the swatch to spot these holes. Then, beginning in the second repeat of the cable (in row 9) we will fill in the gap by working a stitch into that gap. We avoid adding an extra stitch to the count by working that stitch together with the post stitch. This technique is used only on the very first and very last post stitch of the 6-stitch group. Instructions spell out what to do.

Triple-Crossed Cable

I love the look of these triple-crossed cables, worked in fingering-weight yarn on this swatch.

Here are some pointers before you start this swatch:

- The treble post stitches cross a considerable distance, and there may be a tendency for the top loop to stretch out while you work. Counter this by keeping the yarn taut with the yarn-holding hand.

- When working the rows of back post stitches, it can be hard to work into the stitches hiding behind other stitches. Try this: turn the work so you are looking at the front and work across the row in reverse.

- Work into the 3 post stitches in front, then move them out of the way to gain better access to those behind.

- Look at the tops of stitches to see which stitch comes next, and count stitches so that you don't leave out any of the crossed stitches, even those hidden from view.

- In odd-numbered rows after row 3 you will sometimes be working front post stitches around the posts of back post stitches.

BPdc (back post double crochet) Yo, insert hook from back to front around post, yo, draw up a loop, (yo, draw through 2 loops) twice.

· ·

FPdc (front post double crochet) Yo, insert hook around post of designated st, yo, draw up a loop, (yo, draw through 2 loops) twice.

· ·

FPtr (front post treble crochet) Yo twice, insert hook around post of designated st, yo, draw up a loop, (yo, draw through 2 loops) three times.

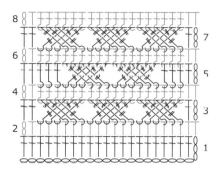

Ch a multiple of 6, plus 4 end sts, plus 2 for tch. (ch 24 for swatch)

Row 1 Dc in 4th ch from hook and in each ch across, turn.

Row 2 Ch 2 (counts as hdc throughout), hdc in each dc across, turn.

Row 3 Ch 3 (counts as dc throughout), dc in next hdc, *sk next 3 hdc, FPtr in next 3 hdc, working in front of post stitches just completed FPtr in 3 sk hdc, rep from * across to last 2 sts, dc in last 2 sts, turn.

Row 4 Ch 2, hdc in next dc, BPdc across to last 2 sts, hdc in last 2 sts, turn.

Row 5 Ch 3, dc in next hdc, FPdc in next 3 hdc, *sk next 3 dc, FPtr in next 3 dc, working behind stitches just made FPtr in 3 sk dc, rep from * to last 5 sts, FPdc in next 3 dc, dc in last 2 sts, turn.

Row 6 Rep row 4

Row 7 Ch 3, dc in next hdc, *sk next 3 dc, FPtr in next 3 dc, working in front of post stitches just completed FPtr in 3 sk dc, rep from * across to last 2 sts, dc in last 2 sts, turn.

Row 8 Rep row 4.

Rep rows 5–8 for pattern ending with a row 6.

Dealing with Row 5

The trickiest maneuver comes in row 5, where you are instructed to work behind post stitches just made. The first time you try this, you may think it's impossible! It really isn't. It'll get easier after a few times. Again, identify the next stitch, move whatever is in the way and remember, crochet stitches are very flexible. Wiggle your hook into place and go for it! Here are some pictures to help you through that row.

Sk 3 dc, FPtr in next 3 dc.

Working behind sts just made

Here is one FPtr made in the first skipped dc.

Cabled Triangles

A wonderful effect can be achieved by working post stitches all over a piece, using front and back posts to create a distinct shape, as is shown in this swatch. A very soft yarn allows this kind of stitch to be used without creating a stiff fabric. Note that the post on the first stitch is omitted since it's not possible when working the turning chain, but it is done on the last stitch of the row. While the earlier cable patterns in this chapter have the cables on the right side only, this pattern looks similar on both sides.

Front

Reverse

Notes

Since the first row of this pattern consists of dc stitches, you can work a row of Foundation dc (see page 62) instead of making a foundation chain and row 1.

FPdc stitches are shown in blue on all even-numbered rows and BPdc are shown in blue on all odd-numbered rows of stitch chart.

....

BPdc (back post double crochet) Yo, insert hook from back to front around post, yo and draw up a loop, (yo, draw through 2 loops) twice.

....

FPdc (front post double crochet) Yo, insert hook around post of designated st, yo and draw up a loop, (yo, draw through 2 loops) twice.

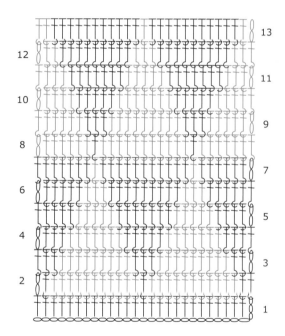

Ch a multiple of 12, plus 2 end sts, plus 3 for tch. *(ch 29 for swatch)*

Row 1 (RS) Dc in 4th ch from hook, dc in each ch across. *(27 dc)*

Row 2 Ch 2 (counts as hdc throughout), *1 BPdc**, 11 FPdc, rep from * across, ending last rep at **, BPdc in tch, turn.

Row 3 Ch 2, 2 FPdc, *9 BPdc, 3 FPdc, rep from * across, turn.

Row 4 Ch 2, 3 BPdc, *7 FPdc**, 5 BPdc, rep from * across, ending last rep at **, 4 BPdc, turn.

Row 5 Ch 2, 4 FPdc, *5 BPdc**, 7 FPdc, rep from * across, ending last rep at **, 5 FPdc, turn.

Row 6 Ch 2, 5 BPdc, *3 FPdc**, 9 BPdc, rep from * across, ending last rep at **, 6 BPdc, turn.

Row 7 Ch 2, 6 FPdc, *1 BPdc**, 11 FPdc, rep from * across, ending last rep at **, 7 FPdc, turn.

Row 8 Rep row 7.

Row 9 Rep row 6.

Row 10 Rep row 5.

Row 11 Rep row 4.

Row 12 Rep row 3.

Rnd 13 Rep row 2.

Rep rows 2–13 for pattern.

The swatch is finished with a row of sc, which is not part of the pattern.

Crocodile Stitch

The crocodile stitch is another wonderful textured stitch. It appears to be a recent — and popular — invention. It's fun, once you overcome a few challenges. Executing the "scales" of the crocodile requires some unusual turning this way and that. The crocodile stitches are usually staggered from one row to the next so that the scales are visible. There are many variations on this stitch, but here's a good one to start with.

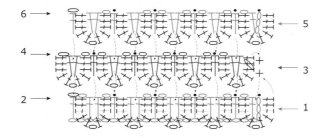

Note

To work around the posts of stitches, insert the hook under the post. This is the same as when working any post stitch, except you will be making several stitches around the same post.

Ch a multiple of 4, plus 2 for tch. (*ch 26 for swatch*)

Row 1 Dc in 4th ch from hook, *ch 1, sk 1 ch, dc in next ch, ch 1, sk 1 ch, dc in next 2 ch, rep from * across, turn.

Note that you have pairs of dc stitches (ready for crocodile stitch) alternating with single dc stitches.

Row 2 Ch 1, *work 5 dc around post of second dc, ch 1, work 5 dc around post of next dc, sl st in next dc (*1 crocodile st made*), rep from * across, work 5 dc around post of last dc, ch 1, work 5 dc around tch, sl st in top of tch, turn.

Row 3 Sc in center of first crocodile st, *ch 1, 2 dc in next dc (there is already a sl st worked into this dc), ch 1, dc in center of next crocodile st, rep from * across, ch 1, 2 dc in last dc, turn.

Row 4 Ch 1, work crocodile st around first 2 dc posts, *sl st to next dc, crocodile st around next 2 posts, rep from * across, sc in sc, turn.

Row 5 Ch 3, dc in first sc, ch 1, *dc in center of next crocodile st, ch 1, 2 dc in next dc, rep from * across, dc in center of next crocodile st, turn.

Row 6 Ch 1, sk first dc, *crocodile st around next 2 dc, sl st in next dc, rep from * across, ending with crocodile st in last 2 sts, turn.

Rep rows 3–6 for pattern.

Making the Scales

The "scales" of this stitch are worked around the posts of paired dc stitches. Work 5 dc around the post of the first dc, going from the top of the post to the bottom (1 and 2), ch 1, work the next 5 dc around the post of the 2nd dc of the pair going from bottom to top (3 and 4), and sl st in next dc.

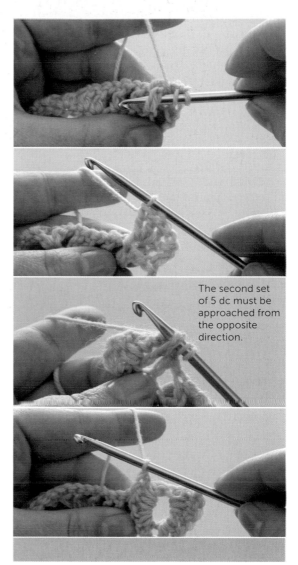

The second set of 5 dc must be approached from the opposite direction.

Crochet Ribbing

Crochet ribbing can be made several ways, either by working into back loops (BL) or using post stitches. Check out the Slouchy Hat project (page 212) to see an example of back loop ribbing. Post stitches, on the other hand, create vertical ribs, so no joining or turning is needed. Each of these ribbing samples has a different look and character, and you may find one suits a particular project more than another.

To use back loop ribs at the bottom of a hat or sweater, you would work the ribbing to the desired length, then sew the last row to the first. From there, you work into the sides of stitches as you work the next row of the project.

It's also possible to work the main body of the project first, then work a separate strip of ribbing and sew the two pieces together.

Post-stitch ribbing can easily be added at the bottom of hats, sweaters, or sleeves since it's worked in the same direction as the main body. It can be worked either flat or in the round.

Back or front loops can also be used to create subtle texture in many other instances. This is the only textured stitch that does not work against drape, but rather enhances it. That's because when only 1 loop of a stitch is picked up, the loop stretches more than when picking up 2, creating a more fluid fabric overall.

Here are patterns for ribbing using single crochet, half double, and double crochet ribbing, each with a different appearance.

Single Crochet Ribbing

Ch any number. (*ch 13 for swatch*)

Row 1 Sc in 2nd ch from hook and in each ch across, turn.

Row 2 Ch 1, BLsc in each sc across, turn.

Rep row 2 for pattern.

Single Crochet/Slip Stitch Ribbing

Note that for this ribbing, it's not necessary to chain 1 on row 2. You'll see that the slip stitches form a ridge along the wrong side of the fabric and push the tops of the single crochet stitches to the right side, making the ribbed look. When you begin row 3, you'll see 2 loops in front and 2 loops in back. Work into the 2 in back.

Ch any number. (*ch 13 for swatch*)

Row 1 (RS) Sc in 2nd chain from hook and in each ch across, turn.

Row 2 Sl st in each sc across, turn.

Row 3 Ch 1, sc in each sl st across, turn.

Rep rows 2 and 3 for pattern.

Half Double Crochet Ribbing

Here is an instance requiring insertion in an unfamiliar place — the loop below the top 2 loops that one finds on half double crochet stitches, formed by the first yarnover in the stitch. Since there is no official terminology for this, it's spelled out below.

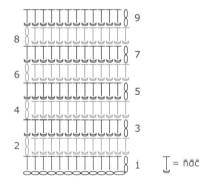

Ch any number, plus 2 for tch. (*ch 14 for swatch*)

Row 1 Hdc in 3rd ch from hook and in each ch across, turn.

Row 2 Ch 2 (counts as hdc), inserting hook in FL and loop below, work hdc across, turn.

Rep row 2 for pattern.

Double and Single Crochet Ribbing

In this ribbing, it is easier to work the first BLsc in the row if you turn counterclockwise at the end of the previous row.

Front Post/Back Post Ribbing

Note that in this ribbing, rows begin with chain-2, instead of chain-3, to better match the height of post stitches. If you want to work this ribbing in the round without turning at the ends of rounds, work all rounds as in row 2 of the instructions.

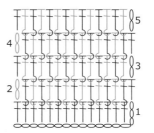

Note

BPdc stitches are shown in blue on all rows of stitch chart.

Ch an even number, plus 3 for tch. (*ch 17 for swatch*)

Row 1 Dc in 4th ch from hook and each ch across, turn.

Row 2 Ch 2 (counts as dc here and throughout), *FPdc in next dc, BPdc in next dc, rep from * across, ending with a dc in last dc, turn.

Row 3 Ch 2, *BPdc in next dc, FPdc in next dc, rep from * across, ending with a dc in last dc, turn.

Repeat rows 2 and 3 until desired length is reached.

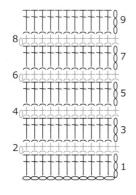

Ch any number of sts. (*ch 14 for swatch*)

Row 1 Dc in 4th ch from hook and in each ch across, turn.

Row 2 Ch 1, BLsc in each dc across, turn.

Row 3 Ch 3, BLdc in each sc across, turn.

Rep rows 2 and 3 for pattern.

9

Crochet in Color

ROCHET CAN BE A TERRIFIC vehicle for colorwork. From simple stripes to patterns that form ripples, shells, and many more designs, the element of color can be a wonderful enhancement to crochet projects. Stitches that extend over additional rows, such as spike and post stitches, provide great opportunities for colorwork. More involved color techniques include intarsia, tapestry crochet, stranded work, and color blocks, each with its own methods for working with multiple colors at a time. We'll look at all these techniques in this chapter.

Changing color in crochet is as simple as changing from one ball of yarn to the other: simply draw the new yarn through the last loop of the last stitch in the previous color (page 57).

But what happens to a color once it's no longer in use? If we cut yarn at the ends of rows often, we have many tails to weave in when the project is done. This is not something most crocheters enjoy, so it's good to know some color patterns that allow us to avoid that.

Carrying Colors along the Side

When two or more colors of yarns are being used in a pattern without being cut, we call this carrying the colors. There are several ways to do it; let's start with the simplest.

Yarns can be carried along the side of the work when the sides will be seamed or covered with an edging. This is a great strategy and works with any stitch patterns where the color can be changed *every other* row. The yarn is carried along the side over only one row. Carrying yarns along the side for more rows is possible, too, as you'll see in the samples below. When using this technique, pay attention to the length of the strands carried on the side — they should be long enough to cover the distance without pulling at the fabric, but not so long that they droop away from the work.

To keep yarns from tangling as you work, keep one ball on your left and the other on your right. When you turn at the ends of rows, alternate the direction you are turning. This will have no detrimental effect at all on the work, and helps keep yarns from twisting around one another. Tangles may still develop and should be undone before things get out of hand, of course.

Any of these stitch patterns can be worked with additional colors, in which case, you will have to cut yarns and weave in ends.

Two-Color Seed Stitch

Front

Reverse

Note

To change color, on the last stitch before the color change, pick up the new color from the side of the work with your hook, and draw it through on the last loop of the stitch.

This swatch is worked with two colors (A and B).

With A, ch an odd number of sts, plus 1 for tch. (*ch 18 for swatch*)

Row 1 Sc in 2nd ch from hook, *ch 1, sk next ch, sc in next ch, rep from * across, change to B, turn. Do not cut A.

Row 2 Sc in first sc, *sc in ch-1 sp, ch 1, sk next sc, rep from * across to last 2 sts, sc in last 2 sts, turn.

Row 3 Sc in first sc, *ch 1, sk next sc, sc in next ch-1 sp, rep from * across, change to A by picking up from row below, turn. Do not cut B.

Rows 4 and 5 Rep rows 2 and 3, change to B, but do not cut A, turn.

Rep rows 2 and 3 for patt, always changing after row 3 and carrying yarn along the side of the work.

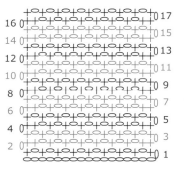

Two-Color Diamond Stitch

Note

To change color, on the last stitch before the color change, pick up the new color from the side of the work with your hook, and draw it through on the last loop of the stitch.

This swatch is worked with two colors (A and B).

With A, ch a multiple of 8, plus 1 end st, plus 1 for tch. (*ch 26 for swatch*)

Row 1 Sc in 2nd ch from hook, *sk 3 ch, 9 dc in next ch, sk 3 ch, sc in next ch, rep from * across, change to B, do not cut A, turn.

Row 2 Ch 3 (counts as dc here and through-out), dc4tog over next 4 dc, *ch 3, sc in next dc, ch 3**, dc9tog over (4 dc, sc, 4 dc), rep from * across, ending last rep at **, dc 5 tog over last 4 dc and sc, turn.

Row 3 Ch 3, 4 dc in dc5tog, *sc in next sc, 9 dc in dc9tog, rep from * across to last st, 5 dc in last st, change to A, do not cut B, turn.

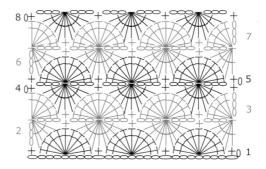

Row 4 Ch 1, sc in first dc, *ch 3, dc9tog over (4 dc, sc, 4 dc), ch 3, sc in next dc, rep from * across, turn.

Row 5 Ch 1, sc in next sc, *9 dc in dc9tog, sc in next sc, rep from * across, turn.

Rep rows 2–5 for patt, carrying colors along the side.

Three-Color Checks

This is a great pattern that allows you to work with three colors (A, B, and C) and still carry yarn. There is some distortion of the color pattern at the edges, but with a seam or edging it should not be obvious.

Note

To change color, on the last stitch before the color change, pick up the new color from the side of the work with your hook, and draw it through on the last loop of the stitch.

With A, ch a multiple of 6, plus 3 end sts, plus 2 for tch. (*ch 29 for swatch*)

Row 1 Dc in 4th ch from hook, dc in next 2 ch, *ch 3, sk 3 ch, dc in next 3 ch, rep from * across, change to B, do not cut A, turn.

Row 2 Ch 3 (does not count as dc), *sk first 3 dc, working over 3 ch of prev row, 3 dc into next 3 ch of starting ch**, ch 3, rep from * ending last rep at **, ch 2, sc in tch, change to C, do not cut B, turn.

Row 3 Ch 2 (counts as dc), sk first sc, working over 2 ch of prev row dc in next 2 dc 2 rows below, *ch 3, sk 3 dc, working over 3 ch of prev row dc in next 3 dc, rep from * across, change to A, do not cut C, turn.

Row 4 Ch 3 (does not count as dc), *sk first 3 dc, working over 3 ch of prev row, 3 dc into next 3 sts 2 rows below**, ch 3, rep from * ending last rep at **, ch 2, sc in tch, change to B, do not cut A, turn.

While cycling through the three-color sequence, rep rows 3 and 4 of patt, always working dc stitches over chains of prev row and into the dc 2 rows below.

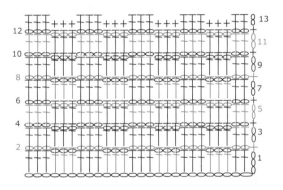

Overlapping Colors

The overlapping color effect is achieved by working over chains in the previous row into stitches 2 rows below — very simple!

Color with Post Stitches

Because post stitches can reach down over rows below, you can change colors in the post stitch row and get overlapping color effects. This pattern is yet another where we can carry colors along the side over several rows. For another color stitch using cables, see Crossed Cables (page 169).

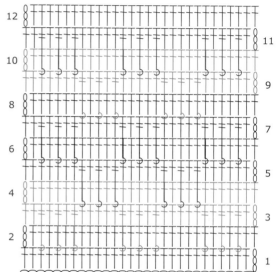

Note

To change color, on the last stitch before the color change, pick up the new color from the side of the work with your hook, and draw it through on the last loop of the stitch.

FPtr (front post treble crochet) Yo twice, insert hook from front to back around post of indicated st, yo and draw up loop, (yo, draw through 2 loops), three times.

This swatch is worked with three colors (A, B, and C).

With A, ch a multiple of 10, plus 9 end sts, plus 2 for tch. (*ch 31 for swatch*)

Row 1 Dc in 4th ch from hook and in each ch across, turn. (*29 dc*)

Row 2 Ch 3 (counts as dc here and through-out), dc in each dc across, change to B, do not cut A, turn.

Row 3 Ch 3, *(dc in next dc, FPtr in next dc 2 rows below) three times, dc in next 4 dc, rep from * across, dc in next dc, dc in tch, turn.

Row 4 Ch 3, dc in each st across, change to C, do not cut B, turn.

Row 5 Ch 3, dc in next 6 dc *(FPtr in next dc 2 rows below, dc) three times, dc in next 4 dc, rep from * across, dc in last dc, dc in tch, turn.

Row 6 Ch 3, dc in each st across, change to A, do not cut C, turn.

Rep rows 3–6 for pattern. If you keep the three colors in the same order, the yarn can be carried over the same number of rows throughout.

Diagonal Box Stitch

This stitch is worked from corner to corner, beginning with one box (see bottom left of diagram); there are 2 boxes in row 2, 3 boxes in row 3, and so on, until the work is the desired size. While the instructions indicate end-of-row turns, it's easier to work the first box of each row without turning, then turn and work into the chain-3 of the previous row's boxes.

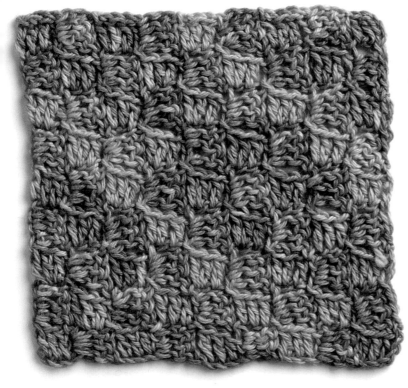

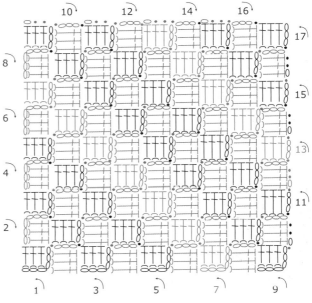

Note

To change color, see note on page 186.

This swatch is worked with two colors (variegated A and solid-color B).

Row 1 With A, ch 6, BLdc in 4th ch from hook, BLdc in next 2 ch, turn. (*1 box*)

Row 2 Ch 6, BLdc in 4th ch from hook, BLdc in next 2 ch, sl st under ch-3 of first box, ch 3, 3 dc around same ch-3 sp, turn. (*2 boxes*)

Row 3 Ch 6, BLdc in 4th ch from hook, BLdc in next 2 ch, *sl st under next ch-3, ch 3, 3 dc around same ch-3 sp, rep from * across. (*3 boxes*)

Rows 4–6 Rep row 3, change to B. (*6 boxes at end of row 6*)

Row 7 Rep row 3, change to A. (*7 boxes*)

Rows 8 and 9 Rep row 3. (*9 boxes at end of row 9*)

Row 10 Ch 1, sk first st, sl st over next 2 dc, *sl st under next ch-3, ch 3, 3 dc around same ch-3 sp, rep from * across, sl st in last ch-3 sp. (*8 boxes*)

Rows 11–12 Rep row 10, change to B. (*6 boxes at end of row 13*)

Row 13 Rep row 10, change to A. (*5 boxes*)

Rows 14–17 Rep row 10, ending with 1 box, fasten off.

Spike Stitches

Spike stitches are single crochet stitches that are elongated by inserting the hook into a row below the current working row. They can be worked into stitches 1, 2, or even more rows below. The color effects are achieved by working the row with spike stitches in a different color than the rows that immediately precede it, and also by varying the height of the spike stitches, as in the next pattern.

Successful Spikes

There are two things to pay close attention to when making spikes: finding a tension that allows the spikes to lie flat on the work without pulling the fabric and finding the exact place to insert the hook.

Pull up loop tail.

Completed spike stitch

Spike stitches add bulk to the fabric, and this, plus the fact that they are generally made over rows of single crochet, means the fabric tends to be stiff rather than drapey. It's a great technique for ornamenting items such as bags, cozies, and belts, where a structured fabric is desirable. The fabric is more fluid if you work with thinner yarns, of course.

Tension control is discussed on page 33. With spikes, check carefully that you've given the stitches sufficient length to stretch over the specified number of rows. Keep your eye on the loop on the hook as well, as it tends to stretch considerably as you work the longer spikes, something to be avoided. Go slow when you start and adjust each stitch until you feel the rhythm of it.

Inserting the hook in lower rows can be tricky because stitches do not align exactly over one another from one row to the next.

Let's be clear about what is meant by "one row below working row." The working row is the one you are in the process of making; the row below is the one you normally work into. When making spike stitches, when it says "work in the row below," you insert the hook at the bottom of that stitch rather than under the top two loops as usual. That's what makes the spike stitch taller than regular single crochet stitches. If it says to make the spike two rows below, here, too, you insert the hook in the bottom of the stitch.

Diagonal Spike

Here's a good pattern for practicing regulating tension and placing the hook correctly. Start with a smooth worsted-weight yarn for this exercise, and follow the notes as you work.

Pause at the end of row 4 to look carefully at the rows and how the stitches align. You'll notice that the odd-numbered rows line up well with each other, and the even-numbered rows line up well with each other, but there appears to be a slight hitch, or offset, between even and odd. I find the easiest way to keep track of where to place the spikes is to use the spike stitch just completed as a guide.

At the end of row 4, turn to get ready for the spike-stitch row 5. The first 2 stitches in the row are normal single crochets, so go ahead and make them. The next is a spike stitch worked 1 row below: insert your hook just under the next stitch and work the spike stitch. You have worked the spike stitch in the *top* of the stitch 1 row below the working row. The next stitch is a spike worked 2 rows below, so insert your hook 1 row farther down than the first spike. The next is worked 3 rows below, so again, 1 row below the spike you just made. The next stitch is a normal single crochet worked as usual, and then we repeat from the first single crochet followed immediately by a spike stitch. If two adjacent spikes look the same, it means you haven't really gone down a row! Not to worry, just work patiently and this will become easier in no time.

After finishing row 5 and turning for the next row, you will see that the backs of the spike stitches look wider in the back than on the fronts. For this reason, to be consistent when using spikes, always work them on the same side. Generally the narrower look seen on the front is considered the right side.

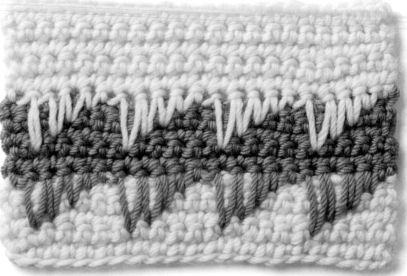

Note

When working spike stitches, always insert hook in bottom of indicated stitch.

This swatch is worked with two colors (A and B).

With A, ch a multiple of 5, plus 1 for end st, plus 1 for tch. (*ch 22 for swatch*)

Row 1 (WS) Ch 1, sc in 2nd ch from hook and in each ch across, turn. (*20 sc*)

Rows 2–4 Ch 1, sc across, turn. At the end of row 4, change to B.

Row 5 Ch 1, sc in first st, *sc in next st, spike 1 row below, spike 2 rows below, spike 3 rows below, sc in next sc, rep from * across, turn.

Rows 6–8 Rep row 2. At the end of row 8, change to A.

Row 9 Rep row 5.

Row 10 Rep row 2.

Rep rows 3–10 for patt.

Spike Wave

It's hard to get spikes to match perfectly, but the overall effect is lovely for colorwork.

16 0 — 15
14 0 — 13
12 0 — 11
10 0 — 9
8 0 — 7
6 0 — 5
4 0 — 3
2 0 — 1

Note

This swatch is worked with three colors (A, B, and C). Fasten off each when no longer in use.

When working spike stitches, always insert hook in bottom of indicated stitch.

With A, ch a multiple of 6, plus 1 end st, plus 1 for tch. (*ch 20 for swatch*)

Row 1 (RS) Sc in 2nd ch from hook and in each ch across, turn. (*19 sc*)

Rows 2–4 Ch 1, sc across, turn. Change color at end of row 4.

Row 5 Ch 1, sc in first sc, *spike 1 row below, spike 2 rows below, spike 3 rows below, spike 2 rows below, spike 1 row below, sc in next sc, rep from * across, turn.

Spike Cluster Tips

One last spike stitch is worth exploring, because it's so pretty and rather unusual. Here are some tips.

- The loop on the hook tends to loosen as you work these long spikes. Tighten it up with a tug from the yarn-holding hand if you see this happening.

- The strands of the cluster obscure the stitches just to the left and right, so make sure to maneuver your hook under them when working the single crochet stitches next to the spikes.

- Count stitches carefully each row to be sure you have maintained the count.

Rows 6–8 Still working with B, rep rows 2–4.

Row 9 Rep row 5.

To continue in patt, rep rows 2–5, always changing colors before row 5.

Spike Cluster

It took me several attempts before these spike clusters looked good, and as usual, it's a question of controlling tension and finding the correct spot to place the hook for each spike. They are so pretty that it's worth the effort. The cluster is worked by drawing up loops to the right, below and left, then finishing the stitch with a chain through all the loops to bring them all together.

With this pattern, the first color can be carried along the back when working the cluster row, so that yarn doesn't have to be cut. It's a bit fiddly when you first try it, but it gets easier with practice. When starting the cluster row, bring color A up so that it can lie flat along the top of the previous row as you work, and work stitches around this strand of yarn. Color B, used in the cluster row, is cut when not in use, although it's possible to carry along the side if you prefer.

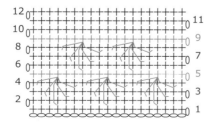

Note

Fasten off spike color when no longer in use.

When working spike stitch, always insert hook in bottom of indicated stitch.

....

Spike Cl Insert hook 2 sts to the right and 1 row below and draw up a loop, insert hook 1 st to the right and 2 rows below and draw up loop, insert hook 3 rows below and draw up loop, insert hook 1 st to the left and 2 rows below and draw up loop, insert hook 2 sts to the left and 1 row below and draw up loop, yo, draw through 6 loops, ch 1 to close tightly. The chain does not count as a stitch and is skipped in the following row. (All directions should be reversed for left-handers.)

....

This swatch is worked with two colors (A and B).

With A, ch a multiple of 6, plus 1 end st, plus 1 for tch. (*ch 20 for swatch*)

Row 1 Sc in 2nd ch from hook and in each chain across, turn. (*19 sc*)

Rows 2–4 Ch 1, sc across. At the end of row 4, change to B, turn.

Row 5 Ch 1, sc in first 3 sc, *work Spike Cl**, sc in next 5 sc, rep from * across, ending last rep at **, sc in last 3 sc, change to A, turn. Cut yarn B.

Row 6 Ch 1, sc in first 3 sc, *sk next ch, sc in Spike Cl**, sc in next 5 sc, rep from * across, ending last rep at **, sc in last 3 sc, turn.

Rows 7 and 8 Rep rows 3 and 4.

Row 9 Ch 1, sc in first 6 sc, *work Spike Cl, sc in next 5 sc, rep from * across to last st, sc in last st, change to A, turn. Cut yarn B.

Row 10 Ch 1, sc in first 6 sc, *sk next ch, sc in Spike Cl, sc in next 5 sc, rep from * across to last st, sc in last st, turn.

Rep rows 3–10 for patt, ending with row 8.

Complex Colorwork

To work more intricate color designs involving several colors in a row, one can use a variety of techniques:

- **Strand the unused color(s)** along the back. Stranded work produces clean color changes, as the unused yarn is carried loosely along the back. Of course, the finished piece is not reversible.

- **Use bobbins.** To avoid carrying yarns altogether, you can use bobbins, tools that hold small amounts of yarn, and leave the bobbins dangling on the back while working other colors. This technique is excellent when using a particular color repeatedly in one area of a project, because there will not be many ends to weave in.

- **Carry unused color(s) along** by working over the unused color in each stitch. This avoids ends, but the unused color is likely to bleed through, an effect that can be attractive at times. It also adds bulk to the work.

Notes

Change color on the last loop of the stitch before the new color begins. Before starting with the new color, cross the strand of the new color over the old to prevent a hole in the fabric where the color is changed. Then drop the old color and continue with the new.

You'll notice that the stitch where the color is changed tends to loosen. Once you've worked the new color and you're ready to pick up the first color again, tug it gently to tighten.

Carry the strands along the back loosely so that the work doesn't bunch up.

To prevent strands on the back that are too long, you can occasionally work 1 stitch over the strand.

Stranded Colorwork

Stranded work is perfect when working in the round, since the right side is always facing and strands naturally end up on the wrong side. In order to do stranded work on a flat piece like this one, with right side facing, cut yarn at the end of each row, and start the next row at the right edge. This results in many ends, to be used as fringe or woven in.

This piece is good practice for reading a stranded work chart. All the stitches are single crochet. To read the chart, simply use one color for the lighter stitches, another for the darker ones. Remember to read this chart from right to left on each row.

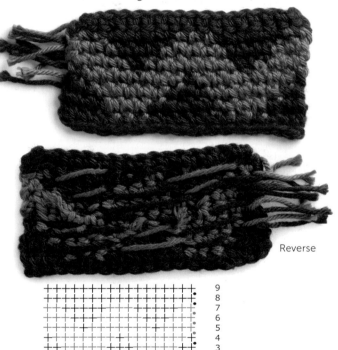

Reverse

Ch 18.

Row 1 Sc in 2nd ch from hook and in each ch across, cut yarn.

Row 2 Join yarn in first sc of row, ch 1, sc in each sc across, cut yarn.

Rep row 2.

Double Crochet Squares

For this pattern in double crochet, on rows involving two colors, carry yarn by working over the original color on each stitch. Carry the unused color by laying it over the top of the stitches you are working into. As you insert your hook into each stitch of the previous row, you will work each stitch around the unused color. The yarn is not carried on rows worked in only one color. To avoid color changes at the side edge on two-color rows, drop the color used in the squares after completing the square without carrying it in the last 3 stitches. See the photo below right for how to pick up the color.

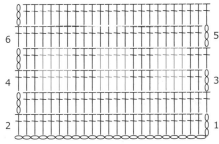

Note

This swatch requires only one extra end to weave in, the one left on the last square.

....

This swatch is worked with two colors (A and B).

With A, ch a multiple of 7, plus 3 end sts, plus 2 for tch. (*ch 26 for swatch*)

Row 1 Dc in 4th ch from hook and in each ch across, turn. (*24 dc*)

Row 2 Ch 3 (counts as dc here and throughout), dc in each dc across, turn.

Row 3 Ch 3, dc in next 2 dc, *change to B, work 4 dc in B, change color, 3 dc in A, rep from * across, continue with A to end of row, turn.

Row 4 Ch 3, rep row 3.

Rows 5 and 6 Rep row 2 with color A only.

Picking Up Old Color

In this photo, when yellow is needed again in the square, with 2 loops of the red on the hook, insert the hook down through the last stitch made with yellow and draw it up through the loops on the hook, then work over the unused color as before.

Tapestry Crochet

Tapestry crochet, which displays clear shapes to wonderful graphic effect, has a rich tradition all over the world. Crochet artists like Carol Ventura are doing amazing things with tapestry crochet, and if you like to create pictures with stitches, this is a great technique to master. To make these well-defined shapes in tapestry crochet, the fronts of stitches are facing at all times. This is done most easily by working in the round. When working flat, you can cut yarn and start again at the right-hand side for each row, but this leaves many ends to weave in. Another alternative, which is easier than you might think, is to crochet backward every other row.

Crochet Backward

1. After turning the work, cross the unused color over the new color.

3. Bring the working yarn in front of the work and insert your hook in the first stitch from back to front.

2. Work the turning chain 1 over the unused color.

4. Yarnover and draw up a loop. Complete the single crochet stitch as usual by yarnover, draw through 2 loops on hook.

Simple Tapestry Crochet

This is a normal single crochet stitch except for the insertion of the hook. Continue working over the unused color in each stitch, tugging on it as necessary to keep the strand at the right tension and enclosed in the stitches.

    If you've never tried this, I encourage you to do so, at first just working with one color to get used to the maneuvers. You can do this for a row or two, and once you feel comfortable, unravel back to row 2 and work it in tapestry crochet pattern, carrying the unused color as before.

    After completing the row working backwards, turn as usual. The unused color can be brought into place without working it in the turning chain, unlike the other side. Just pick it up from the back and place it on top of the row to work over it.

    Start with this pattern to practice tapestry technique. When reading a tapestry crochet chart, read from right to left on one row, then from left to right on the next. To stay on track with the chart, you can put arrows at the sides indicating the direction of work, and move a ruler up to the working line as you go.

Work rows as shown in the diagram, working over the unused color.

Plunge into color. All these color techniques can contribute immeasurably to your projects. Some are more time-consuming than others, and are better used in smaller pieces or very special projects such as gifts. But introducing color into a crochet project can be as simple as making stripes. Now that you know some of the methods involved, take a plunge into your stash and find some good color combos!

10

Finishing Techniques

FINISHING TECHNIQUES ARE important to have in one's toolbox, as they give projects the polished look that turns homemade into handmade. Stitches can be made more even, edges more tidy, fabric softened, and dimensions more precise using the right finishing techniques. Under the rubric of finishing, we include weaving in yarn ends, making edgings, blocking, and executing various seams.

Most of the techniques in this chapter take a little time and practice to be comfortable with. Trial and error are great learning devices, and with experience, you'll find you can fix many crochet problems with good finishing. The important thing is not to rush or panic, but to proceed with care and patience.

Weaving in Ends

Many crocheters weave in tails as they work, and so long as this is done neatly, it's a good practice. To do this, you lay the tail carefully over the tops of stitches in the previous row, and work stitches around them as you go. My caveat with this method is that it can distract you from the stitches you are making, especially if they are challenging or require special attention. Also, if you are changing colors, this method is likely to allow the old color to show on the right side of your work, something to be avoided. In these cases, my recommendation is to weave in ends after completing the work.

Weaving in ends is quicker to do with a tapestry needle (page 32) than a crochet hook.

Thread the tail on a needle and weave in and out of the backs of stitches in one direction.

Then turn and go in the opposite direction. Don't pull the woven strands tight or it can distort the fabric.

If your fabric is open or lacy, you will have to hunt for appropriate places to bury the yarn. Look for places where the stitch is tight, such as the bottom of the stitch, rather than looser strands

in the post, when possible. If no better places are available, you can also weave through chain stitches. I prefer to avoid weaving in ends along the edges, as they may get tangled up in seams or edgings later, but sometimes one must.

Weaving a tail into chain stitches

Hiding a Knot

Pay special attention when weaving in the tail from the slip knot that starts the work. If the knot is visible, pull it to the back of the work by tugging at the tail, but not so tight that the corner is disturbed.

visible knot

knot pulled to back

Sometimes you have a very short end to weave in. You can use a hook for this, but here's a special little trick using a needle.

Thread the end on a needle.

Weave the eye of the needle through, going as far as necessary to use the length of tail you have, then carefully pull the needle out from the top.

Tails can also be used for making small but important tweaks on finished projects. Use them for these tasks:

- Fill in unwanted holes in the fabric. This can occur between the turning chain and 2nd stitch, at seams under the arms, or countless other situations. If you have a tail nearby, work from the wrong side, weaving it in and out of stitches around the hole, mimicking the movement of the strands of yarn in the crochet so that it blends in.

- Secure the ends of seams (see page 202).

- Reinforce fabric under a button to make it stronger. When crocheted fabric is very light and airy, it's hard to sew on a button. Take a tail or separate strand of yarn and with a tapestry needle, working on the wrong side, run the tail back and forth in the small area under the button to create a firmer fabric.

Crochet Seams

Many crocheters profess to hate seams, but I think it's mainly because they have not learned how to do them well. They do require patience, but seaming crochet is much easier than sewing with thread and woven fabric.

Seams can be done with a hook or with a tapestry needle. Hooked seams are thicker and stronger; sewn seams are less visible and more flexible.

Quite often, crochet pieces are joined along the side edges, and our goal is to match row for row along the seam.

Matching row by row

Sometimes, however, as when joining blocks, the two edges are not the same; one may be along the row edge, one along the tops of stitches.

Matching a row edge to a top edge — at left is side edge, and at right is top edge

Slip Stitch Seam

While there are numerous ways to crochet two pieces together, a common way is to work slip stitches through the two edges to be joined. This method is simple and strong.

When joining two pieces, you can begin a slip stitch seam without cutting the yarn on the second piece. Let's call the two pieces side A and side B. Side B is the one in back, with 1 loop on the hook; side A has been fastened off. (The blue yarn is for clarity. In most cases, you would use the project yarn.)

1 Draw the loop through the first stitch in side A. From this step on, you will have side A facing.

2 Holding the two sides together, insert the hook under the next stitch in both sides A and B.

3 Yarnover, and draw a loop through the stitches and the loop on the hook (*1 slip stitch made*). Do not tug or tighten this slip stitch, but let it match the size of the stitches you are working into.

4 Repeat step 2 to the end of the seam. For a less bulky slip stitch seam, you can pick up only one loop from each side, instead of two.

Slip stitch seams can also be used along row edges. In this case, follow the same procedure, picking up one or two loops from each side. You can choose any convenient strand to pick up at the edge, and use your eye to work the slip stitches evenly.

Slip stitch seams work best for items where the seam need not be flexible, such as afghans and heavyweight garments like coats or hats. I often use them at the shoulders of a garment, a seam that bears the weight of the garment and therefore needs to be strong.

Sewn Seams

This is the preferred method for unobtrusive seams that do not add bulk to the fabric. Two types of seams work best for crochet garments, the woven seam and the whipstitch seam. They generally are worked from the right side of the fabric so you can see your final result as you go. Sometimes, because of the yarn or stitch pattern, working from the wrong side may produce a better result, so feel free to experiment. I often work just a few seam stitches and examine each side to see which one looks best.

Before beginning your seam, check that the two edges being joined are the same length. If one side is longer than the other, use skipped stitches on the longer side to adjust the length (see page 202), or reblock the pieces so that they match more closely. An inch or so of extra fabric on one side can be eased in, and we'll cover that a bit farther on.

Pin the two sides together at regular intervals a few inches apart, using safety pins. Break off a length of yarn that is about one and a half times the length of your seam. Thread the yarn on a tapestry needle, leaving a 6-inch tail. When working seams, do not tug each stitch tightly, which causes the fabric to pucker. Yarn and crochet fabric should not be treated like woven fabric and sewing thread. The seam stitches need to match the size of the stitches in your work, and they will do so if you work loosely. It may seem like a loose seam to you, but it will hold together just fine. Remember these are seams to use where there is little or no weight tugging at the seam, such as at the sides of a garment, or between the sleeve and an armhole.

Whipstitch Seam

This seam is simpler than the woven seam, but also more visible.

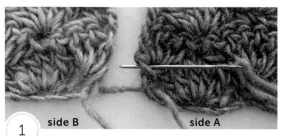

side B   **side A**

1 Insert the needle under two strands from side A. Bring the needle up under two strands on side B. Then bring the yarn over the work, insert the needle again under two strands from side A.

2 Bring the needle up under two strands on side B.

3 Repeat steps 1 and 2 to complete the seam.

Woven Seam

My preferred seam in crochet is the woven seam, because it is the least obtrusive. It's made as follows.

1 Insert the needle under two strands from side A.

4 Bring the needle up under two strands 1 row up on side A.

2 Bring the needle up under two strands on side B.

5 Move up 1 row on side A and bring the needle up under two strands of the matching stitch on side A. Bring the needle up under two strands 1 stitch up on side B.

3 Move up 1 row on side B and bring the needle under two strands of that stitch on side B.

Repeat steps 2–5 to complete the seam.

Reinforcing Seams

With any sewn seam, leave a 6-inch tail at each end and use it to reinforce both ends of the seam on the wrong side of the work, by working back over the seam for an inch or two. Do this on both ends of the seam. After completing the seam, steam it briefly to soften and flatten it.

Reinforce the seam on the wrong side.

Easing in Extra Fabric

Sometimes two pieces must be seamed where the edges are not exactly the same length, and one side has to be eased into the other. On two straight edges only about an inch of fabric can be eased in, but on curved edges, like armholes and sleeve caps, up to 2 inches can be eased in without being noticeable. If the difference is more than that, it's probably wiser to block first so the dimensions of the two pieces are closer. When you are ready to seam, lay the two pieces next to each other and use a safety pin to join them at each end. In order to distribute the excess evenly, pin them again at the center, then at the quarter mark. This way, each quarter has a little of the excess fabric. If working a sewn seam, you will be skipping a stitch here and there on the longer edge; if working a slip stitch or other hooked

skipped stitch

Working a woven seam and skipping 1 stitch on the longer side.

seam, you can either skip stitches on the longer side, or work 2 stitches of the longer edge into 1 stitch on the shorter edge at regular intervals.

Undoing Seams

Undoing seams can be very treacherous! I have had the experience of cutting what I thought was a seam only to find the strand was from a stitch, thus losing a large amount of work. If you are having trouble with your seam, stop before you finish it, pull it out carefully, and try again. If you absolutely must undo a seam after it's done, gently pull apart the two pieces to assist you in identifying those strands of yarn that are actually the seam and not something else.

I urge you to get comfortable with making seams, as they are an important part of the skill set that can bring your crochet to the highest level. Many projects, including throws made of small blocks and garments with set-in sleeves, require good seams. While it takes a little experience, making neat, unobtrusive seams is not out of reach for anyone who devotes some time to building the skill. And seams really make the finished piece look great and last longer!

Edging

Elaborate edgings and trims were very popular in early days of crochet, and many stitch patterns started out as trims for Victorian curtains, pillows, coverlets, shawls, and the like. Today, simpler trims are often used to finish items, while elaborate edgings may be used for large borders on shawls. When complex edgings are used in a pattern, the instructions should specify how to fit the edge stitch into the main fabric.

Evenly Spaced Stitches in Edging

Often a single round of single crochet stitches is used to tidy and firm up all the edges of a work. In this case, a pattern typically specifies where to join the yarn to start your edging, but it may leave the exact placement of stitches up to the crocheter. The phrase used in such situation is to "work evenly spaced" stitches around a particular edge, whether a neckline, hem, or all the way around a throw. This can be puzzling to less experienced crocheter. How do you know how far apart to place stitches?

The answer depends on what part of the stitch you are working the edging into. When working all around a throw, for example, you will be working into the tops of stitches at the top edge, into the foundation chain at the bottom, and into the sides of stitches at the side edges.

Tops of Stitches

You can usually place 1 edging stitch in each stitch. Take care to match the size of the stitches you are working into; a useful guide is that the top of your edging stitch should be the same size as the top of the stitch worked into. If the edging is too tight, you will notice the fabric buckling as you work the edging. If too loose, it will cause the edge to enlarge beyond the intended size, and you may see ruffling of the fabric at the edge.

Foundation Chain

It's not always easy to pick out the base chain under each stitch. Use the stitches of the first row as a guide and work each edging stitch to match, picking up one or two strands of the base chain.

Working into the base chain

Sides of Stitches

The general guideline for working evenly spaced stitches into the sides of the stitches is as follows:

Work	into the side of
1 sc	sc
2 sc	hdc
3 sc	dc
4 sc	tr

You'll note that this is the same as the number of chains used at the beginning of a row to count as a stitch (page 49). These numbers are a general guide. *They don't work in every situation.* What's important when working an edging is not the stitch count, but that the result looks neat and does not distort the edge, either by tightening or loosening it, unless that is the intent (we will discuss how to use edging as a shaping device in a bit). Keep in mind, though, that if you are working two edges that are meant to be the same length (say a side edge and a bottom edge), the number of edging stitches should be the same.

When working into the post of a stitch, you can insert the hook under any two strands, or work around the entire post of the stitch. I prefer the first option, which looks neater. The same is true when working edging into the turning chain — working under two strands and not the whole chain looks better.

A single crochet edging inserting hook under 2 strands instead of working around the whole post

Working Single Crochet Edging around a Group of Chains

Here you may find the 1-to-1 stitch ratio does not work, as the chains are smaller than other stitches. Again, by trial and error, see if you can work 1 or 2 less single crochet stitches than there are chains to keep the edge the same length as the work itself.

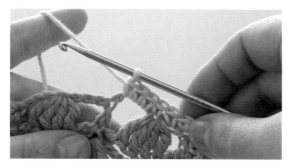

Working sc edging around a group of chains

Working Edging around Corners

Remember the principles learned in True Squares (page 85)? Squares require 2 or 3 single crochet stitches at a corner, and taller stitches will require more — perhaps 5 or 6 if double crochet is used — to go around the corner. If an edging is worked over several rounds, the corners need to continue growing to remain square.

Working 2 sc at corner

If your edge is circular, you should be able to work single crochet stitches without increasing, since the size of the circle does not get much bigger with this short stitch. If you find, however, that there is puckering in the fabric, work an extra stitch at regular intervals; if it's ruffling, skip a stitch at regular intervals. It's trial and error — again.

Working Edging on an Item with a Complex Stitch Pattern

You may find the exact placement of edging stitches can take time to find. Remember, you can adjust the size of your edging stitches, or work extra or fewer stitches as necessary to keep the edge even. Experiment until you find a good solution. Once you have a good sense of how the edge stitches fit into the work — for example, if 5 single crochet fit well into your pattern repeat — then be consistent as you work.

Edging as a Shaping Device

Edging is an excellent tool for tweaking the dimensions of a piece, especially to tighten a neckline, sleeve cuff, bottom of a hat, or waist of a skirt. Here, your goal is to deliberately work the edging row tighter than the piece, but to do so without causing obvious puckering of the fabric.

An excellent technique for this purpose is to work single crochet edging with a smaller hook. Alternatively, you can work with the same size hook but skip 1 stitch every 4, 5, or more stitches, depending on how much smaller you want the end result to be. Trial and error is, as always, the best way to determine this.

If you need to tighten an edge considerably, say more than 2 inches, do it gradually over several rows or rounds of edging, decreasing stitches in each round until you get to the desired result. Decrease at a regular rate, such as every 5 or 10 stitches, spreading decreases across the edge, rather than in any one area.

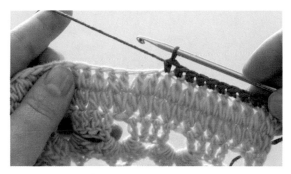

Working at a smaller gauge to tighten the edge

Ruffled Edge

Suppose you want the opposite effect, not a tighter edge, but a ruffled look. This is accomplished by working more stitches into the edge, using taller stitches — double or treble crochet — as shorter stitches are too short to ruffle. How many stitches to add is determined by how deep a ruffle is desired. Pronounced ruffles are appropriate only when working with thin yarns (sport weight or finer), because the thicker fabric produced with heavier yarns will be too bulky to ruffle nicely.

In this swatch, I began by working 3 trebles in every stitch. After working this way for part of the edge, I tried 2 trebles in every stitch. You can see how the ruffle becomes gentler as a result. If you find your ruffle is getting bulky, another alternative is to incorporate chain spaces into the ruffled edge. For example, instead of working 3 trebles in each stitch, you could work (treble, chain 1, treble). The degree of ruffling is very dependent on yarn thickness and gauge, and I mention these variations so you can experiment until you find the effect you like best.

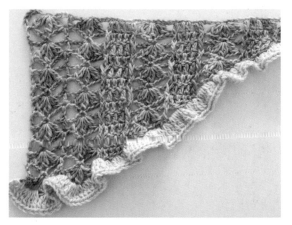

Deeper ruffle along the bottom, where 3 stitches were worked in every stitch

Flattening a Wavy Edge

Certain stitches, such as ripples and some shell patterns, do not end with a flat edge. These curves can be used as a decorative feature in a project, but what if you need to make that edge flat? There's a simple technique in which you work shorter stitches into the upper portion of the curve, and taller stitches into the lower portion.

Smoothing a Rippled Edge

Here is an example with a ripple that has a pronounced curve.

Raised sc Insert hook from front to back in st before working st, bring hook from back to front in working st, yo and draw up a loop, yo, draw through 2 loops. For first st in the row, insert hook from back to front under the 2 top loops of first st.

Ch a multiple of 19, plus 1 end st, plus 2 for tch. (*ch 41 for swatch*)

Row 1 4 dc in 4th ch from hook, *(dc in next ch, sk next ch) eight times, dc in next ch**, (5 dc in next ch) twice, rep from * across, ending last rep at **, 5 dc in last ch, turn.

Row 2 Ch 1, raised sc in each st across, turn.

Row 3 Ch 3, 4 dc in first sc, *(dc in next sc, sk next sc) eight times, dc in next sc**, (5 dc in next sc) twice, rep from * across, ending last rep at **, 5 dc in last sc, turn.

Rows 4 and 5 Rep rows 2 and 3.

Row 6 Rep row 2.

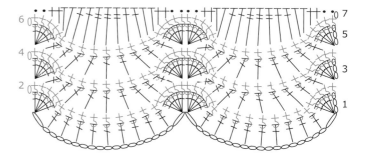

Straight-edge row Ch 1, *sl st in next 2 sts, sc in next 2 sts, hdc in next 2 sts, dc in next 2 sts, tr in next 3 sts, dc in next 2 sts, hdc in next 2 sts, sc in next 2 sts, sl st in next 2 sts, rep from * across.

If you wanted to even out the bottom edge, you could join yarn in the foundation chain and work a straight-edge row, working into the base chain under each stitch. Begin with chain 4 and shorten stitches gradually.

Slip Stitch Edging

Slip stitches can be used effectively to stabilize an edge, a technique that may be necessary if the edge is too flimsy for its function. For example, if the neckline of a piece is lacy, with long groups of chains at the edge, it may benefit from the added strength and stability of a slip stitch edging. When working such slip stitches, make sure not to pull each slip stitch tight, but match them to the stitches you are working into. Unlike a single crochet edging, a slip stitch edging can be nearly invisible, while still providing a neat and durable finish.

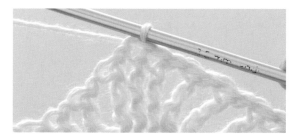

Here, slip stitches reinforce the right edge.

Slip stitch edging can also be very useful when preparing an edge before seaming. If, for example, two edges that will be seamed together do not match each other in length, a slip stitch edging can be used to even them out and will not be noticeable. Since its purpose is to tighten the edge, you will use the slip stitches on the longer piece to make it more closely match its partner. Here you will deliberately make the slip stitches tighter than the stitches you work into. This should be handled subtly, as we always want to avoid visible puckering. An inch or two can be removed from an edge by working slightly tighter slip stitches all along the edge.

Slip stitches shortening an edge

Blocking

There are numerous ways to block work, and each has a different purpose and effect. Blocking can be done using steam or water. These methods are most effective with natural fibers, but acrylic will respond too, though not as well.

Before you block a project, block a swatch using the same yarn and stitch. This way you will know exactly how the yarn behaves and will not have unwanted surprises. Measure your swatch before and after blocking so you know exactly how blocking affects the finished item.

Steam Blocking

Steam blocking is appropriate when you want to relax the stitches and soften the fabric, rather than tweak its dimensions. The steaming process goes very quickly. Hold a steam iron over the work, taking care not to touch the fabric with the iron. You'll find that stiff fabric can be considerably softened with steam. While steaming, the fabric may also enlarge somewhat, but it generally resumes its original size once the fabric cools. As with many other things, this is dependent on the fiber, and you'll find out whether the fabric will shrink back to its original dimension by measuring the swatch once it's cool and dry.

Use care when subjecting acrylic fabric to steam heat, as it burns more easily than natural fibers. Acrylic can be steamed successfully as long as the heat is not too intense. Acrylic can also be deliberately subjected to heat, which is sometimes referred to as "killing" the fabric. This will both soften it and also change the texture and even the color. Use this method with care, and do try it on a swatch first. When done successfully, it's a good trick to know as it can lend more drape to the fabric.

Wet Blocking

When you want to achieve particular dimensions precisely, a full wet block is needed. Many crochet items, especially garments, can benefit from a full wet blocking. Lace work especially should be finished with careful blocking, which opens up the stitches and allows you to really see the lace pattern. Not only does wet blocking allow you to obtain the correct size, but it evens out individual stitches and helps create tidy edges. Some yarns really bloom after wet blocking and look much prettier.

If you know a project will need wet blocking, your gauge swatch should be wet blocked. The pattern should give you the gauge *after* blocking, and your gauge after blocking should match it.

When working an item in several pieces, each piece is blocked to specified dimensions before seaming. Blocking can increase the dimensions of a piece substantially, but you want to avoid stretching fabric to the point where stitches are distorted. When working from a pattern, the desired dimensions for each piece should be given at the start of the pattern or in the schematics.

Immerse each piece in water, then squeeze out excess water by rolling the piece in a towel. Avoid wringing out the fabric, which can cause too much and uneven stretching. Some people put items in their dryer *briefly* on a low setting. Lay out the piece on a blocking board that has a grid showing inches and/or centimeters. Use rustproof or rust-resistant T-pins to pin the piece to the board.

When pinning the wet piece to the blocking board, avoid pulling individual stitches out of shape. To ensure that the stretching is spread throughout the piece, place pins all along the edge, and carefully line up stitches and rows with the lines of the blocking board. You can also place pins within the fabric, in addition to the edges, to make sure the fabric stretches evenly throughout. Pin each piece to the dimensions you want your finished work to be, consulting the schematic when applicable.

If a piece is too large to fit on your blocking board, it can be blocked in sections. Wet the section that does fit, and repeat until every bit has been blocked. If certain parts get wet more than once, that's not a problem. Handle large pieces carefully to avoid unwanted stretching. Some fibers, such as alpaca and cotton, are prone to stretching and must be handled with particular care when wet.

I have also used wet blocking to tighten up work, though this is a rather unconventional use. After wetting the piece in question, place it on the board and push the stitches closer together to reach the desired dimension, then pin in place.

If your goal is to tweak the dimensions of a project just a bit, it's not necessary to soak the pieces — they can be merely dampened. I use this

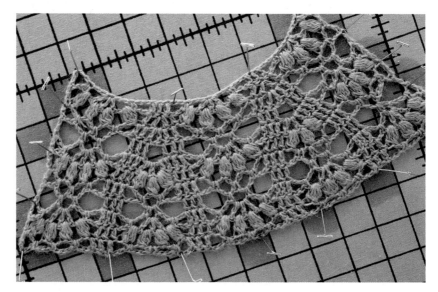

strategy especially when working with fibers that stretch easily. Lay out the piece and spritz both sides with water, then pin it to the blocking board. With this method, you get the benefits of evening out stitches and relaxing the fabric without risking too much stretch. Of course, the piece dries more quickly, too. In such cases, you may not need to pin the item at all, just allow it to dry flat. Or you may only need to pin at corners where there is a tendency for the fabric to curl.

Any items that you intend to hand-wash in the future should have a full wet blocking. That way, you won't get any unwanted surprises. With projects that will need little or no pinning for dimensions, start by measuring the swatch, wetting it, and then allowing it to dry flat with no pins. Measure the swatch when it dries, so that you can have a pre- and post-block gauge. Use the post-block gauge to plan the dimensions of your project. If you're following a pattern, the gauge given will be post blocking, unless otherwise specified. When working the project, work to the pre-block gauge. The finished project can then be soaked, rolled in towels, then dried flat without pins, or perhaps with just a few in crucial places like corners. It should behave like the swatch and change in similar proportions, so that you end up with the correct finished dimensions. If you have any concerns, feel free to pin as necessary when blocking.

If you make large pieces of crochet lace, such as shawls, blocking wires made of flexible metal are another useful tool. These should be rust resistant or rustproof. The advantage of using wires is that they stretch the entire edge, while a pin can exert stretch at only one point. Wires can help you make better-looking edges. The wire is woven in and out of the edge, then pinned at regular intervals on a board to hold the piece in place. You may find it easier to insert the wires when the piece is dry, then lay it down and spritz it.

Care of Crochet

Use caution when laundering crochet. Always follow the directions on the yarn label regarding washing and drying, as many natural fibers should only be hand washed. Items you intend to machine wash should be made with sturdy, washable fiber, with very secure seams.

Hand-dyed yarns can shed color on the first washing; they may even take several washings before they stop bleeding color. Be sure to test an item before washing it with other items. I personally do not put crochet in a washer or dryer, but if you have machines where temperature can be controlled, it should be quite safe when the label says it is. Wash the item by itself so it can't snag, or put it in a mesh bag to protect it.

I tend to spot clean with water and soap any time a crochet piece gets a stain, rather than wash the whole piece. When hand-washing, use gentle soap. Dry the piece flat, and, if it was originally blocked with pins, it should be reblocked after washing to maintain its shape and dimensions.

Most crochet items should be stored folded up rather than on a hanger, as they will stretch over time if hung. I have used a warm iron to remove wrinkles in crochet fabric, but try this first on just a little bit of the fabric to make sure it can stand the heat. Steaming with an iron can also be effective for this purpose.

PART 2

Projects

Slouchy Hat

The rage for slouchy hats shows no signs of abating. This design uses an interesting cluster stitch to create both drape and style. Check out the modifications possible to customize the hat for your own head and tastes. Enjoy the crafty finish to this hat! Instead of shaping, we simply stop when the hat reaches a good height, then gather the fabric at the top using a long foundation chain woven through spaces in the fabric.

LEARN HOW TO

- Control tension on tall stitches
- Make and shape simple crochet ribbing
- Make clusters over stitches that span a distance
- Shape for slouch
- Achieve drape with worsted-weight yarn
- Work a hat from the bottom up
- Finish the top of a hat by gathering fabric

RIBBED BAND

The ribbing on this hat is worked in vertical rows of back loop single crochet stitches (BLsc). I wanted to make the front of the ribbed band wider than the back at the neck so that the slouch would sit farther back on the head. To create that shape, the ribbed band starts at the center back of the head and has gradual increases as it is worked to the front, then gradual decreases working from the front around to the center back again.

shorter rows   longer rows

Note that the shaping is not evenly spaced, as the aim was to increase the band more markedly as it reaches the front of the head. After completing the ribbing, the first and last rows are slip stitched together and the work is turned 90 degrees to begin the body of the hat.

The ribbing fabric is quite stretchy, but unlike knitted fabric, it won't bounce back to its original shape as readily. Make sure the ribbing is very snug when you make it, because it will stretch over time. There is good advice about this at the end of this pattern, under Care.

TWO-LEGGED CLUSTER STITCH

The main body of the head uses a stitch I call a two-legged cluster, a stitch with great texture, but also some bulk, especially with worsted-weight yarn. In order to have good drape for this slouchy hat, it's essential that the cluster stitches be worked loosely.

This is less a matter of hook size than of how loops are drawn up as you create stitches. Each time you make a double crochet stitch that's part of a cluster, after you've inserted your hook and when you are drawing up your first loop, that's the moment to focus your attention. It's this loop that determines the height of the stitch, so please don't skimp; give it a good ¾". If you tend to tug on stitches after making them, tug not! You'll be able to stretch over to the second leg of the stitch much more easily by following this advice, and you'll end with a hat that truly slouches. Because of the span the two-legged cluster covers, this pattern may actually help loosen up on your tension in general. Note that the 2 chains that follow the cluster can be worked tightly, as it is most attractive when chains are being used as connecting lines.

Working the first round of clusters into the ribbing isn't hard to do but is hard to describe in pattern-speak. Here you can see the two-legged clusters worked into the ends of ribbing rows.

Making the Hat

Finished Measurements

Ribbing: 22" in circumference; hat: 9" in diameter at widest point

Yarn

Lorna's Laces Shepherd Worsted (100% superwash wool, 225 yds/4 oz), 2 skeins China Blue

Tools

US H/8 (5 mm) and I/9 (5.5 mm) crochet hooks *or sizes you need to obtain correct gauge*

Stitch marker

Tapestry needle

Gauge

8 sc × 10 rows = 2" × 4" in ribbing with the smaller hook

4 clusters × 2 rows = 4" × 2½" with the larger hook

Cl (cluster) (Yo, insert hook in designated st or space and draw up loop to ¾", yo, draw through 2 loops) twice, (yo, insert hook in next designated st or sp and draw up loop, yo, draw through 2 loops) twice, yo, draw through 5 loops on hook.

dec (decrease) (Insert hook in next st, draw up loop) twice, yo, draw through 3 loops on hook.

RIBBING

Notes

On ribbing, because we are working under the back loop (BL) in the first stitch of each row, the bottom edge can get lumpy. To minimize this, turn the work counterclockwise when starting a new row.

All the shaping stitches are on the upper part of the band.

With smaller hook, ch 9.

Row 1 (RS) Sc in 2nd ch from hook and in each ch across, turn. (*8 sc*)

Row 2 Ch 1, BLsc in each sc across, turn.

Rows 3–10 Rep row 2.

Row 11 Ch 1, BLsc in each sc across, 2 BLsc in last sc, turn. (*9 sc*)

Rows 12–14 Ch 1, BLsc in each sc across, turn.

Row 15 Rep row 11. (*10 sc*)

Rows 16–18 Work even in BLsc, turn.

Row 19 Rep row 11. (*11 sc*)

Row 20–35 Work even in BLsc, turn.

Row 36 Ch1, dec at start of row, BLsc in each sc across, turn. (*10 sc*)

Row 37–39 Work even in BLsc, turn.

Row 40 Rep row 36. (*9 sc*)

Row 41–45 Work even in BLsc, turn.

Row 46 Rep row 36. (*8 sc*)

Rows 47–56 Work even in BLsc, do not fasten off.

Fold band so that first and last row meet. With RS facing, starting with the loop on the hook, work slip stitch seam (see page 199) to join these edges, picking up one strand from each side.

HAT BODY

Turn work 90 degrees and begin working into the top edge of the band, working into ends of sc rows. Make sure that you are working into the edge where the increases and decreases were made; that's the top edge of the band, and the flat edge is the bottom.

The cluster rounds should begin at the top of a rib, every other row. Some of the rows have only a single strand across, so be sure not to work stitches there, but always work into a row where you can pick up two strands.

When finishing rounds of clusters, you will be making the second leg of the last cluster in the same space as the first leg of the first cluster in the round.

Clusters are deliberately offset to accentuate the oblong shape formed by 2 rounds of clusters. Take note of where to start each round.

Change to larger hook.

Rnd 1 Ch 3, yo, insert hook in same row, yo, draw up loop, yo, draw through 2 loops (counts as first leg of Cl), sk next row, work 2nd leg of Cl in next row.

Rnd 2 Insert hook between two legs of Cl directly below and make sl st, ch 3, yo, insert hook in same sp, yo, draw up a loop, yo, draw through 2 loops (counts as first leg of Cl), work second leg in next sp between 2 legs, *ch 2**, Cl beg in same sp as second leg of last Cl, rep from * placing second leg of last Cl in same sp as first leg of first Cl, ending last rep at **, sl st to top of first Cl.

Rnd 3 Sl st in next ch-2 sp, ch 2, dc in same sp (*half Cl made*), work second leg of Cl in next ch-2 sp, *ch 2**, Cl beg in same sp as second leg of last Cl, rep from * around ending last rep at **, sl st to top of first Cl.

Rnd 4 Rep row 2.

Rnds 5–11 Rep rnds 3 and 4 three more times. Then rep rnd 3 once more. Do not fasten off. Pm in last st.

FINISHING

Turn the hat inside out.

Ch 30, fasten off, and leave an 8" tail. Place tail on tapestry needle, and weave the 30 ch through the spaces under each ch-2 in the round. As you proceed, allow the top of the hat to gather, tugging on the chains to move them through. When you arrive at the marker, you have woven through the whole top of the hat. Remove marker. Continue tugging to gather the fabric, closing the top as much as possible. You will have leftover chains that we will unravel, but first pm in the last chain you want to use. Unravel as many chains as necessary to get close to the marker and fasten off. Use the remaining tail to further secure the opening.

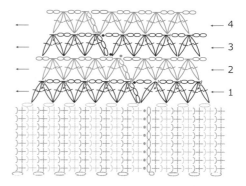

CARE

Hand-wash and dry your hat, or else try a *very gentle* cycle on a washing machine and dryer. If air-drying it flat, squish the ribbing rows close together to retain the original shape.

Keep any leftover yarn handy for future use. Should the ribbing need to be tightened after some time, work a row of slip stitches all around the bottom of the hat from the wrong side. It will be least obvious if you pick up the 2 loops at the very bottom so that the slip stitches are really a line along the bottom of the hat and not too visible on the front. Work these as tightly as necessary to fit head, but at the same time try to avoid bunching up the hat fabric.

Altering the Hat

If this ribbing is too snug, simply add rows as necessary. You will end up with more stitches in the rounds above the ribbing, too, which is suitable for a larger head.

If you like the size of the ribbing but would like a slouchier hat, work additional rounds before fastening off, then follow Finishing instructions.

To make this hat fuller in circumference in the upper portion only, without making the ribbing longer, is a bit trickier. You have two choices: (1) in the first round of the hat body, you can easily add extra stitches between other stitches; if you intend to add several, space them evenly around the hat, though they needn't be exact, or (2) expand the circumference after the first round in an odd-numbered row, placing new clusters between other clusters.

Naturally, the hat can be made smaller by starting out with fewer rows of ribbing. Measure the circumference of the head you want to fit and make the ribbing about 2 inches shorter in length, since it will stretch. After that, you can follow the pattern as written, but you'll have different stitch counts.

Marguerite Cowl

The marguerite stitch is so pretty, but it's not seen enough in designs, probably because it's traditionally worked at a dense gauge. The stitch really shines when worked at this looser gauge. This is a quick project once you get all the details down.

LEARN HOW TO

- Work the marguerite (aka star) stitch (see page 77)

- Control and change tension when working different stitches

- Adjust a pattern stitch when working in the round

- Count stitches when working in the round

- Start a project with foundation single crochet

- Apply reverse single crochet edging

The yarn used in this project is a worsted with some fuzz, so it can be considered similar in thickness to a bulky yarn, but very soft and flexible. I used a large hook and made the loops of the marguerite much larger than the hook's shaft. You could choose an even larger hook, but note that the stitch pattern has an alternating row of half double crochet stitches, and it may be difficult to get to the proper size with a giant-sized hook. Instead, practice tension control by drawing up each loop of the marguerite nice and tall, and make all the loops close to each other in size. Then work the rows of half double crochet stitches at a normal gauge. This is definitely one to practice on a swatch before embarking on the project!

If you're new to marguerite stitch, practice flat first, following the directions for the gauge swatch, without worrying about the foundation single crochet (Fsc) start. Use the yarn you intend to use for this project and aim to get the correct gauge. Once you can get gauge, you can begin the project and be more assured of a good outcome.

If the gauge eludes you, in order to make a cowl that fits, you can redo the stitch and row counts, as explained in chapter 5, using the circumference of the cowl at the top as your starting point for the dimension. Adjusting a pattern for your gauge is another excellent skill to cultivate!

Making the Cowl

Finished Measurements

About 20" in circumference at the top, 34" in circumference at the bottom, and 9" deep

Yarn

Blue Sky Techno (68% baby alpaca, 10% extra fine merino, 22% silk, 120 yds/50 g), CYC#4 medium, 2 skeins #1972 Suede

Tools

US M-N/13 (9 mm) crochet hook *or size needed to obtain correct gauge*

Tapestry needle

Gauge

5 marguerites and 5 rows = 4¾" × 4" (see Marguerite Gauge Swatch on next page)

Fsc (foundation single crochet) Please refer to the step-by-step instructions for foundation single crochet on page 61. When making this stitch, the base chain is formed by the ch-1 made after inserting the hook and pulling up a loop. Make each ch-1 larger than the hook's shaft so that the base chain is not tight. Use the size of the top loops in the hdc row on your gauge swatch as a guide to how large these stitches should be.

Rsc (reverse single crochet) Edging See the step-by-step tutorial on page 76. When applying the edging, it's important not to make it too tight. Because the edging stitches are dense, they may need steaming to relax them.

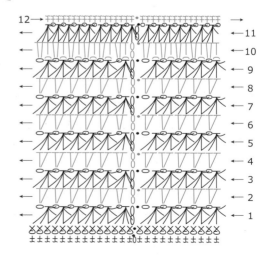

Notes

Count stitches at end of each round. It's easy to mistakenly make extra half double crochet stitches. If you're short by only one and have no place to put last loop of last marguerite, work it into the chain-2 at the beginning of the round, so long as you have the correct number of marguerites at the end of round. For larger errors, better to unravel! For a traditional starting chain, chain 43 to begin and work 42 sc in round 1.

MARGUERITE GAUGE SWATCH

Ch 14.

Row 1 Draw up a loop in 2nd ch from hook, draw up a loop in each of the next 4 ch, yo, draw through 6 loops on hook, ch 1 (*marguerite made*), *draw up a loop in ch-1 just made, draw up a loop in last loop of previous marguerite, draw up a loop in same ch as last loop of previous marguerite, draw up a loop in next 2 ch, yo, draw through 6 loops on hook, ch 1 (*marguerite made*), rep from * across, hdc in last ch, turn. (*5 marguerites*)

Row 2 Ch 2 (counts as st on even rows only), * sk hdc, 2 hdc in next ch (eye of marguerite), rep from * across, hdc in top of tch, turn. (*12 hdc*)

Row 3 Ch 2, draw up a loop in FL of 2nd ch from hook, draw up a loop in BL of 2nd ch from hook, draw up a loop in first hdc, draw up a loop in next 2 hdc, yo, draw through 6 loops on hook, ch 1 (*marguerite made*), *draw up a loop in ch-1 just made, draw up a loop under last loop of prev marguerite, draw up a loop in same hdc as last loop of prev marguerite, draw up a loop in each of the next 2 hdc, yo, draw through 6 loops on hook, ch 1, rep from * across, hdc in same st as last loop of last marguerite, turn.

Rows 4 and 5 Rep rows 2 and 3.

Swatch should measure 4¾" wide and 4" long.

COWL

Setup Ch 2, insert hook in 2nd ch and draw up loop, ch 1, yo, draw through 2 loops (*Fsc made*), *insert hook in base ch of first Fsc and draw up loop, ch 1, yo, draw through 2 loops. Repeat from *across 40 more times (*42 Fsc made*), sl st to top of first Fsc in rnd.

Rnd 1 Ch 2, draw up a loop in 2nd ch from hook, draw up a loop in each of the next 4 fsc, yo, draw through 6 loops on hook, ch 1 (marguerite made), *draw up a loop in ch-1 just made, draw up a loop

in last loop of prev marguerite, draw up a loop in same fsc as last loop of prev marguerite, draw up a loop in next 2 fsc, yo, draw through 6 loops on hook, ch 1 (marguerite made), rep from * across, for last marguerite in rnd, after drawing yarn through 6 loops, do not ch 1, but instead sl st to first loop of first marguerite in rnd. (*21 marguerites*)

Rnd 2 Ch 2, *2 hdc in eye of marguerite, rep from * across, sl st to top of ch-2. (*42 hdc*)

Rnd 3 Ch 2, draw up a loop in back loop only of 2nd ch from hook, draw up a loop in front loop only of 2nd ch from hook, draw up a loop in next 3 hdc, yo, draw through 6 loops on hook, ch 1, *draw up a loop in ch-1 just made, draw up a loop in last loop of prev marguerite, draw up a loop in same hdc as last loop of prev marguerite, draw up a loop in next 2 hdc, yo, draw through 6 loops on hook, ch 1, rep from * across, for last marguerite in rnd, after drawing yarn through 6 loops, do not ch 1, but instead sl st to first loop of first marguerite in rnd.

Rnd 4 Rep rnd 2.

Rnds 5–8 Rep rnds 3 and 4.

Rnd 9 Rep rnd 1.

Rnd 10 (inc rnd) Ch 2, *hdc in upper loop of next marguerite, 2 hdc in eye, rep from * across, sl st to top of ch-2. (*62 hdc*)

Rnd 11 Ch 2, work marguerite at around, sl st to top of ch-2. (*36 marguerites*)

Rnd 12 1 Rsc in same sl, *1 Rsc in eye, 1 Rsc in loop next to eye, rep from * around, working the last Rsc in the first st of the rnd, then sl st to the WS in any convenient strand of the first Rsc. Fasten off.

FINISHING

With RS facing, join yarn in first Fsc, ch 1, 1 Rsc in same st as join, 1 Rsc in each ch around. Fasten off. Weave in all ends.

Steam the bottom edge briefly to relax the fabric.

Colorwork Bag

Post stitches combined with color provide a great opportunity for exciting colorwork. This is a great pattern for getting comfortable with post stitches and for training your counting skills when working in the round. For the color effect to work, in each round the sequence of stitches is moved 1 stitch over, and accuracy is crucial. The last group in each round will help you keep track of where you are in the stitch pattern.

LEARN HOW TO

- Count stitches
- Join rounds
- Use stitch markers
- Change colors
- Work finishing details on a bag
- Make crochet I-cord

Making the Bag

Finished Measurements

About 19" in circumference and 12" long; strap 20" long

Yarn

Knit Picks Shine Sport (60% pima cotton, 40% Modal, 110 yds/50 g), 2 balls Currant (color A), 1 ball each Wisteria (color B), Hydrangea (color C), French Blue (color D), and Pageant (color E)

Tools and Materials

US E/4 (3.5 mm) crochet hook *or size needed to obtain correct gauge*

US 7 (4.5 mm) crochet hook (for strap only)

2 stitch markers

Ruler or tape measure

Scissors

Steam iron

Straight pins

Tapestry needle

Paper

¼ yd of ultrafirm interfacing

¼ yd of fusible interfacing

1 medium-sized magnetic snap with prongs and back plate

Gauge

8 sts and 4 rows in patt = 2" × 1½", blocked

Notes

The bag is finished with a crochet I-cord strap made with two strands of yarn. The cord inserts into the top rim of the bag, which is made with small holes for this purpose. The end of the cord is sewn inside the rim, then the rim is reinforced with interfacing to maintain its stability. Finally, the rim is folded in half and sewn down inside the bag.

The instructions also include a base for the bag that will help keep its shape. We've made it removable, so that the bag could be washed separately.

FPdc (front post double crochet) Yo, insert hook from front to back around post of designated stitch, yo and draw up a loop, (yo, draw through 2 loops) twice.

BPdc (back post double crochet) Yo, insert hook from back to front around post of designated st, yo and draw up a loop, (yo, draw through 2 loops) twice.

Stitch markers are used in this project to help keep track of where to increase when making the bottom of the bag. You can use a safety pin as your marker. When the pattern tells you to mark the last stitch made, put your safety pin anywhere in the top of the stitch just after completing it; it doesn't matter exactly where, as long as you can see it when you get to the next round.

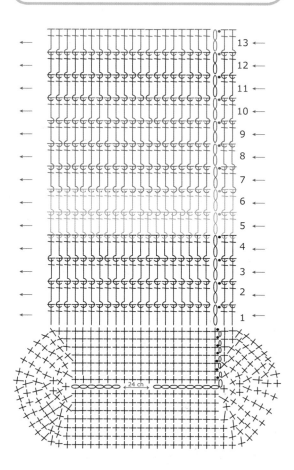

BAG BOTTOM

With A, ch 34.

Rnd 1 Sc in 2nd ch and in each ch across to last ch, 3 sc in last ch, working now in base of foundation ch (there is already a st in first sc, so beg in 2nd), sc in next 22 sts, 2 sc in last sc, sl st to first sc. (*48 sc*)

Rnd 2 Ch 1, sc in next 22 sc, (2 sc in next sc), pm in last st made, (2 sc in next sc) twice, sc in next 21 sc, (2 sc in next sc), pm in last st made, (2 sc in next sc), sc in same st as first sc of rnd, sl st to first sc. (*54 sc*)

Rnd 3 Ch 1, *sc in each sc to marker, 2 sc in marked st, move marker to last st made, sc in next sc, 2 sc in next sc**, 2 sc in next sc, rep from * to **, sc in same st as first sc in rnd, sl st to first sc. (*60 sc*)

Rnd 4 Ch 1, *sc in each sc to st before marker, 2 sc in next sc, move marker to last st made**, (sc in next 2 sc, 2 sc in next sc) twice, rep from * to **, sc in next 2 sc, 2 sc in next sc, sc in next 2 sc, 2 sc in last sc, sl st to first sc. (*66 sc*)

Rnd 5 Ch 1, *sc in each sc to marker, 2 sc in marked st, move marker to last st made, (sc in next 3 sc, 2 sc in next sc) twice, rep from * around, slip stitch to first sc. (*72 sc*)

Rnd 6 Ch 1, *sc in each sc to st before marker, 2 sc in next sc, move marker to last st made**, (sc in next 4 sc, 2 sc in next sc) twice, rep from * sc in last sc, sl st to first sc. (*78 sc*)

Rnd 7 Ch 1, *sc in each sc to marker, 2 sc in marked st, move marker to last st made, (sc in next 5 sc, 2 sc in next sc) twice, rep from * around, sc in last sc, sl st to first sc. (*84 sc*)

BAG BODY

Rnd 1 Ch 2 (counts as dc), dc in each sc around, sl st to top of ch-2. (*84 dc*)

Rnd 2 Ch 2, FPdc in next 5 dc, *BPdc in next 6 sts, FPdc in next 6 sts, rep from * around to last 6 sts, BPdc in next 6 dc, sl st to top of ch-2.

Rnd 3 Ch 2, *FPdc in next 6 sts, BPdc in next 6 sts, rep from * around to last 11 sts, FPdc in next 6 sts, BPdc in next 5 sts, sl st to top of ch-2.

Rnd 4 Ch 2, BPdc in next FPdc, *FPdc in next 6 sts, BPdc in next 6 sts, rep from * around to last 10 sts, FPdc in next 6 sts, BPdc in next 4 sts, sl st to top of ch-2, change to B.

Rnd 5 Ch 2, BPdc in next 2 FPdc, *FPdc in next 6 sts, BPdc in next 6 sts, rep from * around to last 9 sts, FPdc in next 6 sts, BPdc in next 3 sts, sl st to top of ch-2.

Rnd 6 Ch 2, BPdc in next 3 FPdc, *FPdc in next 6 sts, BPdc in next 6 sts, rep from * around to last 8 sts, FPdc in next 6 sts, BPdc in last 2 sts, sl st to top of ch-2, change to C.

Rnd 7 Ch 2, BPdc in next 4 sts, *FPdc in next 6 sts, BPdc in next 6 sts, rep from * around to last 7 sts, FPdc in next 6 sts, BPdc in last st, sl st to top of ch-2.

Rnd 8 Ch 2, BPdc in next 5 sts, *FPdc in next 6 sts, BPdc in next 6 sts, rep from * around to last 6 sts, FPdc in next 6 sts, sl st to top of ch-2, change to D.

Rnd 9 Ch 2, *BPdc in next 6 sts, FPdc in next 6 sts, rep from * around to last 11 sts, BPdc in next 6 sts, FPdc in next 5 sts, sl st to top of ch-2.

Rnd 10 Ch 2, FPdc in next st, *BPdc in next 6 sts, FPdc in next 6 sts, rep from * around to last 10 sts, BPdc in next 6 sts, FPdc in next 4 sts, sl st to top of ch-2, change to E.

Rnd 11 Ch 2, FPdc in next 2 sts, *BPdc in next 6 sts, FPdc in next 6 sts, rep from * around to last 9 sts, BPdc in next 6 sts, FPdc in next 3 sts, sl st to top of ch-2.

Rnd 12 Ch 2, FPdc in next 3 sts, *BPdc in next 6 sts, FPdc in next 6 sts, rep from * around to last 8 sts, BPdc in next 6 sts, FPdc in next 2 sts, sl st to top of ch-2, change to C.

Rnd 13 Ch 2, FPdc in next 4 sts, *BPdc in next 6 sts, FPdc in next 6 sts, rep from * around to last 7 sts, BPdc in next 6 sts, FPdc in next st, sl st to top of ch-2.

Rnds 14–61 Rep rnds 2–12 four more times following color sequence: 2 rnds C, 2 rnds B, 4 rnds A, 2 rnds B, 2 rnds C, 2 rnds D, 2 rnds E, 2 rnds C, 2 rnds B, 4 rnds A.

Continue with A.

CLOSURE BAND

Rnds 62–65 Ch 1, sc in each st around, sl st to ch-1.

Rnd 66 Ch 1, sc in next 28 sc, ch 2, sk 2 sc, sc in next 9 sc, ch 2, sk 2 sc, rep from * once, sl st to ch-1. (Note that the last skipped sc are last 2 sts of round.)

Rnds 67–70 Rep rnd 62. Fasten off.

CROCHET I-CORD STRAP (MAKE 2)

This is an interesting method for creating a tubular cord with sufficient heft for a bag strap.

With the larger hook, holding together colors D and E, ch 3, yo, draw up loop in 2nd ch from hook, yo, draw up loop in 3rd ch from hook. (*3 loops on hook*)

*Remove hook from last 2 ch made and pinch them with your yarn-holding hand so they don't unravel. Insert hook in first dropped ch, ch 1, insert hook in 2nd dropped ch, ch 1 (*3 loops on hook*). Rep from * until strap is desired length. Fasten off by yo, draw through all 3 loops on hook, and cut yarn.

BAG BASE

Measure the length and width of the bottom of the bag. Draw a bag base on paper using these measurements, rounding the edges, and adding ¼" around the template; it should be a little bit larger than your bag so that you can trim it to fit.

Cut out one bag base from the ultrafirm interfacing. Place it in the bottom of the bag to check the fit and trim as needed. Once it fits nicely, use it as your final template and cut out two more bag bases from the ultrafirm interfacing.

Cut two pieces of fusible interfacing that are 2" wider and 2" longer than your bag base. Stack the three bag bases and tack the four corners with a pin to keep them stable. Place the bag base in the middle of one sheet of the fusible interfacing, then place the other sheet on top. Using a steam iron, press the fusible interfacing to the bag base top, sides, and bottom. Trim excess interfacing, leaving ¼".

FINISHING

Cut a piece of fusible interfacing measuring the width and length of the band facing at the top of the bag, plus 1" more in each direction. Lay the fusible interfacing strip on the inside of the band facing at the top of the bag and fuse with a steam iron. Cut open the strap opening in the interfacing to match the skipped stitches in rnd 66.

Fold the band facing in half and pin to the bag. Take one end of the strap and slide it though the opening until the end of the strap is concealed under the band facing. Using matching yarn and a tapestry needle, secure the strap by sewing it though all layers of the bag. Slide the other end of the strap through the corresponding strap opening and repeat. Repeat for a second strap on the other side.

Center the female half of the magnetic snap inside the band facing. Push the snap prongs through the bag facing, place the back plate over the prongs, and press each prong down facing outward. Repeat the same process for the male half of the snap, making sure to match the placement of the male snap to the female snap.

Sew the entire bag band in place. Weave in and trim all ends.

Lace Capelet

This pretty and versatile wrap can dress up many outfits and provide warmth on a spring or fall day. It's also a great example of some of the shaping concepts explored in chapter 7.

LEARN HOW TO

- Work with fingering-weight yarn
- Use sophisticated shaping techniques
- Work evenly spaced crochet edging
- Crochet simple cords to close a garment

Shaping concepts discussed on page 147 are used in this shawl. The design begins with a reduced version of the stitch pattern, with only 1 double crochet between fans instead of 3. From rows 1–5, 2 more double crochet stitches are added to each pattern repetition. Beginning at row 6, the double crochet panel opens up, and another pattern repetition is introduced between double crochet panels. The pattern repetition reaches its full size in row 12, and the remainder is worked even.

When working the edging, if you find the stitch counts given are not producing the desired result, feel free to change them. Small differences in gauge can affect how edging stitches fit into edges, and this design gives you an opportunity to refine your edging technique.

For the last bobble in the group of 4, you may wish to make 1 extra chain to close the bobble tightly. This is optional: try it with and without to see which you prefer. If you do choose this option, make sure this extra chain is tight and not noticeable.

Making the Capelet

Finished Measurements

About 30" at neck edge, 64" at bottom edge, and 10" long at center front

Yarn

Manos del Uruguay Serena (60% alpaca, 40% pima cotton, 170 yds/50 g), fingering weight, 2 skeins color #2020

Tools

US D/3 (3.25 mm) crochet hook *or size needed to obtain correct gauge*

Tapestry needle

Gauge

For swatch, ch 30 and work first 4 rows. 2 patt reps = 5"; rows 1–4 = 4½"

Bobble (Yo, insert hook in designated sp, yo and draw up a loop, yo, draw through 2 loops) four times in same ch-1 sp, yo, draw through 5 loops on hook.

Ch 150 (12 × 12 + 6).

Row 1 Sc in 9th ch from hook, *ch 1, sk 2 ch, (dc, ch 1) three times in next ch, sk 2 ch, sc in next ch, ch 2, sk 2 ch, dc in next ch, ch 2, sk 2 ch, sc in next ch, rep from * across, ch 2, sk 2 ch, dc in last ch, turn. (*12 patt reps*)

Row 2 Ch 3 (counts as dc throughout), sk (2 ch, sc), *(bobble in next ch-1 sp, ch 3) three times, bobble in next ch-1 sp, sk 2 ch, dc in next dc, rep from * across, placing last dc in 6th ch of tch, turn.

Row 3 Ch 5 (counts as dc, ch 2 throughout), *(sc in next ch-3 sp, ch 3) twice, sc in next ch-3 sp, ch 2**, dc in next dc, ch 2, rep from * across, ending last rep at **, dc in tch, turn.

Row 4 Ch 8 (counts as dc, ch 5 throughout), *sk (ch 2, sc), sc in next ch-3 sp, ch 3, sc in next ch-3 sp, ch 5**, 3 dc in next dc, ch 5, rep from * across, ending last rep at **, dc in 3rd ch of tch, turn.

Row 5 Ch 5, *sc in next ch-5 sp, (ch 1, dc) three times in next ch-3 sp, ch 1, sc in next ch-5 sp, ch 2**, dc in next 3 dc, ch 2, rep from * across, ending last rep at **, dc in 3rd ch of tch, turn.

Row 6 Ch 3, *sk (ch 2, sc), (bobble in next ch-1 sp, ch 4) three times, bobble in next ch-1 sp**, sk 2 ch, dc in next dc, (dc, ch 1, dc) in next dc, dc in next dc, rep from * across, ending last rep at **, dc in 3rd ch of tch, turn.

Row 7 Ch 5, *(sc in next ch-4 sp, ch 3) twice, sc in next ch-4 sp, ch 2**, dc in next 2 dc, (dc, ch 1, dc) in next ch-1 sp, dc in next 2 dc, ch 2, rep from * across, ending last rep at **, dc in tch, turn.

Row 8 Ch 8, *sk (ch 2, sc), sc in next ch-3 sp, ch 3, sc in next ch-3 sp, ch 5**, dc in next 3 dc, ch 3, dc in next 3 dc, ch 5, rep from * across, ending last rep at **, dc in 3rd ch of tch, turn.

Row 9 Ch 5, *sc in next ch-5 sp, (ch 1, dc) three times in next ch-3 sp, ch 1, sc in next ch-5 sp, ch 2**, dc in next 3 dc, (dc, ch 1) 2 times in next ch-3 sp, dc in same ch-3 sp, dc in next 3 dc, ch 2, rep from * across, ending last rep at **, dc in 3rd ch of tch, turn.

Row 10 Ch 3, *sk (ch 2, sc), (bobble in next ch-1 space, ch 4) three times, bobble in next ch-1 sp**, sk 2 ch, dc in next 3 dc, sk next dc, bobble in next ch-1 sp, ch 4, bobble in next dc, ch 4, bobble in next ch-1 sp, sk next dc, dc in next 3 dc, rep from * across, ending last rep at **, dc in 3rd ch of tch, turn.

Row 11 Ch 5, *(sc in next ch-4 sp, ch 3) twice, sc in next ch-4 sp, ch 2**, dc in next 3 dc, ch 2, sc in next ch-4 sp, ch 3, sc in next bobble, ch 3, sc in next ch-4 sp, ch 2, dc in next 3 dc, ch 2, rep from * across, ending last rep at **, dc in tch, turn.

Row 12 Ch 8, *sk (ch 2, sc), sc in next ch-3 sp, ch 3, sc in next ch-3 sp, ch 5, sk ch-2 sp**, dc in next 3 dc, ch 5, rep from * across, ending last rep at ** dc in 3rd ch of tch, turn.

Row 13 Rep row 5.

Row 14 Ch 3, *(bobble in next ch-1 sp, ch 4) three times, bobble in next ch-1 sp**, sk 2 ch, dc in next 3 dc, rep from * across, ending last rep at **, dc in tch.

Row 15 Ch 5 (counts as dc, ch 2), *(sc in next ch-4 sp, ch 3) twice, sc in next ch-4 sp, ch 2**, dc in next 3 dc, ch 2, rep from * across, ending last rep at **, dc in tch, turn. (9 sc, 8 dc, 12 ch-sps)

Row 16 Ch 8 (counts as dc, ch 5), *sk (ch 2, sc), sc in next ch-3 sp, ch 3, sc in next ch-3 sp, ch 5, sk 2 ch**, dc in next 3 dc, ch 5, rep from * across, ending last rep at **, dc in next ch, turn. (6 sc, 8 dc, 9 ch-sps)

Row 17 Ch 5 (counts as dc, ch 2), *sc in ch-5 sp, ch 1, (dc, ch 1, dc, ch 1, dc) in next ch-3 sp, ch 1, sc in next ch-5 sp, ch 2**, dc in next 3 dc, ch 2, rep from * across, ending last rep at **, dc in 3rd ch of tch, turn. (6 sc, 17 dc, 18 ch-sps)

Rows 18–25 Rep rows 14-17 twice.

Do not fasten off.

FINISHING

Front edging first side Ch 1, starting at bottom and working along center front edge of wrap, work 44 evenly spaced sc (2 sc per row) to the top of the front edge. Make sure that the size of the sc does not cause this edge to enlarge; a little tight is better than loose, as the stitches can be relaxed with steaming. At top corner, make the tie.

Tie Ch 30, inserting hook in BL of ch, slip st in 2nd ch and in each ch, matching size of slip sts to chains, then continue to top edging

Top and front edging Sc in corner, work 2 sc around each ch-2 space and work sc in base of each st across; work at a tension that does not enlarge this edge. At the opposite end, work the second tie. Before continuing with opposite front edge, check that both ties are close in length, then continue down opposite front edge, working the same as first front edge. Fasten off.

Weave in ends. Steam entire piece to relax the fabric.

Cabled Lace Scarf

The lovely stitch pattern used here combines the delicacy of lace with the eye-catching texture of cables and bobbles. The design can be worked as a basic rectangular scarf, or as a cowl that drapes around the next once or twice (shown on facing page).

LEARN HOW TO

- Select a yarn that drapes well with textured stitches

- Perfect front and back post stitches

- Make bobbles that pop from the fabric

- Work a slip stitch seam

Post stitches and bobbles are textured stitches that create density in our crochet fabric, and density works against drape. That's why it's important to choose the right yarn and fiber for this project. Please refer to pages 15–17 for fibers that are soft and flexible. Working at the right gauge is another significant factor for drape. If your yarn is a bit stiffer, you can try working with a bigger hook at a slightly larger gauge for more drape.

For help with post stitches, see page 164.

For help with bobbles, see page 159.

For help with seaming, see page 198.

Making the Scarf

Finished Measurements

Cowl: 48" in circumference and 8½" deep

Scarf: 60" long and 8½" wide

Yarn

LB Collection Cashmere (100% cashmere, 82 yds/25 g), DK weight, 4 balls Terra Cotta

Tools

US E/4 (3.5 mm) crochet hook *or size needed to obtain correct gauge*

Tapestry needle

Gauge

Rows 1–4 in pattern = 8½" × 1¾" (length measured from row 1 at bottom of bobble)

Bobble (Yo, insert hook in designated st, yo, draw up loop, yo and draw through 2 loops) five times in same stitch, yo, draw through 6 loops on hook.

FPdc (front post double crochet) Yo, insert hook from front to back around post of designated stitch, yo and draw up a loop, (yo, draw through 2 loops) twice.

BPdc (back post double crochet) Yo, insert hook from back to front around post of designated st, yo and draw up a loop, (yo, draw through 2 loops) twice.

Ch 47 (multiple of 14 plus 5).

Row 1 (WS) Dc in 7th ch from hook (counts as 2 ch on base ch, 3 ch for dc, 1 ch on row 1), ch 1, sk next ch, *dc in next 3 ch, bobble in next ch, dc in next 3 ch**, (sk next ch, ch 1, dc in next ch) three times, sk next ch, ch 1, rep from * across, ending last rep at **, (sk next ch, ch 1, dc in next ch) twice, turn. (3 patt reps)

Row 2 Ch 3 (counts as dc throughout), dc in first dc, *ch 1, FPdc in next dc, ch 1, sk next ch, dc2tog, dc in next 3 sts, dc2tog, ch 1, FPdc in next dc, ch 1**, 3 dc in next dc, rep from * across, ending last rep at **, 2 dc in 5th ch of starting ch, turn.

Row 3 Ch 3, 2 dc in next dc, *ch 1, BPdc in next dc, ch 1, sk next ch, dc2tog, dc in next dc, dc2tog, ch 1, BPdc in next dc, ch 1, 2 dc in next dc**, dc in next dc, 2 dc in next dc, rep from * across, ending last rep at **, dc in tch, turn.

Row 4 Ch 3, dc in next dc, 2 dc in next dc, *ch 1, FPdc in next dc, ch 1, sk next ch, dc3tog, ch 1, FPdc in next dc, ch 1, 2 dc in next dc**, dc in next 3 dc, 2 dc in next dc, rep from * across, ending last rep at **, dc in next dc, dc in tch, turn.

Row 5 Ch 3, dc in next 3 dc, *ch 1, BPdc in next dc, ch 1, dc in next dc, ch 1, BPdc in next dc, ch 1, dc in next 3 dc**, bobble in next dc, dc in next 3 dc, rep from * across, ending last rep at **, dc in tch, turn.

Row 6 Ch 3, dc in next dc, dc2tog, *ch 1, FPdc in next dc, ch 1, 3 dc in next dc, ch 1, FPdc in next dc, ch 1, sk next ch, dc2tog**, dc in next 3 sts, dc2tog, rep from * across, ending last rep at **, dc in next dc, dc in tch, turn.

Row 7 Ch 3, dc2tog, *ch 1, BPdc in next dc, ch 1, 2 dc in next dc, dc in next dc, 2 dc in next dc, ch 1, BPdc in next dc, ch 1, dc2tog**, dc in next dc, dc2tog, rep from * across, ending last rep at **, dc in tch, turn.

Row 8 Ch 2, dc in next dc (counts as dc2tog), *ch 1, FPdc in next dc, ch 1, 2 dc in next dc, dc in next 3 dc, 2 dc in next dc, ch 1, FPdc in next dc, ch 1**, dc3tog, rep from * across, ending last rep at **, dc2tog, turn.

Row 9 Ch 4 (counts as dc, ch 1) *BPdc in next dc, ch 1, dc in next 3 dc, bobble in next dc, dc in next 3 dc, ch 1, BPdc in next dc, ch 1, dc in next st**, ch 1, rep from * across, ending last rep at **, turn.

COWL

Rows 10–103 Rep rows 2–9 twelve more times, then repeat rows 2–8 once more, continue to Finishing.

SCARF

Rep rows 2–9 until desired length, fasten off.

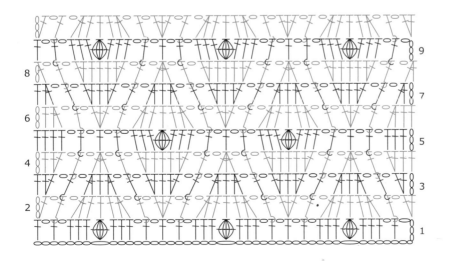

FINISHING

For the cowl only Remove hook from the last loop and fold piece in half, with WS together. Hold the starting row and the last row together. With RS and starting row facing, draw loop through base ch of first st. Work a slip stitch seam across by inserting hook under 2 loops in next base ch of starting row and next st on last row and drawing yarn through. Do not work these slip stitches tightly, but rather use your eye as a guide so that the seam stitches are the same size as the stitches being joined. The seam should not pucker the fabric at all. When done working slip stitches across, cut yarn. For more help with this seam, see Slip Stitch Seam finishing, page 199.

Steam the seam to relax fabric if necessary.

Pattern Reading

American-style pattern instructions are meant to tell crocheters every stitch they have to make, and where to insert the hook for each one. Most published patterns are exceedingly detailed. In order to cram this much information on a printed page, instructions assume knowledge of certain conventions and abbreviations. None of them are terribly difficult, but when you are starting out with instruction reading and have to keep looking up abbreviations and meanings, it can be daunting!

Nevertheless, if you're patient and persistent, you can learn to read patterns very proficiently, and even start writing them yourself. In fact, I highly recommend that you practice writing out instructions for anything that you are crocheting without a pattern. That way, you will know exactly what you did, and at the same time you'll learn something about how crochet instructions are written. Doing something yourself is the best teacher of all!

Publishers vary in the details of their format, but most patterns begin with general information at the top, including the following:

- Name of the pattern

- Name of the designer

- Materials needed to make the pattern, including the brand and type of yarn (for example, worsted or fingering weight), the color name and/or number, and the weight and yardage of one ball or skein of the yarn. If you are using a different yarn, be sure to check the yardage so you are getting the correct quantities. Publishers generally do not give exact yardage; if a partial ball is used in a pattern, it is rounded up and counted as another ball. Notions, such as buttons or beads, are also listed.

- Finished size of the project

- Skill level

- Gauge

After this you may find pattern notes, which are very important. Here is where the designer puts any special instructions that don't conveniently fit into the instruction format. Be sure to read this section carefully, even making notations in the pattern where it will help you work the project as intended by the designer.

The pattern notes may or may not explain how the project is constructed, what pieces come first, and how they are joined and/or finished. If they do not, read through the pattern carefully to help you better understand the project and how its various sections fit together.

Next you'll find definitions for any special stitches used in the project. Publishers assume that the crocheter knows the basic stitches, but will define and describe such things as how stitches are worked together, special stitches such as clusters, puffs, bobbles, or post stitches, and any other elements beyond the most basic needed to make the project.

If a stitch pattern is used, it will usually be spelled out before the pattern begins. This is where you can tell how many stitches and rows or rounds are required to make a pattern repeat. It's crucial information for making your gauge swatch. Always make your swatch with the stitch pattern used in the project.

If the project has several sections, instructions may be given for each section under a separate heading. For example, a garment pattern generally separates the instructions for the body from the sleeve, or a bag pattern might separate the front and back pieces. The numbering of rows or rounds may restart in each section, though sometimes they do not.

Finishing instructions come at the end of the pattern and may include any edgings to be made, whether to block pieces, and how they are seamed.

Pattern reading can get tricky because of the use of symbols such as asterisks, parentheses, and brackets. Let's look at a typical a line of instructions:

Ch 1, (sc, dc) in first sc, *sc in next dc, dc in next sc, rep from * across, turn.

Commas are used to separate one action from the next. For this line of instructions, the first is to make a chain-1. The next action is to work the stitches in the parenthesis — in this case, a single crochet and a double crochet; where to place them is specified after the parenthesis. Here they are both worked into the first single crochet of the row. The next action is to work a single crochet in the next double crochet, followed by a double crochet in the next single crochet. Because these two actions are repeated across the row, there is an asterisk placed before the repeated action, and the pattern tells you to repeat the actions after the asterisk (but not those before it) until you come to the end of the row or round.

This line gets a bit more complex:

Ch 1, (sc, dc) in first sc, *(sc in next dc, dc in next sc) three times, (2 sc in next dc, 2 dc in next sc), rep from * across, turn.

Let's focus on the instructions after the asterisk, where you see two sets of parentheses. We are told to make a single crochet in the next double crochet and a double crochet in the next single crochet, and after the parenthesis we are told to do that three times. The next set of parenthesis tells us to follow those three repetitions with other actions: work 2 single crochet stitches into the next double crochet and work 2 double crochet stitches in the next single crochet. This is done once, and then we go back to the asterisk and do all of that again, until we come to the end of the row. The difference between this line and the earlier one is that there are several different actions to be repeated across the row, and some of these actions are themselves repeated before going on to the next action.

It's important to read instruction text carefully. Notice the difference within the second set of parentheses from the previous example:

Ch 1, (sc, dc) in first sc, *(sc in next dc, dc in same dc) three times

Within the second set of parentheses, the single crochet stitch is worked into the next stitch, and the double crochet is worked into the *same* stitch where you worked the single crochet just before. Make sure you pay attention to whether the instructions say "next" or "same." It really matters!

In crochet, repeated actions within a larger repeated series of actions are quite common. The actions in themselves may not be difficult, but notating them conveniently can be cumbersome. In such cases, brackets can be used to enclose the larger repeat, while smaller repeated actions remain within parentheses, as in this example:

Ch 1, (sc, dc) in first sc, *[(sc in next dc, dc in next sc), (2 sc in next dc) twice] four times, rep from * across, turn.

Let's be clear about what is done two times and what is done four times. All the moves within the brackets are done four times. Within the brackets, you have two sets of parentheses. But "twice" refers only to the stitches in the parentheses immediately preceding.

Another element you may see is a double asterisk, as shown here:

Ch 1, (sc, dc) in first sc, *(sc in next dc, dc in next sc) three times**, (2 sc in next dc) twice, rep from * across, ending last rep at **, dc in last dc.

This is used when a series of stitches is repeated across the row, but the last repeat leaves out some of the stitches. The double asterisk tells you where to stop the last repetition.

Another variation for the end of the row or round may tell you to stop at a specific point, as follows:

> Ch 1, (sc, dc) in first sc, *(sc in next dc, dc in next sc) three times, (2 sc in next dc) twice, rep from * across to within last 3 stitches, dc in next 3 sts, turn.

This simply means that having worked all the stitches in the last repeat, there will be 3 more stitches to work, and it tells you what to do for those 3 stitches.

Stitches that are not worked into are called skipped stitches. Generally, patterns spell out which stitches to skip, as in this example:

> Ch 1, (sc, dc) in first sc, *(sc in next dc, dc in next sc) three times, sk 3 sc, rep from * across.

As you can see in the example above, skipping stitches can also be part of the actions to be repeated across a row. You will also find that some patterns don't mention all the skipped stitches. Generally this practice is used when the skipped stitches are obvious, or to save space in a complex pattern.

When a series of chains is part of a pattern stitch, you will find instructions that look like this:

> **Row 1** Sc in 2nd ch, ch 5, sk 3 ch, sc in next ch, rep from * across, turn.
>
> **Row 2** Ch 5 (counts as dc, ch 2), *sc in ch-5 sp**, ch 5, rep from * across, ending last rep at **, ch 2, dc in sc.

In row 1 of the above pattern, you are working a series of single crochet stitches connected by 5 chains, and skipping 3 chains on the foundation chain for each repetition. In the next row, the 5 chains are referred to as ch-5 space. If there had been a different number of chains used between single crochet stitches, that would be reflected in the instructions for the next row, for example, ch 3 becomes a ch-3 space, ch 2 becomes a ch-2 space.

Note also, in the beginning of row 2 above, the initial chain-5 is explained in parentheses. This helps the crocheter understand what part of the initial chains stands for a stitch, and which of them are chains between stitches.

For patterns that begin with a foundation chain, the number of chains to start is given. Stitch counts are generally given at the end of the first row or round as well. Thereafter, stitch counts should be given wherever the number of stitches changes due to an increase or decrease.

Glossary

Base chain: Foundation chain underlying stitch

Bias: Rows worked diagonally by increasing on one end and decreasing on the other; these rows run at an angle to the edges of the work.

Block: Finishing touches applied to crochet pieces using steam or water to even out stitches, relax fabric, and achieve precise dimensions. Note that the term *block* can also refer to a crochet square.

Chart: Schematic of stitches showing when to change color or stitch

Cluster: A group of stitches worked together

Construction: Direction of work and arrangement of pieces

Decrease: Remove stitches in a row or round

Decrease row: Row in which stitches are removed

Diagram (as in "stitch diagram"): Symbolic representation of stitches

Even (as in "work even"): The number of stitches remains the same; the pattern stitch or motif in use remains constant. Not to be confused with "even-numbered" rows, the opposite of odd-numbered.

Eye: A small hole within a stitch pattern usually created by working many stitches into one space, followed by a chain-1.

Filet: Traditional crochet openwork created by alternating double crochet stitch and 1 or 2 chains

Flexible tension: The ability to adjust the size and tightness of stitches

Foundation chain: Series of chains that begin the work

Foundation stitches: Technique that makes the base chain and first row of stitches simultaneously

Gauge: Given number of stitches and rows equated with a given measurement

Gauge equation: The equation stating the above

In the round: Working in a circular direction

Increase: Adding stitches in a row or round

Increase row: Row in which stitches are added

Internal shaping: Increasing or decreasing within the row or round rather than at the outside edges

Marguerite (aka star stitch): A flowerlike traditional crochet stitch consisting of a series of loops drawn together

Mitered corner: An angle created by increases or decreases made in a series of rows

Mitered square: Square created by making 45-degree angles using mitered corners

Multiple: Number of stitches in a pattern repeat

Pattern repeat: Series of stitches grouped together and used repeatedly across a row or round

Post: Vertical portion of a stitch, sometimes called a "stem"

Post stitch: Stitch worked around the post

Rate of increase: Number of stitches increased in a series of rows or rounds

Row ends: Stitches at the beginnings or ends of rows

Schematic: Drawing showing measurement of pieces in project

Shaping: Adding or subtracting stitches (or rows) to achieve a particular shape

Short Row: Rows that are shorter than those that precede and follow

Solomon's knot (aka lovers' knot): Elongated chains locked in place with a single crochet (the "knot")

Spin: Process used to manufacture yarn

Split clusters: Stitches worked together with several stitches in between them.

Stem: Vertical portion of a stitch (also called *post*)

Stitch count: Number of stitches in a row or round

Tail: Several inches of yarn left at start and end of work

Tunisian crochet: A special technique worked with a long or cabled hook, considered a cross between knitting and crochet.

Turning chain: Chain made at the beginning of a row to stand for the first stitch

Weave in: Hiding tails by working them through strands on back of work

Working stitch: Current stitch being made

Yoke: Upper portion of garment from neck to underarm

Key Stitch Guide

O	adjustable ring
•	slip stitch
○	chain
⌢	back loop only
⌢	2 back loops of hdc
⌣	front loop only
+	single crochet
┼	extended single crochet
Ŧ	reverse single crochet
✗	foundation single crochet
✕✕	single crochet 2 together
T	half double crochet
T	extended half double crochet
T	foundation half double crochet
✝	double crochet
✝	extended double crochet
✝	foundation double crochet
✝	linked double crochet
✝	treble crochet
✝	linked treble crochet
✝	double treble crochet

✝	front post double crochet
✝	back post double crochet
ʒ	front post single crochet
ʓ	back post single crochet
⸙	spike stitch
✝	loop stitch
✝	short knot st
✝	long knot st
⩜	single-double crochet decrease
⩙	multiple double crochet decrease
⋀	double crochet 2 together
⋀	forked cluster
◍	puff
⬡	bobble
⬡	popcorn
⩜	marguerite stitch
⋀	split cluster

Abbreviations and Basic Stitches

beg: beginning

BL (back loop): Referring to the 2 loops at the top of a stitch, this is the one at the back of the work. In instructions, it means to insert hook under the back loop of the stitch named, not both top loops. For example, for BLsc, work 1 sc into the back loop only.

BP (back post): Work into the back post of the stitch named. For example, for BPdc, yo, insert hook from back to front around post, yo and draw up a loop, (yo, draw through 2 loops) twice.

ch (chain): Yarn over and draw through loop on hook.

ch-sp: chain space. This can mean any number of consecutive chains, for example, ch 3 or ch 5, used in a pattern.

Cl (cluster): A group of stitches worked together by pulling the last loop through several partially worked stitches

cont: continue

crab st: *See* rsc.

dc (double crochet): Yo, insert hook in designated st, yo and draw up a loop (3 loops on hook), (yo, draw through 2 loops) twice.

dec: decrease

dtr (double treble crochet): Yo 3 times, insert hook in designated st, yo and draw up a loop (5 loops on hook), (yo, draw through 2 loops) four times.

E (extended stitch): An extra chain is made after inserting the hook and drawing yarn through the first time, and before working off the loops on the hook, with the purpose of elongating the st. For example, for Edc, yo, insert hook in designated st, yo, and draw up a loop, ch 1, (yo, draw through 2 loops on hook) twice.

F (foundation stitch): A method of making the first row of stitches and the starting chain at the same time. For example, for Fdc, yo, insert hook in base ch of previous st, yo and draw up a loop, ch 1, (yo, draw through 2 loops) twice.

FL (front loop): Referring to the 2 loops at the top of a stitch, this is the one at the front of the work. In instructions, it means to insert hook under the front loop of the stitch named, not both top loops. For example, for FLsc, work 1 sc into the front loop only.

FP (front post): Work into the front post of the stitch named. For example, for FPdc, yo, insert hook from front to back around post, yo and draw up a loop, (yo, draw through 2 loops) twice.

hdc (half double crochet): Yo, insert hook in designated st, yo and draw up a loop (3 loops on hook), yo, draw through all loops on hook.

inc: increase

patt rep: pattern repeat

pm: place marker

prev: previous

rep: repeat

RS: right side, the side meant to be shown

rnd: round

rsc (reverse single crochet): aka crab stitch, single crochet stitches worked in the "wrong" direction as an edging, producing a decorative twist

sc (single crochet): Insert hook in designated st or sp, yo and draw up a loop, yo, draw through 2 loops.

sk (skip): Skip 1 or more stitches (as indicated) before inserting your hook to make the next stitch.

Sl st (slip stitch): Insert hook in designated st, yo and draw loop through st and loop on hook.

sp: space created by making chain stitches

tog: together

tr (treble crochet): Yo twice, insert hook in designated st, yo and draw up a loop (4 loops on hook), (yo, draw through 2 loops) three times.

tch (turning chain): Chain stitches made at the start of a new row or round with the purpose of bringing hook up to the proper height for the stitches that will follow.

tr (treble crochet): Also called *triple crochet*. Yo twice, insert hook in designated st, yo and draw up loop, (yo, draw through 2 loops) twice.

WS: wrong side, or back of the work, not meant to be shown

Yo (yarnover): Wrap the yarn counterclockwise from back to front over the hook.

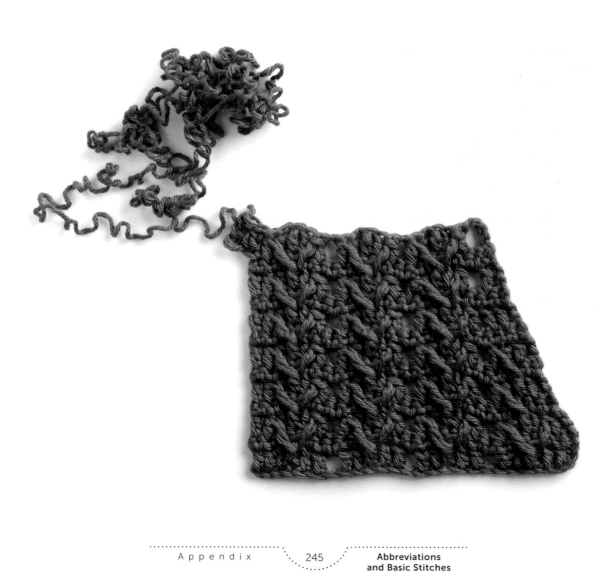

Resources

We thank the yarn companies listed here who generously provided their beautiful yarns for swatches and projects in this book.

Blue Sky Alpacas
888-460-8862
www.blueskyalpacas.com

Knit Picks
800-574-1323
www.knitpicks.com

Lion Brand Yarn
800-661-7551
www.lionbrand.com

Lorna's Laces
773-935-3803
www.lornaslaces.net

Manos del Uruguay
Fairmount Fibers, Ltd.
888-566-9970
www.fairmountfibers.com

Rowan
+44-0-1484-681881
www.knitrowan.com

Trendsetter Yarns
800-446-2425
www.trendsetteryarns.com

Acknowledgments

Thank you to James Walters, whose 1979 book *Crochet Workshop* served as both an inspiration and model for me in this endeavor. I have learned a great deal from you about crochet techniques, even though we have never met. Thank you for sharing your wisdom in a way that makes it accessible even to those of us who are not math wizards! Many thanks as well to Charles Voth, my tech editor; Pam Thompson, my book editor; and everyone at Storey Publishing — what a great crew of people to work with! Thanks also to Karin Skacel of Skacel Knitting for supplying the gorgeous Addi Click interchangeable crochet hooks we've used in the photos.

Index

Page numbers in *Italic* indicate photos or illustrations; page numbers in **bold** indicate charts.

Other Storey Titles You Will Enjoy

Christmas Crochet for Hearth, Home & Tree by Edie Eckman
A collection of 18 fresh projects for making stockings, ornaments, a tree skirt, and other decorations for the home.
184 pages. Paper. ISBN 978-1-61212-329-5.

The Crochet Answer Book by Edie Eckman (new edition available January 2015)
All the information a crocheter could need to unsnarl any project.
320 pages. Flexibind with cloth spine. ISBN 978-1-58017-598-2.

Crochet One-Skein Wonders edited by Judith Durant and Edie Eckman
The one-skein craze meets crochet with 101 designs for bags, scarves, gloves, toys, hats, and more, each using just a single skein of yarn.
288 pages. Paper. ISBN 978-1-61212-042-3.

Hooked on Crochet by Candi Jensen
Step-by-step instructions and 20 sassy projects for beginners.
144 pages. Paper. ISBN 978-1-58017-547-0.

And if you like to knit, try these other Storey titles:

Cast On, Bind Off by Leslie Ann Bestor
A one-of-a-kind reference for more than 50 ways to cast on and bind off, featuring step-by-step photography and detailed instructions.
216 pages. Paper with partially concealed wire-o. ISBN 978-1-60342-724-1.

Circular Knitting Workshop by Margaret Radcliffe
Detailed photographic sequences for every classic technique on circular knitting needles, plus 35 demonstration projects.
320 pages. Paper. ISBN 978-1-60342-999-3.

The Knowledgeable Knitter by Margaret Radcliffe
Learn the "whys" and "hows" behind knitting techniques to make every project a success.
296 pages. Paper. ISBN 978-1-61212-040-9. Hardcover. ISBN 978-1-61212-414-8.

These and other books from Storey Publishing are available wherever quality books are sold or by calling 1-800-441-5700.

Visit us at *www.storey.com* or sign up for our newsletter at *www.storey.com/signup*.